Patterns of Soviet Thought

Patterns of Soviet Thought

*The Origins and Development of
Dialectical and Historical Materialism*

Richard T. De George

Ann Arbor
The University of Michigan Press

Copyright © by The University of Michigan 1966
All rights reserved
Library of Congress Catalog Card No. 66-17026
Published in the United States of America by
The University of Michigan Press and simultaneously
in Toronto, Canada, by Ambassador Books Limited

Paperback ISBN: 978-0-472-75093-1

Preface

Every widely held system of thought is more or less viable and more or less adequate to accommodate the facts of everyday life; otherwise, the fact that it is widely held would be incomprehensible. This is true of Soviet thought, and to assume anything else is to hide one's head in the sand. The importance of understanding the school of thought dominant in such a large part of the world scarcely needs to be emphasized here. Yet to understand Soviet thought is not necessarily to agree with it. It is permeated with ambiguities, difficulties, and mistakes which form its philosophical Achilles' heel but which, paradoxically, sometimes help make up its characteristic pattern and supply it with its resiliency in the face of facts. This book is based on the assumption that only by understanding Soviet thought can one know to what extent—and why—one agrees or disagrees with it.

I have attempted to avoid the threefold error of rendering systematic a body of thought which has been and still is in the process of change, of dealing with only the Marxist classics on the false assumption that Soviet thought and classical Marxism coincide, and of describing only the present-day positions on the equally false assumptions that they are intelligible without a knowledge of the Marxist classics or that they are the last word of a stagnant or atrophying position. The process of development is part of the pattern of Soviet thought, the use of the Marxist classics is part of its pattern, and the utilization and development of classic doctrines by the Party to fit changing conditions is part of its pattern.

The terms in which problems are stated, the categories and concepts utilized, form part of the characteristics of any thought. In Soviet thought these have been forged out of the Marxist and Leninist writings, which are still widely read and studied in the Soviet Union. The present volume not only makes available in summary fashion the contents of the philosophically significant works of Marx, Engels, and Lenin and provides the requisite background for understanding them, but it distills out of them and highlights the basic patterns which have come to characterize the contemporary Marxist-Leninist world view. I have dealt with both dialectical and historical materialism, for both together provide the philosophical basis for Soviet thought. In addition to the classics I have also utilized contemporary Soviet writings, translated and untranslated, popular and technical. While I have attempted no full-scale critique, I have pointed out difficulties and have shown the part they play in the development of Soviet thought. For those interested in a more detailed treatment of a particular point or in a critical analysis from a particular point of view, I have indicated in the notes and in the Bibliography where these may be found.

Without aid from many sources and many people this work would never have been completed. I wish to express my thanks to the Foreign Area Fellowship Program, administered by a joint committee of the Social Sciences Research Council and the American Council of Learned Societies, for enabling me to devote a year to study and research at the Institute of East European Studies in Fribourg, Switzerland, and to spend a month in the Soviet Union meeting philosophers and ordinary Soviet citizens. I also wish to thank Professor J. M. Bochenski and his colleagues at the Institute for their encouragement and criticisms; the University of Kansas, which provided me with free time, materials, and the secretarial assistance necessary to produce the manuscript; and my students for their enthusiastic response and challenging questions as this material was presented to them in various courses on Marxism, Leninism, and Soviet philosophy. Special thanks go

Preface vii

to my wife for her tireless criticism of style and her constant encouragement.

Note on Transliteration and Permissions

In transliterating Russian names and titles I have used the Library of Congress system (less diacritical marks), except where there is a different, commonly used form of a proper name in English.

When books cited in the notes are also listed in the Bibliography, I have given only a short reference in the notes, followed by a bracketed number which refers to the full entry in the Bibliography.

In citing or quoting the works of Marx, Engels, or Lenin I refer first to the standard collections of their works and then to an English translation—where possible in a popular and available edition. I would like to express my thanks to Lawrence and Wishart for permission to quote from *Marx, Engels, Marxism: A Collection of Articles by V. I. Lenin* (London, 1936); and to International Publishers Co. Inc. for permission to quote from Karl Marx and Friedrich Engels, *The German Ideology* (New York, 1947), and from Joseph Stalin, *Marxism and Linguistics* (New York, 1951).

Contents

I. *Introduction: Marxism, Leninism, and Soviet Philosophy* 1

PART ONE: Marxism

II. *The Philosophical Background* 9
HEGEL 9
    Importance for Marxism-Leninism 9
    Hegel and Theology 10
    Idealism 11
    The Dialectical Method 13
    Philosophy of History 16
    Hegel's Contribution to Marxism 18
THE YOUNG HEGELIANS AND LUDWIG FEUERBACH 18
    The Young Hegelians 18
    Feuerbach vs. Hegel 22
    The Essence of Christianity 24
    Marx's "Theses on Feuerbach" 29

III. *Young Marx: The Forging of a Philosophical Framework* 31
    Approach to Marxist Interpretation 31
    Life and Writings 33
    Marx's Doctoral Dissertation 37
    Contribution to the Critique of Hegel's *Philosophy of Right* 39
    Economic and Philosophic Manuscripts of 1844 41
    The Holy Family 44
    The German Ideology 46
    Basic Patterns and Beliefs 52

IV. *Marx and Political Economy* 55
   The Poverty of Philosophy 55
   The Communist *Manifesto* 57
   The Critique of Political Economy 63
   Capital 67
   Critique of the Gotha Program 71
   Mature Marxism 72

V. *Engels and Marxist Theory* 77
   The Place of Engels 77
   Life and Writings 78
   Anti-Dühring 80
   Ludwig Feuerbach and the End of Classical German Philosophy 93
   Dialectics of Nature 102
   Engels' Contribution to Soviet Thought 107
   Marxism and Revisionism 108

PART TWO: Leninism

VI. *The Russian Background* 113
   RUSSIAN PHILOSOPHY IN THE NINETEENTH CENTURY 113
      The Slavophiles and Westernizers 114
      Narodnichestvo 115
      Russian Marxism 117
   PLEKHANOV 119
      Life and Works 119
      Monistic View of History 120
      The Individual and History 122
      Geography, Art, and Knowledge 125
      Contribution to Marxism-Leninism 127

VII. *Lenin and the Party* 128
   V. I. Ulianov (Lenin): Life and Works 128
   What Is to Be Done? 131
   The Party and Partymindedness 135
   The Party and Determinism 138
   The State and Revolution 140

VIII. *Materialism and Empirio-Criticism* 146
   Idealism, Realism, and Materialism 147

Contents xi

    The Copy Theory of Knowledge   151
    Truth   154
    Matter   157

IX. *Lenin's Philosophical Legacy*   161
    The Essentials of Marxism   161
    Philosophical Notebooks   164
    Ethics and Militant Materialism   171
    Lenin's Contribution to Soviet Thought   174

PART THREE: Soviet Philosophy and Ideology

X. *The Development of Soviet Thought*   179
    Mechanism versus Deborinism   179
    Stalin's Consolidation   184
    History of the CPSU(b): Short Course   189
    Linguistics and the Superstructure   194
    Stalin's Contribution to Soviet Thought   198
    The New Program of the CPSU   201

XI. *Fundamentals of Contemporary Soviet Philosophy*   206
    Matter, Mind, and Modern Physics   207
    Categories and Laws of Dialectics   210
    Logic and Theory of Knowledge   213
    Historical Materialism   216
    Class Struggle and Social Development   219
    Social Consciousness, Individuals, and the Masses   222

XII. *Contemporary Practice and Future Prospects*   226
    Philosophy and Ideology   226
    Theory, Practice, and Propaganda   233
    Open Areas and Lines of Future Development   239
    Philosophical Criticism and the Confrontation of Ideologies   245

Notes   249
Annotated Bibliography   273
Index   283

Chapter I
Introduction: Marxism, Leninism, and Soviet Philosophy

Soviet thought has developed from Marx to Lenin and from Lenin to the present day. It is still developing, for development forms part of its pattern. The structure of Soviet thought is at once rigid in certain basic assumptions, dogmatic in its adherence to the writings of Marx, Engels, and Lenin, and flexible in its ability to accommodate itself to change in times and circumstances. It is both romantic and prosaic, materialistic and full of ideals.

To understand Soviet thought is in part to understand the approach of many of the ordinary educated Soviet citizens to the problems of life, history, and society. It is also to understand their presuppositions, their way of conceiving of the world, the concepts they use in framing problems, and the approaches they characteristically use to solve them. Such terms as "freedom," "truth," and "democracy" take on different meanings in Soviet and in contemporary Western thought; others, such as "dialectics," are household words in Soviet though not in Western discourse; and still others, such as "communism," represent good for one side and evil for the other. A large number of the Soviet people who have been educated and trained in the Soviet Union from youth to maturity accept certain presuppositions which they have imbibed almost with the air they breathe. It is important to realize that all peoples hold certain presuppositions and that those of a large and influential portion of the Soviet people differ in many respects from those most current in the West. All this must be remembered if we are to understand the Soviet people and if we are to follow intelligently not only Soviet foreign policy but also the internal developments taking place within Soviet society. A people's presuppositions—their view of what they are and of what their society should be like—are significant factors in how their society operates and develops.

To try to understand either Soviet society or Soviet policy without a knowledge of the foundations of Soviet thought is in many respects like trying to understand the Middle Ages without a knowledge of Christianity. The role of the Party, the drive toward collectivization in many aspects of life, and the pride of the Soviet people in the morality of their social system become fully comprehensible only when the theoretical bases for them are understood. This does not necessarily mean that all Soviet citizens are willing to sacrifice present pleasure or comfort for the development of a glorious future society, even though theory and the Party tell them they should. There is often a discrepancy between what people are told they should do and what they believe they should do, as well as between what they believe they should do and what they actually do. The study of theory takes one only so far, yet the importance of studying the theoretical foundations of Soviet thought—found in the writings of Marx, Engels, and Lenin, as interpreted by the Communist Party of the Soviet Union—can scarcely be overemphasized. Marxist-Leninist philosophy is the most assiduously propagated philosophy in the world, and its role in providing a view of the world for many members of Soviet society is without parallel in pluralistic Western societies. Its conceptual adequacy or inadequacy in dealing with reality must be appreciated to confront communism intelligently, but to a certain extent its adequacy or inadequacy, and its truth or falsity, are beside the point if we wish to see how a great many of the people raised in this view at least *tend* to conceive the world.

Marxist-Leninist philosophy, known also as dialectical and historical materialism, is taught in all Soviet schools; it is required in all college, university, and technical programs of instruction. Marxism-Leninism[1] is the world view upon which the Soviet educational system is built, and it infuses educational theory and practice more completely than Dewey's philosophy ever did in America. Soviet children learn Marxism-Leninism indirectly and in a sense unwittingly in their elementary school training. In schools comparable to our junior and senior high schools, courses in historical materialism are required, and Marxism-Leninism permeates the history, the literature, and the natural and social science courses, among others. In colleges, professional schools, and even technical schools all students must take courses in Marxism-Leninism based on the history of the Communist Party of the Soviet Union. In universities they must take courses in dialectical and historical materialism to help them see the philosophical implications of their chosen discipline and to prepare them the better to aid the spread of communism.[2]

Marxism-Leninism is expected to infuse all learning, all research, and all practical activity. A striking example is afforded by the physical sciences, which in the West are usually considered immune from ideological encroachment. In the Soviet Union dialectical materialism provides a methodological foundation for the sciences. It also makes quasi-scientific assertions (e.g., that the universe is infinite) which must be accepted. Any theory which goes counter to these assertions is rejected not on the basis of experimental data, but on the basis that it contradicts dialectical materialism, the truth of which is guaranteed by the Party. Thus, both quantum mechanics and relativity theory were at one time attacked because of their apparent incompatibility with certain doctrines of dialectical materialism. Only after several years of debate was it decided that these theories could be interpreted not only as compatible with dialectical materialism, but so as to prove it. Not until then were they completely accepted. It should also be noted that the scientists and philosophers who defended these theories for scientific reasons never attempted to do so by denying the validity of dialectical materialism or by attacking it as false. In a similar manner the Lysenko theory of the inheritance of acquired characteristics was long in high favor, not because it had been scientifically established, but primarily because it accorded so well with the dialectical unity of environment and organism.[3]

The pervasiveness of Marxism-Leninism in Soviet society, moreover, is not limited to education and science. As the guiding tool of the Communist Party[4] it infuses all official party publications, the Party Program, the five-year plans, and the legal system, as well as newspapers, radio and TV programs, the movies, and much of art and literature. The leaders of the Soviet Union claim that Marxism-Leninism contains the only correct and objectively true world outlook. They go to great lengths not only to propagate this view but also to keep the Soviet people, as far as possible, insulated from other points of view.[5] The Central Committee of the Communist Party of the Soviet Union is a philosophical watchdog, correcting philosophical errors or deviations of Soviet philosophers and guarding the purity of Marxist-Leninist doctrine.[6] All religious, idealistic, or bourgeois views are systematically refuted and scarcely any attack on Marxism-Leninism goes unanswered.

Add to all this the collectivist structure of Soviet society in which people live and work closely together and carry on many of their activities in organized groups or collectives and in which each man is expected to consider himself his brother's keeper, and the impetus for nonconformity or originality in thought is seen to be extremely small indeed. Even for those so inclined the possibilities for extended systematic contact with other thought are limited, and the task of self-education under such conditions difficult. The achievement of communism may appear to some Soviet citizens as utopian, at least during their lifetime, but capitalism with its implied values and with its individualism certainly does not seem to be the alternative which any significant portion of the Soviet population seeks. Marxism-Leninism is what they have been taught, what they know, what they are constantly exposed to; and it cannot help but influence and structure their thought.

That many students give evidence of finding their philosophical studies boring or uninteresting or merely learn by rote and shrug off official propaganda does not preclude the fact that it is in terms of dialectical materialism that they learn to see the world, that they learn to think about the philosophical problems of their discipline, and that they learn the stock answers which form the basis for their patterns of thought. This is not surprising, for, as the history of philosophy has shown, it is extremely difficult for anyone to develop true originality in thought. Great philosophers have always had to struggle against what they had been taught before they could forge their own way of conceiving reality or of approaching problems. Only the exceptional person can break out of the framework of categories in which he has been educated and which pervades his environment. The vast majority of mankind has neither the time nor the ability to pursue such a struggle. This is true of our own, as well as of Soviet, society, though perhaps, because of the pluralistic nature of our society, our own conformity and timidity in thought is less obvious to us. In a society like that of the USSR, in which original philosophical thought outside the Marxist-Leninist framework is frowned upon, it is even less surprising that extremely few people engage in it, and that few of those who do, let others know it.

Marxism-Leninism has a basic appeal for a large part of Soviet society, moreover, which should not be overlooked. It claims to be scientific and to be based on scientifically demonstrable laws of nature and history. In a century when the prestige of science is high, it is reassuring for the Soviet people to be told that their world view is the only scientific one there is. The claim to science implies verifiability; but just as most people do not attempt to verify what they are told with respect to the physical sciences, so most of the Soviet people do not attempt to verify those claims of dialectical and historical materialism which they have been taught have been scientifically established. The claim to science bolsters the claim that the triumph of communism is inevitable, thus making it for many worth working for. This is the more true as the appeal of communism is this-worldly, even though in the future. For what communism promises is a good life for all in an opulent society in which there will be no poor, no abused, and no exploited people. It is thus dynamic, future-oriented, and calls for noble self-sacrifice for a greater good. Furthermore, a great part of Marxism-Leninism's appeal is moral. Marxism is rooted in moral indignation against capitalism and the exploitation it involves. Though this was often lost or submerged in the writings of Lenin and Stalin, the moral claims of Marxism are loudly voiced again today. That the United States is wealthy and that wealth is desirable is not denied even by the Soviet leaders. But a wealthy society is not necessarily a moral one. It is for the basic immorality of its social structure and not for its wealth that Marxism-Leninism condemns capitalism. It is both for its wealth and for its morality that a communist society as a moral ideal has the attraction it does for so many both in and out of the Soviet Union.

Since the Communist Party of the Soviet Union claims to know the truth and claims that the truth is found in the writings of Marx, Engels, and Lenin (referred to as the "classics"), these works are not to be challenged in the USSR. This is the most characteristic aspect of the pattern of Soviet thought. Imposed upon it is the pattern of "change from above," a right which devolves upon the leaders of the Communist Party of the Soviet Union and which enables them to reinterpret and develop classical positions in the light of historical exigencies. Lenin interpreted and developed the doctrine of Marx and Engels, and Stalin did the same to Lenin's doctrine. Contemporary Soviet thought in its turn is synonymous with neither classical Marxism nor Leninism, yet it cannot be understood without knowing the works of Marx, Engels, and Lenin.

As the basis of Marxism-Leninism, Soviet philosophy is a factor in Soviet life which deserves close attention. The Soviet insistence on the importance of philosophy continues a tradition which goes back to Marx, a trained philosopher who originally intended to pursue a career as a university professor in philosophy. Lenin, despite his active career, was a devoted student of philosophy and studied closely not only the writings of Marx, but those of Hegel, Aristotle, and others as well. He clearly pointed out the importance of philosophy to the triumph of communism.[7] Stalin was no less insistent on the importance of philosophy for communism,[8] and Khrushchev reiterated again and again the necessity of guarding the purity of Marxism-Leninism as the basis for communist theory and practice. The new Program of the Communist Party of the Soviet Union adopted in 1961 as the guide for the development of Soviet society for the next twenty years continues a pattern when it states: ". . . it is of prime importance that a scientific world outlook be shaped in all working people of Soviet society on the basis of Marxism-Leninism, an integral and harmonious system of philosophical, economic, and sociopolitical views."[9]

Our study, concerned primarily with the philosophical basis of Marxism-Leninism, is divided into three parts. The first is concerned with Marxism. Marx presented no systematic body of thought. Though he formulated the basic tenets of

Marxist doctrine, his ideas developed and changed during his lifetime. Consequently, to understand his contribution to Soviet thought we must be careful to avoid the danger of systematizing his writings. The same is true of an approach to Engels' works. The positions of Marx and Engels vary, change, and develop, and must be seen as developing and not as static. We must also take into consideration their immediate predecessors, especially Hegel and Feuerbach, the stamp of each of whom is still to be found on contemporary Soviet thought. Marx, Engels, and their predecessors form the Western sources from which the Soviet philosophical doctrine developed.

Lenin interpreted Marx and Engels; he accepted some of their ideas, added some of his own, and adapted Marxism to the Russian philosophical tradition and to Russian economic conditions. The result is Leninism, a selective dogmatization and interpretation of Marxist theory. Although based on Marxism it is no more identical with it than with contemporary Soviet thought. Leninism is the concern of the second part of this study.

Neither Marx nor Engels nor Lenin addressed their philosophical works exclusively to the professional philosopher. Their works were directed to a somewhat broader audience, and, consequently, much in their writings is polemical and often lacking in technical philosophical precision. Since problems and solutions were hastily formulated under the pressure of controversy, the task of interpreting these works poses no little difficulty. The resultant ambiguities, difficulties, and mistakes themselves help form the pattern of Soviet thought. In each case the task of clarification and interpretation is part of the intellectual inheritance. Ambiguities have led to divergent interpretations of doctrine, difficulties to ingenious explanations and new theories, mistakes either to dogmatism, self-deception, or embarrassment.

The third part of this volume deals with contemporary Soviet thought, which we shall consider to have begun roughly in 1922 with the appearance of the journal *Under the Banner of Marxism* and with the expulsion of non-Marxist philosophers from the Russian universities. During the period of his reign Stalin dominated the philosophical scene, and Marxist-Leninist doctrine, which had moved into the universities, at last became consolidated and to some extent systematized. Though Marxist-Leninist philosophy became the official Soviet philosophy and the only one tolerated in the USSR, its ambiguous Marxist-Leninist inheritance remained open both to interpretation and to change from above. The Soviet period is marked by selective dogmatization and interpretation of Leninist doctrine, by the subordination of philosophy to the Party, and by the adaptation of theory to the changing conditions of the USSR. But when controversy is allowed, the nonsystematic make-up of the Marxist-Leninist classics provides Soviet philosophers some leeway in the presentation and solution of some philosophical problems. Because dogmatism and development are both intrinsic parts of the pattern of Soviet thought, the intrinsic interest of Soviet philosophical writings is paradoxically proportional to the ambiguity of the writings of Marx, Engels, and Lenin. Where the classics are least clear and explicit, Soviet philosophers have the greatest opportunity for creative interpretation and originality within the Marxist-Leninist framework.

Part 1: Marxism

Chapter II
The Philosophical Background

Hegel

Importance for Marxism-Leninism

The seeds of Marxism were scattered in a very real sense early in the nineteenth century, though it is only later that the fruits were reaped by Marx and changed to the finished product that nurtured his successors. The early nineteenth-century is dominated by Georg Wilhelm Friedrich Hegel (1770-1831). Marx does not dominate but rather shares the latter half of the century with several others who like himself bear the imprint of Hegel either as disciple or opponent. Marx was both a disciple and an opponent. As a university student he immersed himself in Hegel's writings and emerged a convinced Hegelian. His doctoral dissertation was clearly Hegelian, and even as he turned from Hegelian idealism to materialism he did not shake off Hegel completely. He remained convinced that Hegel was partly right, that he had discovered something true, important, and worth preserving, despite his enormous mistakes and illusions. If we were to summarize this something in one word it would be *dialectics,* though we might just as easily say *method.* Even in repudiating Hegel, Marx admits this debt to him.

It is not without justification, then, that we begin a study of Marxism-Leninism by briefly examining certain aspects of Hegel's philosophy. His influence on Marx is so central that

Lenin remarked in his *Philosophical Notebooks:* "It is impossible completely to understand Marx's *Capital,* and especially its first chapter, without having thoroughly studied and understood the *whole* of Hegel's *Logic.* Consequently, half a century later none of the Marxists understood Marx!"[1] Hegel's influence on Engels was equally large, and Lenin clearly admired Hegel and studied his works carefully, though he approached them from a materialistic point of view.[2] Soviet thought today, which follows Marx, Engels, and Lenin, is consequently often strongly flavored with Hegel, and Hegelianism has played a not insignificant role in the internal tensions that still characterize the development of dialectical and historical materialism in the Soviet Union. *Kommunist,* the official organ of the Central Committee of the Communist Party of the Soviet Union, after the unmasking of Stalin in 1956, indicated that philosophers should pay more attention to Hegel and that they —unlike Lenin—had been underestimating to their detriment the importance of studying Hegel's works.[3]

The greatness of Hegelian philosophy consists in the strength and unity of its vision, the comprehensive interrelated grasp which it presents of all of reality. But the beauty and simplicity of the whole is marred by the extreme complexity of the parts coupled with language so abstract and abstruse as to be often unintelligible. Far from condemning his philosophy to obscurity, however, these very traits seem to have increased its influence. It was so abstruse as to be open to divergent interpretations and so abstract as to move many readers to revolt against it and to seek a more concrete approach to reality. Marx was among those who both interpreted and reacted. Although a complete exposition of Hegel is beyond the scope of this book, yet some understanding of his approach to theology and of his idealism, his use and exposition of the dialectical method, and his notion of history are central to an appreciation both of Marx and of Soviet thought today.

Hegel and Theology

Hegel was educated at the Theological Seminary of the University of Tübingen. Both by early training and by interest he was a theologian, but a rationalistic theologian who was concerned with interpreting theology philosophically. After receiving his degree from Tübingen he wrote various minor

The Philosophical Background 11

works in which he began developing his philosophical interpretation of Christianity. In *A Life of Jesus* he presents Jesus as a rationalistic thinker who preaches a Kantian-type morality, and in the *Spirit of Christianity* Hegel interprets the doctrines of Christianity in terms of a rationalistic philosophy picturing man's relation to God as one of alienation which is to be overcome by the union of love. These early works are significant both because they foreshadow Hegel's later treatment of religion and because they provide a key to an interpretation of his philosophy. In later works Hegel presents religion as one of the highest stages of consciousness, superseded only by philosophy.

Christianity teaches that God is a Spirit, that man is also basically spiritual (has a soul), that God became Man. But in Christianity the truth of philosophy is grasped not clearly and rationally but through representations and figuratively. Creation, for instance, is for Hegel nothing other than a representational way of describing the transition of the Idea into its opposite—Nature. The Incarnation represents for Hegel his claim that man is actually part of God, that God is man and man is God. Redemption, fraternity, and all Christian doctrines are given similar rationalistic interpretations and are depicted by Hegel as necessary steps in the development of the Absolute's consciousness of itself, which is reached in its plenitude only in philosophy. In philosophy one rids oneself of the pictures or representations which mask the truth in religion.

Hegel thus rationalized religion, subordinated it to philosophy, and robbed it of its supernatural character. His view of religion was not for him an attack on religion. But given this view it is not surprising that Marx and the Young Hegelians rejected religion. Hegel laid the foundation for the war against religion which his followers did in fact wage. It was on the religious front that the Young Hegelians were to launch their first attacks. Marx joined them in the enterprise. With Lenin atheism became militant; and the nonexistence of God remains a postulate of Soviet thought today.

Idealism

Hegel's first major work, the work which contains most of the ideas which he was later to develop and the work which most strongly influenced Marx, was the *Phenomenology of*

Mind (1807). In it Hegel starts from what can be called ordinary experience. But his analysis of ordinary everyday objects and of how they appear to us leads him to a view which is in many ways opposed to a common sense view of the world. It leads to a philosophical position known as objective idealism, which according to one interpretation (and the one that Marx, Engels, Lenin, and the present-day Soviet philosophers hold) means that in some sense the realm of thought or consciousness is more real, more basic, more primary than the realm of matter. We shall examine the claim and its meaning more closely when we investigate Marx's attack on idealism. But we can here distinguish three main elements in Hegel's idealism.

1) Hegel begins his analysis with any individual object of consciousness considered as part of the non-self or as independent of the knower. But in order to understand it he finds it necessary to go beyond the object in its individuality to the realm of science which deals with generalizations and laws. The realm of science and its laws are more general, more intelligible, and so for Hegel more real than the realm of individual objects. But the realm of science is the realm of thought. Thus, the realm of thought is more real than the realm of sense in that it is both more fundamental and more inclusive. The reality of an object necessarily implies a mind or consciousness which contains the object and which is more real than the object. Thus, *the existence of the object is mind-dependent.* This is the first element of Hegel's idealism.

2) Consciousness does not equal *my* consciousness, for I know that others of whom I am conscious are also conscious of me. Each of us and the consciousness of each is thus very partial, part of a total or universal consciousness or spirit. I am part of a total consciousness which contains in it and which is identical with the totality of objects. To this *total consciousness or mind of which I—and everything—am a part*, Hegel gives the name of the *Absolute*. This spirit or mind in its totality (the Absolute) is or exhausts all reality.

3) The third element of Hegel's idealism is that reality forms a total, comprehensive, coherent whole and that truth consists in and is the same as this coherent whole. Reality is consequently systematic and the adequate expression of reality must also be systematic or form a system. Consequently, the development of Hegel's philosophy proceeds via the development of the concept or notion. Any concept is a partial

The Philosophical Background 13

affirmation calling forth another concept which will be an attempt to make up for the deficiencies of the first. This in turn will call for another until a fully sufficient concept, the absolute concept, is unfolded. This unfolding of the concept develops from the abstract to become more and more inclusive or "concrete" and is actually nothing other than the development of self-consciousness itself. Hegel gives a presentation of this self-development in his *Logic*. Insofar as the self-developing idea becomes an ever-more "concrete" concept, Hegel's *Logic* is not an abstract formal logic but is the same as metaphysics or an analysis of reality. Moreover, the development of the Spirit in time (or the autobiography of the Absolute becoming aware of itself) is world history, and its *alienation* from itself and its development in space is Nature.

Marx, following Feuerbach, rejects all three elements of Hegel's idealism. He rejects Hegel's initial analysis, his equation of intelligibility with reality, and his notion of an all-inclusive Absolute. His rejection of Hegel, however, both colors his own position and raises a number of problems. For though he rejects Hegel's idealism he adapts Hegel's method to his own purposes. The dialectical method at once constitutes Marx's greatest debt to Hegel and is a source of many of his most serious philosophical difficulties.

The Dialectical Method

Dialectics forms the heart of both Hegel's and Marx's thought, though the one is idealistic and the other materialistic in approach. Their differences and similarities will become clear in due course.

In the *Phenomenology* Hegel started by analyzing a given object and his analysis soon led him to difficulties which he could not resolve without going beyond the object in its individuality and without leaving the realm of sense experience for the realm of theoretical laws. The difficulty was resolved by rising to a higher level of discourse, where the concepts employed were both more general and more inclusive of individual instances. He followed this technique from level to level until finally he arrived at the concept of the Absolute, the most inclusive or "concrete" of all concepts, which embodies and coincides with all of reality. To this method, which is to a greater or lesser extent charactertistic of all his works, Hegel gives the name "dialectics." But his use of this method often differs from place to place, and unfortunately what he says about his method in his discussions of the dialectic as such does not always coincide with his use of the method.

In the "Introduction" to the *Science of Logic*—the work which Lenin so admired and in which Hegel presented his system—Hegel discusses his method at some length.

To deal with things from a fixed point of view is permissible for mathematics, he tells us, and suffices for ordinary life as well as for empirical philosophy. However, since such concepts are static and abstract, they distort reality and are incomplete; as such they demand completion or fuller development. Any statement insofar as it is incomplete or is only partly true demands or calls forth what it leaves out. One can, for instance, talk about the desk being solid and stable from the viewpoint of common sense, and from the viewpoint of science one can also hold it is a mass of moving electrons. There is no contradiction so long as we remain on either level or speak from either point of view. Yet it is true that the table is both solid and not solid at the same time. If we want to seize the table as it is we have to include the fact that at the same time it is both mobile and immobile. Hegel attempts to resolve such "contradictions" by going beyond them to some sort of identity-in-difference which unites various aspects while still maintaining the differences. He also attempts to do justice to the fact that reality as we know it is moving through time. Any given object changes from second to second if only in the fact that it is a second older. This fact of movement or motion is ignored when we ordinarily speak of the table. But if we are to grasp reality we cannot do so with static concepts, for reality is not static but fluid, moving, changing. What is finite is necessarily transitory, time-toned and changeable. Everything that surrounds us is in movement, and dialectic is the principle of this movement and activity. Insofar as it is in movement or changing, an object is both what it is and is not what it is. Insofar as it is incomplete it calls forth what it is not. The motive force for all change is contradiction, the contradiction inherent in finite reality. Reason goes beyond both sides of the contradiction showing that they require each other and that they can be superseded and reconciled by a type of identity-in-difference. The solution contains the contradictions but contains them in a higher stage. As reality is in movement so must the concept which

The Philosophical Background 15

embodies reality be in movement. As reality is dialectical so must philosophy be dialectical. On this both Marx and Hegel agree.

There are three moments or stages in the dialectic. The initial stage of the dialectical movement is positive and stable. We start with a finite concept. Since the concept is necessarily partial, it leads to a second, contradictory, stage in which what has been posited is negated. The negation itself is only partial and so it in turn must also be negated. This third stage, which is a negation of the negation, annuls the claim of each of the two previous stages to be complete; it preserves the positive aspect of the two previous stages; and it elevates them to a higher level.[4] The third stage is consequently richer than the two previous stages since it contains the positive aspects of both. It should be noted that the terms thesis, antithesis, synthesis—often used by later Hegelians and Marxists to designate these three stages of the dialectic—come not from Hegel but from Fichte. This dialectical process of positing a *concept*, negating it, and then negating the negation, however, is found throughout Hegel's works, which are divided and subdivided triadically in great part. For Hegel the stages of the dialectic arise necessarily. We do not determine them; they determine themselves. All we do in philosophy is follow out the development of the dialectic. We can look for the dialectical development of spirit in experience, but it is something we find there, not something we impose upon experience. Dialectical movement is not a mathematical deduction but an ever more and more inclusive development. For Hegel "the Method is no-ways different from its object and content; for it is the content in itself, *the Dialectic which it has in itself*, that moves it on. It is clear that no expositions can be regarded as scientific which do not follow the course of this Method, and which are not conformable to its simple rhythm, for that is the course of the thing itself."[5] This view of the dialectic is crucial, for Marx will attempt to separate the dialectical method from Hegel's content. Hegel begins his system with simple immediacy, complete abstraction, or in his terms with "being-in-general," which, since it is without content, is indistinguishable from nothing (its opposite or negation). Each leads to or passes into the other and this "passing into" (negation of the negation) Hegel calls "becoming." The dialectical process continues in the *Logic* until

Hegel finally arrives at the all-inclusive concept of the absolute. Marx will attempt to deal not with concepts but with things, objects of experience, actual men in their real circumstances. He thus claims that his dialectical method "is not only different from the Hegelian, but is its direct opposite."[6] He will be forced to justify this separation of method and content, of dialectic and idealism, and to explain what it is that moves the dialectic on.

Philosophy of History

For Hegel reason rules the world and consequently the events in world history happen according to reason. Just as reason stands behind or grounds or makes intelligible the material world, so it presents itself in world history as well. We must take history as it is, however, and consequently it is an empirical and not an a priori discipline. In history we find the absolute in its temporal development. We must try to see events as instances or movements of the Absolute. We must go beyond the particular to the reality—Reason—of which it is a manifestation in order to comprehend the development of reason in time. This development *is* history. What we are to look for, therefore, is the spirit behind or in history which manifests itself as human spirit. Just as electricity manifests itself as sparks or lightning, the Absolute Spirit manifests itself in human consciousness, and the total development of human consciousness constitutes the development of the Absolute's consciousness. When man comes to know he is part of the Absolute, the Absolute comes to know itself. When man sees that man is essentially free, the Absolute becomes conscious of what it is. This insight leads Hegel to an analysis of three topics: (*a*) the nature of spirit; (*b*) the means it uses to realize itself; and (*c*) its realized form (the state).

a) The essence of spirit, Hegel tells us, is freedom. Spirit is opposed to matter; matter is composite and extended, while spirit is in itself or self-contained. Since it is self-contained it determines itself and it is consequently both freedom and consciousness. Spirit makes itself what it is by bringing to actuality what it is in itself potentially, just as an acorn brings forth the oak. World history is the spirit striving to become conscious of itself and of its nature (i.e., of its freedom and consciousness). Thus, world history has as its object a study of the development of the consciousness of freedom, and the end of history is the actualization of this consciousness.

b) The Absolute becomes conscious of itself through the actions of men, conscious individuals. Individuals act for their own interests or passions, for their own particular ends. But the Absolute utilizes these particulars in order to reach its own end. For man by his action produces more than he intends, and it is this surplus that is utilized by spirit. Julius Caesar, for instance, was interested only in maintaining his own position. In order to do so, he had to fight and conquer his various opponents. But in so doing, he actually brought about the unity of the Roman Empire, a consequence which he did not directly envisage and which was beyond his immediate aim. This unity, however, was necessary for the development of the Absolute, and the Absolute is thus seen to work through Caesar.

c) The state is the realization of the idea in human society. Man is an end in himself insofar as he is divine or has reason and freedom, and insofar as he shares in the rational end of the Absolute. In the state the individual enjoys his freedom in willing and knowing the universal. The state is the union of the universal and subjective will, for in the state the objects of both coincide. One must view the state, therefore, as a "concrete universal" encompassing its two parts either of which can be separated from or made subservient to the other. It should be noted, however, that the state of which Hegel speaks is not any particular state, but the idea of the state which manifests itself in successive developments in history. In obeying laws, the spirit obeys itself, and thus it is free. Consequently, men are free when they recognize and follow law as rational and necessary. In doing so, subjective and objective aims coincide.

The march of world history thus has a direction: the development toward the goal of greater and greater self-consciousness or freedom; its development is organic, and it is transindividual.

Marx retains Hegel's organic view of history though he denies its teleological end. He must thus face the problem of whether and how one can know the direction of history; the role of the individual in history likewise becomes a problem with which he must deal—as do the questions of freedom and necessity.

Hegel's Contribution to Marxism

Marx's large debt to Hegel is one which he himself acknowledges. The same can be said with respect to Engels, who formalized the principles of what has come to be known as dialectical materialism. Whatever they took from Hegel, however, they necessarily modified, for Hegel's system was idealistic while the orientation of the philosophy of Marx and Engels was materialistic. No idea was taken over whole or without change, development, or materialistic inversion. Many of Marxism's problems thus had their source in Hegelianism. To take part of a system which was as closely developed and internally consistent as Hegel's could not be done without some resultant difficulties. The extent to which these difficulties were satisfactorily resolved is still a question of dispute.

The Hegelian source of the following, which were adapted and interpreted materialistically by Marxism (as we shall see later at greater length), should be noted:

1) the dialectical method;
2) the recognition of the active role of man (or mind) in knowledge and in the world;
3) the notion of alienation;
4) the integral view of history as a process and as independent of individual interests;
5) the notion of freedom and determinism;
6) the notion of dialectical logic;
7) the equation of logic with theory of knowledge and with dialectics;
8) the rejection of static or old metaphysics;
9) the optimistic view of the development and constant improvement of society throughout history; and
10) the monistic view of nature, of man and of society.

The way Hegel's inheritance was used and the difficulties that this indebtedness caused form an important part of the history of both Marxism and Marxism-Leninism.

The Young Hegelians and Ludwig Feuerbach

The Young Hegelians

Hegelianism continued to dominate German philosophy even after Hegel's death. His followers split into two main groups: the Right (conservative) Hegelians and the Left (radical) or

The Philosophical Background 19

Young Hegelians. As a student Marx was associated with the latter group, but early in his career he gained his intellectual independence and developed his own views by vigorously attacking not only Hegel but the Left-Hegelians as well.

For Hegel spirit manifests itself most clearly and objectively in the world of institutions—in law, society, morality, ethics, history, the state. These are the means by which spirit becomes effective in the world. History is the autobiography of the Absolute unfolding itself, necessarily and rationally and becoming aware of itself in time. The state is the highest expression of the Absolute as objective spirit. In the preface to his work *The Philosophy of Right and Law* (of which Marx wrote a detailed criticism) Hegel makes the statement: "The rational is actual; and the actual is rational." Its meaning as derived from its context is quite clear. What are real for Hegel are concepts, and it is in this sense that reality is rational. The concept of the state, for instance, includes all its individual instances and so is both more real and "concrete" (or inclusive) than any of its instances. A concept appears in many forms or instances, and in order to see the real in what is passing and temporal one must look for the eternal concept which is immanent beneath it. The particular is united to, but is only part of, the universal behind it. The apparently simple statement, however, was interpreted in different ways by the "Left" and by the "Right."

The Right Hegelians took as their theme Hegel's dictum "The actual is rational." For them this was the vindication of the status quo. According to their line of thinking, whatever exists or is in fact the case must be rational since it is a phase in the development of spirit. Their conservatism showed itself in support of the existing Prussian state, in adherence to the established Lutheran church, and in defense of the content of Hegelian idealism which men like Karl Göschel and Karl Michelet claimed was compatible with Christian theology.[7]

The Left-Hegelians,[8] on the other hand, seized on the Hegelian dictum "The rational is actual." They argued that obviously everything did not end with Hegel: life and thought continue; there is still movement and motion; the dialectical process has not come to an end. They therefore rejected the static content of Hegelian thought, which seemed to uphold the status quo, but they preserved its method. In politics, the

Left-Hegelians opposed the existing regime and were generally socialists, liberals, or radicals. In religious matters they attacked orthodox Christianity, and in the development of philosophy they usually adhered to the method rather than content of Hegelian idealism. It should be noted that there were degrees of Left-Hegelianism and no particular man necessarily held the extreme position in all three domains.

The Left or Young Hegelians who played a main part in Marx's development were David Strauss, Bruno Bauer, Arnold Ruge, Max Stirner, Mikhail Bakunin, and Ludwig Feuerbach (a Left-Hegelian before the development of his materialism). Since they held that the dialectical method involves continual progress and that no state of affairs is final, they preached a philosophy of action, though Marx and Engels in *The German Ideology* later characterized their struggle as merely a fight against phases.[9] The Young Hegelians extended their notions of concrete action into the field of politics and social activity. But this is not where they began. They began initially by attacking the church and Christian doctrine in general.

David Strauss (1808-74) begins the onslaught in his *Leben Jesu*, in which he attacks the Gospels as contradictory. He does not reject religion entirely and in fact he remains a Christian, but he characterizes the Gospels as myths and traces the development of dogma from myth through naive belief, symbolic representation, and the formulation of doctrines to fixed dogma. Like Hegel, he holds, however, that the Gospels are an adequate symbol of the truths of philosophy. What he undermines is the dogmatic authority of the church. Strauss remains an idealist, for he sees the strength of idealism in explaining cultural and spiritual life. But he admits that idealism has difficulty in handling matter and the physical sciences. It is not surprising then that in *The German Ideology*, Marx and Engels criticize Strauss for remaining too idealistic and too religious even in his criticism.

Bruno Bauer (1809-82), a privatdozent at Berlin and later at Bonn University, was a teacher of Marx and had a considerable influence on him in Marx's youth. Bauer's doctrine, referred to as "critical self-consciousness," specifically states that the dialectical process does not end. From this he concludes that there is no definitive truth and that truth is necessarily partial and developing. Bauer thus has an excellent

The Philosophical Background 21

tool to undermine absolutistic and institutional authority. With respect to the Gospels, he continues the work of Strauss. He goes further than Strauss, however, and denies even their symbolic truth. According to Bauer the Gospels were not myth but a fabrication and an invention—a story, he claims, made up initially by St. Mark. His attack on religious institutions was an attack in principle on all dogmatic authority, and this applied to the government as well as to religion. In his thinking Bauer remains an idealist, though it is clear that he rejects the theological implications developed by Hegel. For Bauer ideals are still the most important reality and ideas—not the masses—are what form history. Marx criticizes Bauer most bitterly and sarcastically in *The Holy Family* and argues that ideas alone are insufficient to change history.

Arnold Ruge (1802-80), coeditor for a short period with Marx of the *Deutsch-Französische Jarhbücher* applied the Hegelian dialectic to the practical political order and claimed that if there was to be progress within the state, then the state which occupied the position of thesis must necessarily have an antithesis. This antithesis, he claimed, should take the form of a political opposition, and since its purpose was to bring about progress in the state, such political opposition should be given legal status. His hope was that the resulting synthesis would bring about the rise of a radical political democracy. He envisaged, moreover, that this would take place and would be possible by ordinary political activity. Marx differed from him on the latter two points.

Max Stirner (1806-56), perhaps the most radical of all the Young Hegelians, was opposed to abstractions of any type. He claimed he brought to a conclusion the work begun by Strauss and continued by Bauer. Just as they attacked Christian doctrine as myth and fabrication, so he attacks adherence to any ideal, be it religious or to an ideal of Man, as adherence to an illusion. For Man or moral obligation are as much illusions as is God. Stirner denied adherence to such abstractions and wished to free himself from such illusions as God and Man in order to concentrate on his own personal reality. Marx, ironically, attacks Stirner's notion of the "ego" as itself being an abstraction since Stirner considered it apart from and independent of any relation to its social and economic environment.

The Russian defender of anarchism, Mikhail Bakunin (1814-76), was also associated for a while with the Young Hegelians. He drew revolutionary conclusions from Hegel's dialectic, and he emphasized negation and destruction. But he did so in the name of freedom, seeking harmony through "creative destruction." Though he later translated the Communist *Manifesto* into Russian and began a translation of *Capital*, and though he both influenced and was influenced by Marx, Bakunin and Marx each harshly denounced the tactics and character of the other, and they clashed over leadership of the International Working Men's Association.

Moses Hess (1812-75), the chief theoretician of the German movement called "true Socialism," should also be mentioned here. Though Hess collaborated with Marx and Engels in writing part of *The German Ideology*, he held different positions at different periods of his life. In particular he elaborated a doctrine of extreme communism which was attacked by Marx because of the extreme revolutionary strategy which it advocated.

Of all the Young Hegelians, Ludwig Feuerbach (1804-72) is probably the best known and certainly exerted the greatest philosophical influence on both Marx and Engels. A simplification of the case would be to present their position, which came to be known as "dialectical materialism," as a synthesis arising from Hegel's dialectical idealism and Feuerbach's materialism. It was through Feuerbach's teaching more than through that of any other individual figure that Marx and Engels were able to free themselves from the domination of Hegelian idealism. Moreover, Feuerbach's analysis of the alienation of man from himself in religion foreshadows Marx's analysis of man's alienation from himself in society. To grasp the one is to go a long way toward understanding the other.

Feuerbach vs. Hegel

Ludwig Feuerbach was born in Landshut. He studied theology at the University of Heidelberg and philosophy in Berlin under Hegel for the two years 1824-26. In 1828 he became a privatdozent in philosophy at Erlangen, but he soon gave up teaching and retired to a life of study and writing. His works have been collected in ten volumes. Of these the most important are his *Critique of the Philosophy of Hegel* (1839), in which appear his major criticisms of Hegel, and

The Philosophical Background   23

The Essence of Christianity (1841), which is undoubtedly his most important work and the one which most strongly influenced Marx and Engels. The former is predominantly negative in content; the latter is a positive presentation of Feuerbach's own interpretation of religion.

Feuerbach's attack on Hegel can be summarized under three main headings: (1) he attacks Hegel's starting point, (2) he attacks his theory of perception, and (3) he attacks his notion of the Absolute.

1) Feuerbach argues that Hegel has his whole system in his starting point. For "being" includes all of reality. It is not surprising, therefore, that he is able to deduce all that he does. Furthermore, since Hegel's starting point is an idea—the concept of pure being—he quite consistently ends up with the claim that all of being is a concept. But if this is true, Feuerbach argues, then Hegel does not really *deduce* the Absolute at all, but he merely presupposes it from the very beginning. Where one should begin philosophy, Feuerbach claims, is not with an abstract concept but with what is given us in our actual experience: that is, one should begin with man as he is and as he is experienced.

2) Feuerbach next attacks Hegel's theory of sense perception as a weak point in Hegel's system and one which must be rejected. According to Feuerbach, Hegel begins not with an object which is the real term of our experience, but with the "thought of the other-than-thought," or with the object-as-thought-of. But the object-as-thought-of is not what is given us in our experience. Rather, we experience the object first, and then think it. Feuerbach then shows where Hegel's analysis is defective. Hegel's analysis hinged upon the fact that if we look at any object it will appear as a "this" which is "here" and "now." But "here" and "now" are universal terms, that is, they are capable of application to an unlimited number of instances. All adjectives and common nouns are universals. But since an object is nothing but all its qualities taken together, the object *is* in fact nothing but an intersection of the universals of which it is composed. For Feuerbach, however, universals merely point to existing reality; they do not compose objects. In fact our ability to recognize or pick out universals presupposes sense perception of really existing, independent objects. We must have experienced a "this" and a "that" to be able to distinguish and to compare them. Hegel's

"here" and "there" are not the "here" and "there" that belong to the objects, but rather to the logical "here" and "there" which I attribute to the objects. Thus, Feuerbach tells us in *The Essence of Christianity,* "I differ *toto coelo* from those philosophers who pluck out their eyes that they may see better; for *my* thought I require the senses, especially sight. . . ."[10] For Feuerbach reality *begins* with individuals and nature. Hegel, he says, is unable adequately to explain nature for he is unable to derive it a priori by deduction. From an idea you cannot derive the contingent concrete individuals found in nature. Thus, Hegel's difficulty in accounting for nature should be sufficient evidence that nature is neither derived from nor the result of ideas; rather, ideas are derived from nature.

3) The third prong of Feuerbach's attack on Hegelianism is directed against the Absolute. According to Feuerbach, Hegelianism is "the last refuge, the last rational support of theology." Feuerbach here rejects the concept of the Absolute as that which is ultimately real. Hegel, he claims, has gone somewhat beyond ordinary theology by holding the union of man and of God in the Absolute. The truth of the matter is that God and man are one, but since God for Feuerbach is an abstraction, if man be part of Him man must be an abstraction. This is contrary to our experience, and so Hegel's position must be wrong.

The Essence of Christianity

Feuerbach, then, differs fundamentally with Hegel, and he is often portrayed as being diametrically opposed to him. There can be no doubt that Feuerbach does reject the greater part of Hegelianism, and in this he paves the way for Marx. Yet Feuerbach remains a Hegelian in some important aspects. His notion of alienation remains basically Hegelian; his respect for ideas and ideals is scarcely less strong than Hegel's; and the Hegelian dialectic plays a significant role in his writings.

Feuerbach presents the positive aspects of his thought in *The Essence of Christianity,* which can be considered under the three headings: (1) materialism; (2) anthropology, and (3) humanism.

1) Feuerbach rejects idealism and is a materialist, but he is far from a crude or crass materialist. He goes beyond sensa-

The Philosophical Background 25

tionalism, for he admits the importance of man, of consciousness, and of values. The first tenet of his materialism consists in stating that objects exist independently of mind. An object for him is not something derived from thought but rather *that alone* is an object "which has an existence beyond one's own brain."[11] This doctrine in itself is a statement usually identified with *realism* and by itself does not make him a materialist, though it does place him in opposition to epistemological idealism. A second feature of his materialism is his claim that all knowledge is derived from the senses. And a third feature is his denial of the existence of spiritual beings. Existence, he claims, can be proved only by the senses[12] and therefore a spiritual entity which cannot be sensually perceived is a contradiction. (Unfortunately, he makes no attempt to prove these claims which he takes as self-evident.) These three claims agree with materialism of the crude type. According to Feuerbach, however, crude materialism is unable to explain ideas, spirit, and history. A fourth element is necessary to remedy the defects of earlier materialisms and this tenet is his claim that ideas and ideals exist and are important. He finds these in his experience as man, and he correctly holds that any philosophy is unsatisfactory insofar as it is unable to handle them. But, unfortunately, as Marx later noted, Feuerbach's explanation of history, ideas, and ideals was not materialistic, and his materialism with its exclusive emphasis on sense knowledge was unable to handle them.[13] A rudimentary and inconsistent synthesis is what we find in Feuerbach and to his materialism we might give the name "idealistic materialism."

2) Feuerbach, an avowed materialist, is primarily concerned with explaining the origin and function of religion, and his theme in *The Essence of Christianity* is religion and theology. The former he accepts as containing truth; the latter he rejects as contradictory and false. His analysis of religion and of Christianity in particular ends not in a rejection but in a reversal of religion. His message is "God is Man; Man is God." He humanizes religion and divinizes humanity. For him, true theology is anthropology, and it is to this aspect of his work that we next turn.

Feuerbach analyzes the nature of man and discovers that the attributes of God are also the attributes of man. Consequently, God and man must both be the same. Although he claims that in the religion of his time the appearance of religion has been substituted for religion itself, he nevertheless takes for his analysis the Christ of religion. For Christ is a "product and reflex of the supernatural human mind."[14]

What is religion? In order to answer the question, Feuerbach must determine what man is and what distinguishes him from the brute. What separates the two, Feuerbach claims, is consciousness. Man alone is able to consider his species as an object of thought; man alone can put himself in the place of another; man alone is both an I and a Thou. The ability to do all this is proof of his consciousness. Moreover, man is conscious of the infinite for he can draw no lines to his consciousness. Using an almost Hegelian argument, Feuerbach argues that any attempt to draw a limit to human consciousness puts one beyond the limit; and to have no limit to consciousness is to have infinite consciousness.

Yet certainly man sees himself as limited. If he is limited, with respect to what is he limited? The answer is that he is limited only with respect to what he sees other men are capable of, that is, he is limited with respect to fulfillment of the capabilities of human nature. If man were truly limited, he could not know his limitations. Since he knows his limitations he is able to go beyond them; and the way he is able to go beyond them is by means of his species. If he imagines a being higher than he is, the predicates he attributes to this being must necessarily be drawn from himself. For there is nowhere else he could get them. Since a man cannot get beyond himself, the attributes which he gives to his God are necessarily attributes derived from his own experience. What is God? God is "human nature purified, freed from the limits of the individual man, made objective—i.e., contemplated and revered as another, a distinct being."[15] God is my nature, human nature, freed from the limitations imposed by any individual instance of human nature. Man is the measure of all things; the divine predicates are inexhaustible because human nature is infinitely variable and inexhaustible. God is real; He exists and His qualities are the qualities of man. "Religion is that conception of the nature of the world and of man which is essential to, i.e., identical with, a man's nature."[16] God's attributes are man's attributes. If this be so, Feuerbach goes on, then it must follow that God is human nature.

In support of his claim that God's attributes are man's, Feuerbach analyzes the various attributes that religion claims to give to God. Psychologically, whatever religion denies, it attributes unconsciously to God. If man denies his reason in religion, God becomes all-knowing; if man gives up his personality, God becomes an infinite person. If man is poor, then God is rich. If man is finite, God is infinite; if man is imperfect, God is perfect. If man is temporal, God is eternal. The poorer a man is, the richer is his God. Once we realize that God's predicates are man's, a further proof that the divine nature is the same as man's is that we make the disjunctives finite-infinite, perfect-imperfect, eternal-temporal that we do make. For if God's nature were not the same as man's there would be no basis for these disjunctives.

In theology man disunites or alienates his own attributes from himself. He then sets God before himself as the antithesis of himself, as something alien to himself, before which he bows down—"God is not what man is—man is not what God is."[17] Since man is accustomed to thinking of objects as separate from himself, it is not surprising that when he thinks of human nature, he separates this also from himself, making God an object for him which is independent of himself. But man's great mistake is that in this process of alienation he bows down before a false object, a product of his own nature, which through theology comes to dominate him, restrict him, and to which he becomes subservient. But in seeing this truth he can overcome the alienation.

Man, according to Feuerbach, is love as well as consciousness, and religion has its basis in both an emotional and an intellectual need. These needs explain the origin and purpose of religion. God's highest attribute in the eyes of Christianity is his moral perfection; he is all good. But measured against this law, which is the perfection of humanity, man sees that he is a failure, a sinner. It is only through God as loving that he is saved from condemnation. Man is reconciled to God through love, and the consciousness of this love is the Incarnation. But man's love of God is in actuality love of man. For God to suffer for man is equivalent to a statement that to suffer for others is divine.[18] To love moreover, is to express a need for another, and in religion, man, conscious of himself in his actual or living totality, sees that in order for him to be self-conscious, he must be united as an "I" to a "Thou." Religion thus fulfills man's needs.

Man's notions of the ought and of perfection also come

from his notion of humanity, for "only men taken together are what man should and can be."[19] The race is perfect because the essence of man is one and the infinity of individuals reciprocally compensate for one another. Man's notion of the good is derived from his notion of humanity. His will seeks to do the good. One's fellowman, in fact, is his objective conscience. As with morality, so with truth, each man is for himself only a subjective standard. It is what each thinks in accordance with the standard of the species, in accordance with law as every man must think it, that anything is objectively true or good. "That is true which agrees with the nature of the species."[20] Faith in the future is faith in man. "The beginning, middle and end of religion is MAN."[21] "The end of religion is the welfare, the salvation, the ultimate felicity of man."[22]

3) In his claim that theology is anthropology and in his discussion of the nature of man, Feuerbach's humanism follows as an almost automatic corollary. For man is what deserves man's attention; it is humanity that is infinite; it is humanity that is all good; it is humanity in a word that is God. The true notion of religion has therefore been made manifest, Feuerbach claims, by bringing the knowledge to man that God is human nature.

Man, now freed from theology and from false religion, can devote and dedicate himself not to false abstractions before which he becomes subservient, but to the true God, to humanity, to man.

Marx, as we shall see, places strictures on Feuerbach's thought, but there are strictures other than Marx's which may be mentioned in passing. Feuerbach rejected Hegel's starting point and claimed that we must start with what we are given, with the actually experienced. But his defense of his starting point is as inadequate as he claims Hegel's is, for the concept is given as surely as is the object. Realism is no more self-evident as a starting point than idealism, though it is perhaps more naïve. Either should be the conclusion of an argument and of an analysis of the totality of experience, not the starting point; otherwise, as Feuerbach correctly claims of Hegel, one presupposes the conclusions to be proved. This weakens his general position. Undoubtedly, Feuerbach gives many insights into the psychology of some people's notions of God, and he is certainly correct in stating that our predicates of God are derived from human experience, for there is nowhere else from whence they could come. His consequent claim, however, that therefore God cannot exist independently of man, is valid only if one accepts the view that only material objects exist and that immaterial beings cannot exist. This claim, however, since it is unsupported by Feuerbach, is as dogmatic on his part as many of the premises he says Hegel asserts or presupposes without proof.

It is not on this point however that Marx differs from Feuerbach. Marx agrees with him in rejecting Hegel's idealism, his a priori method in epistemology, and his doctrine of the absolute in metaphysics. Marx accepts to a modified extent Feuerbach's materialistic humanism and also accepts his critique of religion. In the latter he sees a truth that he will develop and expand. Religion, according to Feuerbach, is a result of man's alienation from human nature, and it is the expression of and compensation for a want and a need. Likewise, Marx will say, the state is a result of man's alienation from society, a false projection of his social being.

Marx's "Theses on Feuerbach"

Though Marx took much from Feuerbach and initially depended upon him in his rejection of Hegelianism, he considered Feuerbach's position as a whole unacceptable. Marx's main criticism is given in his eleven "Theses on Feuerbach" and in a joint effort with Engels, *The German Ideology*. His position in the "Theses" can be summarized as follows: (1) Marx attacks Feuerbach's theory of knowledge. Feuerbach and all other materialists, according to Marx, consider objects only insofar as they exist objectively and independently of man. But such treatment of a thing allows for no *activity* on the part of the knowing subject. The value of idealism is that it stresses, though abstractly, the active role of reason in knowledge (Thesis I). If Feuerbach's notion of a thing is correct, how can one really explain man's knowledge? Marx sees this as an essential difficulty unless the mind has some active role to play in the knowing process. (2) Feuerbach, Marx claims, regards man's essential activity as theoretical. He ignores man's practical activities. This is seen both in his notion of truth, which for Feuerbach is theoretical and not practical, and in his analysis of religion. He shows that religion has a secular basis, but he does not take the essential step of advocating means by which this contradiction in society is to be eliminated. Reconceptualization by itself is not enough (Theses I, II, III, VIII). (3) Feuerbach, according to Marx, is much too abstract. He changes the religious essence into the human essence; but this too is an abstraction. Marx argues that one must analyze the reality of social relations in which each individual is bound up, for man is not an abstract essence but a product of, or the ensemble of, social relations. Not civil society but human society must be the object of study. Feuerbach claims that the basis of his philosophy is man, but in fact its basis is the abstraction "MAN." He deals with abstract humanity and not with the actually living man involved in his society, in his means of production, and in his concrete historical and social environment (Theses VI, VII, IX, X). (4) Marx tells us that "philosophers have only interpreted the world." Feuerbach has given us a *reconceptualization* of the world; but Marx goes on, "the point is to *change* it." Exposing man to the origin of religion does not change anything. One must get at the source of man's lack and need, at the source of alienation, and then *change society* if one is really to overcome the alienation that Feuerbach has shown. Thought, reconception, philosophy are secondary to man's physical and economic needs. Interpretation is not enough; action is what is called for (Thesis IV, XI).

Feuerbach's materialism was insufficiently dynamic and too abstract. Both Hegel and Feuerbach had to be corrected and completed, and it is this task which Marx attempts initially to accomplish.

Chapter III
Young Marx: The Forging of a Philosophical Framework

Approach to Marxist Interpretation

The pitfalls of tracing the historical development of Marxism are legion, but, fortunately, for our purposes they are not insurmountable. The numerous varying and contradictory interpretations of Marx's writings all claim with some justification to be based on Marxian texts. This is possible for several reasons: (1) Since the writings of Marx are not systematic, there are many areas, such as ethics, aesthetics, theory of knowledge and so on which are never fully developed, and sometimes not even explicitly touched on. The interpolations which different followers of Marx develop on these questions consequently vary. (2) Even on questions with which Marx dealt specifically there is often room for divergent interpretations, largely because many of Marx's writings—especially his philosophical writings—are polemical, being addressed not to professional philosophers but to a wider intellectual audience, and consequently not always as precise and unambiguous as one would expect in a technical presentation of philosophy. (3) Marx's position developed and was never static. Early in life he was a Hegelian, then he was influenced by Bauer, and was for a short while a Feuerbachian; he developed his own position gradually. Moreover, his emphasis shifts from philosophy to economics. Whether he had evolved his philosophical position sufficiently to use it as a framework for economic research or whether he forsook the one for the other is debated.

there being much diversity of opinion about which works state Marx's "real" or "final" philosophical views. (4) Another reason for diverging interpretations is that many of the early manuscripts of Marx were not available to many Marxists.[1] The *Economic and Philosophic Manuscripts of 1844*, for instance, is an unfinished work first published in part in 1927 and in its entirety only in 1932. Interpretations of Marx's later writings based on knowledge of this work are sometimes different from interpretations which ignore or were unable to take account of it. (5) As certain aspects of Marxism have appealed to some Marxists while different aspects have appealed to others, many differences of interpretation are due to differences of emphasis. (6) Some interpreters who accept much of Marx's writings and claim to be Marxists have felt either that he was mistaken in certain doctrines, which should be corrected or revised, or that his writings should be rethought and his basic insights applied to solving problems of their own times.

Since our aim is to understand Marxism primarily as a source for the development of Marxism-Leninism and for the patterns of present-day Soviet thought we need not completely solve the historical puzzle and search for the "real" Marx. The Soviets tend primarily to interpret the early works in terms of the later ones, using these as the basis of Marxism. They turned their attention to the early works only after other interpreters—such as Lukács (by anticipation) and Marcuse—brought attention to them and used them as the basis for interpreting the later works of Marx. Some of the early writings were unknown to Lenin and played no role in his interpretation or development of Marxism. We shall examine each of Marx's philosophical works in turn and attempt to indicate its impact on Soviet thought.

Another controversy in Marxist literature concerns the relationship of the works of Engels to those of Marx. Engels explicitly discusses the laws of dialectics and applies them to nature—as well as to history—in a way which Marx never does. Some interpreters, consequently, carefully differentiate the writings of Marx from those of Engels and claim that some elements in Engels' works are foreign to Marx and should not be confused with Marxism. Others, however, point out that Marx and Engels were close collaborators throughout their lives and that Engels can be taken—as he tells us—as the interpreter of Marx who added nothing new to the doctrine but merely faithfully presented Marx's own views. For our purposes we should note that both Lenin and the Soviets considered Engels' writings as authoritative as those of Marx. That this causes Soviet philosophers difficulties and, as we shall see, in some instances embarrassment, is beside the point. For an understanding of what the Soviets hold we should keep in mind not only that they accept the works of Engels *in toto* as orthodox Marxism, but also that in questions of philosophy they more frequently quote Engels than Marx, partly because Engels deals with many philosophical questions not explicitly discussed by Marx. In the following chapters we shall accordingly give equal stress to the works of Engels and to those of Marx.

Life and Writings

Karl Marx was born May 5, 1818, in Trier, Prussia. His father was a lawyer who converted to Lutheranism from Judaism. When Karl was about six years old, he and the other children of the family were brought into the Lutheran church and they were raised in a liberal Protestant tradition. Karl Marx attended the local gymnasium in Trier and at the age of seventeen went to the University of Bonn, where he studied law. After a year, however, in 1836 he transferred to the University of Berlin. There he encountered the Young Hegelians. The greatest initial influence on him came perhaps from Gans, his Hegelian professor of jurisprudence. Marx immersed himself in Hegel's writings and emerged his convinced follower.

Marx soon abandoned law for the study of philosophy and planned to become a teacher of philosophy. In Berlin he had become a close associate of Bruno Bauer, who had moved from Berlin to the University of Bonn in 1839, where Marx expected to follow him as a colleague after finishing his studies. Unfortunately, before this became possible, the Minister of Education condemned the work of Bauer, and he was expelled from the university. Marx, who had collaborated with him on a minor work, lost all chance of gaining a position at Bonn. To avoid difficulties with a hostile administration Marx submitted his doctoral dissertation to the University of Jena, from which he received his doctorate in 1841. The title of his dissertation was *The Distinction Between the Democritian and Epicurean Philosophies of Nature*. It is a clearly Hegelian work in the history of philosophy, and in it Marx interprets and defends Epicurus' philosophy as a dialectical advance over that of Democritus. With an academic life closed to him Marx did not publish his dissertation.

All was not lost, however, and Marx was soon invited to contribute to the journal *Rheinische Zeitung*. In October 1842 he became its editor. The journal was censored by the government, and though for a time Marx managed to get most of his material through, he was forced to resign in March 1843. During this period he became involved in practical political studies and recognized the need for the study of political economy. This involvement with the actual world of politics, in addition to reading Feuerbach's writings (*The Essence of Christianity* appeared in 1841, "Preliminary Theses in The Reform of Philosophy" in 1842), enabled Marx to divest himself of his Hegelian idealism.

In 1843 Marx married Jenny von Westphalen, to whom he had been engaged since 1837 despite the protest of many in the girl's family who felt their social status was above that of the Marxes. Financial difficulties and hard times began almost immediately for the couple. In the autumn of 1843 Marx took his young bride to Paris, where he was to publish with Ruge the *Deutsch-französische Jahrbücher*. But the first issue (Feb. 1844) was the only one of this publication to appear. It included two contributions by Marx: "On the Jewish Question," which was a critique of two books by Bruno Bauer, and "Contribution to the Critique of Hegel's *Philosophy of Right*, Introduction." The former is a reduction of religious questions to social ones. The latter does not actually present a criticism of Hegel, but it does enunciate an early version of the revolutionary role of the proletariat which Marx was later to develop.

In Paris Marx steeped himself in the French and British thinkers and made the acquaintance of the works of Quesnay, Adam Smith, Ricardo, and Proudhon. From April to August 1844 Marx completed four manuscripts which were preserved in part and later published as *Economic and Philosophic Manuscripts of 1844*.[2] Though still somewhat Hegelian and Feuerbachian in terminology they mark an important stage in his development and already contain the ingredients of his materialist conception of history. The manuscripts include excerpts from and comments on an impressive number of writings of political economists, Marx's most detailed presenta-

Young Marx 35

tion of the alienation of labor, and a critique of Hegel's *Philosophy of Right*.

It was in Paris in September 1844 that Marx met Friedrich Engels, and from this meeting developed a friendship that was to last for the rest of their lives. Both men found themselves engaged in revolutionary activity; both were dedicated to this work; both had been Hegelians and were reacting against Hegel's philosophy. Engels, who had been collecting material on England's economic and social history, supplied details of actual economic conditions and Marx supplied the theoretical framework he had developed in which to place these details. They collaborated on a number of works including *The Holy Family* (1844) and *The German Ideology* (completed in 1846). In the first the theories of the Bauer brothers —Bruno, Edgar, and Egbert—are attacked. The second not only contains a critique of the Bauers, Ruge, Stirner, and Feuerbach, but it also—and more importantly—gives a developed presentation of the materialist interpretation of history. Marx's "Theses on Feuerbach," later published by Engels, also date from this period. The friendship of Marx and Engels remained close and fruitful throughout their lives. Engels willingly assumed a secondary role as an expounder of Marx's doctrine and throughout his life contributed substantially and continuously toward the support of Marx and his family.

In January 1845 Marx, with other German fugitives, was banished from Paris as a dangerous revolutionary. He moved to Brussels, where Engels joined him. In 1846 Proudhon, a well-known French political economist whom Marx had met in Paris, sent him a copy of his book *The System of Economic Contradictions: The Philosophy of Poverty*. Marx wrote a devastating attack on it entitled *The Poverty of Philosophy* (1847), revealing the insufficiency both of its economic theories and of its pseudo-Hegelianism. Marx also develops his theory of history in his work.

In Brussels Marx and Engels developed and circulated their ideas concerning the laws of history and the inevitable triumph of communism. In January 1847 they were invited to join an organization called the League of the Just, which in the summer of that year was renamed the Communist League. Marx soon became an organizer and leader of this organization and together with Engels was commissioned in December 1847 to write a statement of its aims. The result was the famous

Manifesto of the Communist Party, which appeared in February 1848. Upon its appearance the Belgian government expelled Marx who with his family went to Paris and thence to Cologne, where he edited the *Neue rheinische Zeitung.* It was in this journal that the article "Wage, Labor, and Capital" appeared. This journal, too, was soon suppressed, and Marx issued the last number in red ink. Tried for sedition, he was first acquitted, then expelled from Germany in May 1849.

In August 1849, with many of the capitals of the world closed to him, Marx moved to London where he was to stay until his death. There he spent most of his time pursuing his economic research in the British Museum. Two articles, "The Class Struggles in France 1848-1850" and "The Eighteenth Brumaire of Louis Bonaparte," both of which are analyses of the revolution of the Second Republic and excellent examples of the application of historical materialism to specific historical events, appeared at this time. Although Marx was busy with his research and was carrying on correspondence with Engels and other revolutionaries, he was close to starvation. He was hounded by creditors, he and his family suffered eviction, and within five years three of his children died. That the family survived at all was only because of the money which Engels was able to send them. In 1852 Marx became a part-time correspondent on European affairs for the *New York Tribune.* Though this was to be a source of some revenue for almost ten years it was certainly not enough to live on. His first article for the *Tribune* was to be on the nature of warfare. Since he knew little about it and did not have sufficient command of the English language at the time, Engels wrote the article and signed Marx's name.

In 1859 Marx published *A Contribution to the Critique of Political Economy,* containing some of the main theses of his major work, *Capital.* In 1864 the International Working Men's Association was founded in London (the first International), and Marx was the driving force behind it. He wrote the Inaugural Address and many of the International's declarations and resolutions; he also helped direct the working-class movement in various countries. But internal conflicts developed within the association, and as a tactical move Marx had its headquarters moved to the United States, where it finally dissolved in 1876. In 1867, after many years of painstaking research, Marx finally published the first volume of *Capital,*

Young Marx 37

which uncovers and describes the economic laws, Marx claimed, that capitalist society is built on and that supposedly govern the historical development of classes. Little noticed in England, it was better received in Germany and the rest of continental Europe; it created the greatest stir in Russia.

The international labor movement in Germany fell under the control of Ferdinand Lassalle and his followers; Marxist groups held sway elsewhere. An attempt at reconciliation of the groups at Gotha was made in the form of a program which was submitted to Marx, who severely criticized it in his "Critique of the Gotha Program." The movement grew nonetheless and received impetus from the work of Eugene Dühring, a lecturer in economics at the University of Berlin. Dühring's influence was counteracted by Engel's work, *Anti-Dühring*, which Marx is said to have approved of.

Capital was hotly discussed in Russia, and as a result Marx received a great many inquiries from Russian revolutionaries concerning tactics. In order to reply to these inquiries, Marx devoted himself to learning Russian and in six months was able to carry on a correspondence in it. In answer to questions from the Russian revolutionaries he made some changes in doctrine and agreed that, given Russia's circumstances, communism might possibly develop there without the country's going through a capitalist phase, providing that communism were to spread simultaneously in the rest of Europe.

In 1881 Marx's wife died of cancer; he himself was sick and two years later died peacefully in his armchair. Engels brought out volumes II and III of *Capital*. The manuscripts were in rather poor condition, and on the whole the level of the later volumes is inferior to that of volume I. Karl Kautsky was responsible for volume IV, consisting mainly of posthumous material on related issues. Also published after Marx's death were his "Critique of the Gotha Program," the speech he delivered in English on June 26, 1865, called "Value, Price, and Profit," and four volumes of correspondence between Marx and Engels.

Marx's Doctoral Dissertation

Marx's dissertation, "The Distinction Between the Democritean and Epicurean Philosophies of Nature," is significant not as a contribution to philosophy but as proof of Marx's masterly use of Hegelian dialectics and as evidence of his early conversion to Hegelianism. The dissertation is an attempt to complete a portion of the history of philosophy insufficiently treated by the master. Marx contends that contrary to the common interpretations of Epicurus as merely a follower of Democritus, there is an essential difference between the physics of Epicurus and of Democritus, a difference exemplified in even the smallest details. According to Marx Epicurus dialectically solved the contradictions inherent in Democritus' views. Marx records the details of atoms, void, and the swerve of atoms given by Epicurus and provides a dialectical interpretation. In this study of materialist doctrines, he raised—and solved—some of the problems of materialism which will concern us in the study of Marxism. The primary problem was that of the validity of knowledge. Epicurus' solution, according to Marx, is based on an insight into the activity of consciousness, an activity which Marx had learned to appreciate from Hegel and which he preserved as a distinguishing feature of his own materialism.

Marx tells us that Democritus presents a contradiction concerning the nature of truth which he does not resolve. According to Democritus atoms are the ultimate constituents of reality, but they are unknowable as such. What we perceive, and therefore all that we know, is phenomena or appearances. Consequently, what we know is not real and what is real cannot be known. Likewise, atoms have no qualities and are changeless; but, contradictorily, the world of appearance is saturated with qualities and changes constantly. A good Hegelian does not worry about contradiction, however; he goes beyond it. Epicurus does precisely this, Marx tells us, for he accepts the contradictions of Democritus and rises above them to a synthesis, the details of which need not concern us here. The upshot, however, is that from an empirical point of view atoms make up the phenomenal world which is apprehended by the senses; but atoms considered in their purity, that is, as having no weight, shape, or size, are the object not of empirical but of abstract reason. The final synthesis of the two points of view takes place when material emanations reach a conscious being who sees and unites in himself both worlds and who thus both reflects and overcomes the independence exhibited by nature.

Marx's dialectical prowess, exemplified in his dissertation, remained with him throughout his development, but he was not long in throwing off Hegelian idealism and in turning to the more practical and empirical study of society.

Contribution to the Critique of Hegel's Philosophy of Right

Feuerbach's *The Essence of Christianity* appeared in 1841. In the same year Marx began to write a paragraph by paragraph critical commentary on Hegel's *Philosophy of Right*.[3] Though he decided against completing the work,[4] his notes, comprising more than 150 pages in the MEGA edition, were preserved and first published in 1932. The essence of Marx's criticism is primarily Feuerbachian in that he applies to Hegel's conception of the state and society the same type of attack which Feuerbach applied to religion. Society is prior to the state, he argues, because human beings, not concepts, are the fundamental reality. Ideas do not produce institutions, and insofar as Hegel remains on the level of ideas he illegitimately introduces institutions into his system. In the autumn of 1843 and the early weeks of 1844 Marx wrote his "Introduction" to the unfinished work. This was published in February 1844 in the *Deutsch-französiche Jahrbücher*.

Marx begins his "Introduction" with the statement that for Germany the criticism of religion which consists in showing that man makes religion, not religion man, has been largely completed. States and societies produce religion, an invertedworld consciousness, because they are an inverted world. Religion "is the *opium* of the people,"[5] it is man's illusory happiness, and to abolish it is to demand man's *real* happiness. Now that human self-alienation has been unmasked in its sacred form it must be unmasked in its secular form. The criticism of religion and theology must become criticism of law and politics. Furthermore, criticism must be viewed not as an end but as a means. Since material force can be overthrown only by material force, criticism can become effective only if it is seized by the masses. The criticism of religion ends with the doctrine that man is the supreme being for man. This must be followed by the emancipation of man and by the overthrow of the conditions which lead to man's abasement, abandonment, and enslavement.

From these premises Marx outlines a theory of revolution. Revolutions need both a material base—the people—and a theory which they adopt. But a theory will be adopted by the people only insofar as it fulfills their real needs. Traditionally, only a section of civil society has emancipated itself and in its turn has dominated other sections of society. As a whole, society can be emancipated only when (1) the whole of society is in the same situation as the revolutionary class, that is, only where there are but two classes, the rulers and the ruled, and the ruled revolt as a whole; (2) the aims of the revolutionary class are the aims of society itself, otherwise one section of society would set itself in opposition to another; and (3) the one class concentrates all evils in itself, so that in freeing itself of these evils it frees all mankind of them. The triumph of this class thus becomes the dissolution of all classes and in emancipating itself it emancipates all humanity.

Here is the conceptual, dialectical structure of what is needed to liberate mankind. The sharp dichotomy of two antagonistic classes bears the stamp of a dialectical division; and the equation of one class with all of humanity suggests a Feuerbachian notion of humanity. All three conditions are arrived at seemingly a priori, and whether any concrete meaning can be given to the terms is at best problematic. But this is only half the task. The next step is the practical one of finding the class which embodies these essential traits. Is there a real possibility of emancipation in Germany? Marx's reply is: "A class must be formed which has *radical chains*, . . . a sphere of society which has a universal character because its sufferings are universal. . . ."[6] This class, according to Marx, is the proletariat, which as a result of the industrial movement is beginning to form itself in Germany. Thus, in the struggle for the emancipation of man, philosophy finds its material weapon in the proletariat just as the proletariat finds its intellectual weapon in philosophy.

Whether Marx's judgment that the proletariat could or would bring about the ultimate emancipation of mankind was correct, history alone would tell. But much of Marx's later writings can be read as an attempt to demonstrate that capitalism by its nature will inevitably lead to the creation of a proletariat which fulfills the three above-mentioned criteria and that through a proletarian revolution mankind will be made free. This is the vision that inspires Marx's continued research and leads both to his developed philosophical position and to his painstaking economic investigations.

Young Marx 41

Economic and Philosophic Manuscripts of 1844

The four unfinished and unedited manuscripts were written by Marx from April to August 1844. In recent years they have been one of the most discussed and quoted early works of Marx because they contain the fullest treatment of the concepts of alienation and of man to be found in Marx's writings. Alienation, furthermore, is here linked with revolution, the emancipation of all men, and the rise of communism.

The first three sections of the first manuscript, containing many extracts from the works of Adam Smith, Jean-Baptiste Say, and E. Burat deal primarily with an analysis of labor and capital "based on a conscientious critical study of political economy."[7] Marx's indignation at the level to which the worker has been reduced is clear throughout in such statements as "the worker has become a commodity,"[8] "the worker has sunk to the level of a machine,"[9] and so on. Marx defines the proletarian here as "the man who, being without capital and rent lives purely by labor, and by a one-sided, abstract labor."[10] The fourth section carries the moral indignation of the earlier sections, but the topic rather abruptly changes to a consideration of alienated labor.

Marx claims that political economy presupposes private property, the separation of labor and capital, the division of labor, and so on. But it cannot explain why these exist any more than theology, by asserting man's fall, can explain the origin of evil. Marx starts, therefore, from the fact that the human world decreases in value directly as the world of things increases in value. The more objects the worker creates the poorer his inner world becomes. Just as, according to Feuerbach, man made God an object independent of himself whom he worshipped, so in political economy man makes objects which are separate from himself, objects which are thus alien to himself, but which contain part of himself, part of his reality—the part of him which went into their production. "Alienation" thus becomes for Marx a value word to describe at the same time a basic fact and a basic evil of political economy, since it robs man of his reality, prevents his development and self-expression, and reduces him from a human being to an object or a machine.

Marx distinguishes three different aspects of alienation: the alienation of the worker from the products of his labor, the alienation of the worker from his productive activity, and the alienation of man from his species-life—from nature and other men. Implied in these descriptions are Marx's views of the proper relationship of man to his labor, to nature, and to other men.

The alienation of the worker from the product of his labor takes place when the object of his labor becomes external to him and is no longer an extension or expression of himself. Not only does it exist outside of him but it becomes a power which confronts him as hostile and alien. Moreover, he soon becomes the slave of his object both because the labor saps his strength and because he comes to live for the objects (such as wages) which make it possible for him to live.

The worker is likewise alienated from himself or from his productive activity insofar as he does not develop his mind and body by his labor but stunts his growth, does not affirm himself in his work but denies himself, and does not express his essential being in his labor, which is something external to himself. When a worker's labor is forced, moreover, it is not done, as it ought to be, to satisfy a need. It is not done freely, spontaneously, as an extension of himself. And it is not so done because it is not truly his own labor; it belongs to another. It is not a worker's if he sells it to another and so separates it from himself, selling part of himself to another in a very real sense.

The third aspect of alienation follows from the other two. Man (Marx here follows Feuerbach) differs from other animals because of his consciousness, through which he treats himself as a living species, as a universal and so a free being. As such he sees his unity with his species and he sees nature as his, an extension of himself. But in alienation the free conscious activity, which is the species character of man, is denied, for man produces as man only when he is free from physical need. In forcing his labor, in separating him from the object of his production, alienated labor separates him from nature (his product), separates him from his mental or human life, and so separates him from other men to whom he becomes related by alienation.

Practically speaking, if my life activity and the objects of my labor do not belong to me, they must belong to another; they must be his property, not mine. Private property is both a product of alienated labor and the means by which labor is alienated. To do away with either is to do away with the other. Thus, the emancipation of the worker and of all mankind consists for Marx in ridding man of his alienation, and he sees this as practically possible by ridding the world of private property.

We have here the basis for Marx's indictment of private property—the claim that it is a correlate of alienation, which in his terms is seen to be unnatural at best, evil at worst, and undesirable in all events. Any system built on private property is necessarily built on alienation and is undesirable, unnatural, and immoral. This is the basis for the later condemnation of capitalism. But it should be noted that the necessary relation claimed by Marx between alienation and private property is nowhere shown to be necessary and not accidental and that furthermore the very descriptive terms used in describing alienation are themselves value terms of a negative sort.

From here the jump to communism is a short one.

The second manuscript contains only four pages. In the third manuscript Marx discusses communism and ends with a critique of Hegel. Communism is "the positive expression of annulled private property."[11] Marx distinguishes three forms. The first is crude communism. This consists in universalizing the ownership relation in which the community becomes the universal capitalist and owner of property; the role of the worker is extended to all men, and everything which cannot be possessed by all, such as talent, is eliminated by force.[12] In the second form, still political in nature, the state is not yet abolished, and alienation is not yet completely superseded. Finally, the third form is the positive abolition of private property and of self-alienation and the recapture by man of his true, social nature. Thus, communism becomes a humanism —a theme which the Soviets have recently been emphasizing. Man is only human when he is social man. "The individual is *the social being*."[13]

The appeal of Marx consists in his vision of a society in which man is free to engage in his own creative self-development, in which he dominates objects instead of being dominated by them and relates to his fellow men by a mutual sharing, and in which each delights in the happiness and success of others. Marx's vision has been termed by some a society of artists, by others a heaven on earth. But the appeal is real and corresponds to the actual desires of men; when joined to a concrete plan of action supposedly guaranteed successful by the laws of history, it is not hard to understand its widespread attractiveness. At bottom it presents a moral condemnation of the existing order based on a certain view of what man can and should be.

The last part of the third manuscript is entitled "Critique of the Hegelian Dialectic and Philosophy as a Whole." The fourth manuscript covers the same ground in summary form. The essence of Marx's critique consists of two main points: (1) Hegel deals only with the realm of thought. Consequently, alienation for him is only the alienation of thought; wealth, state, law, and so on are considered only as thought-entities, the alienation of abstract thought. Therefore, insofar as they are superseded in Hegel's system they are not essentially changed. But man's alienation is not only mental but takes place in the physical world and must be overcome not in thought but in activity, by acting in the physical world. (2) For Hegel the essence of man is mind or self-consciousness. But on the contrary man is a corporeal, natural, active being who expresses his life through objects and so has his nature outside himself (though since he is a "species-being" he is also a being for himself).

The influence and terminology of Feuerbach (in such terms as "species-man" are clearly evident; but this work is solidly anti-idealistic. Marx's divorce from Hegel's idealism here becomes complete and he emerges as a thoroughgoing materialist.

The Holy Family

The Holy Family or *The Critique of Critical Critique,* the first joint work of Marx and Engels, was written in the autumn of 1844 and published in 1845. Engels said later that in this book Marx begins replacing Feuerbach's cult of abstract man by the science of real men and their historical development. By far the larger part of the work is written by Marx. The major portion of it consists of polemical attacks on Young Hegelianism and on the mystical elements of idealism still held by those who, unlike Marx and Engels, did not follow Feuerbach into materialism. Largely polemical, the work is full of parody, satire, and ad hominem attacks—a style often taken up by Lenin and some Soviet writers. Its positive elements include Marx's discussion of the role of the masses and of the inevitability of communism and his brief history of French materialism.

In opposition to the "critical critics," Bruno, Edgar, and Egbert Bauer—for whom the masses made up the material, passive, dull, unhistorical element of history and for whom selected individuals were the vehicles of Spirit and so the makers of history—Marx claimed that the masses are the real makers of history. This doctrine was later emphasized by Lenin, who paradoxically seems by his action to have demonstrated just the opposite.

Marx continues to develop the concern for the proletariat which he displayed in the "Contribution to the Critique of Hegel's *Philosophy of Right.*" The proletariat, he tells us, is the abstraction of all humanity and is *necessarily* driven to revolt against all inhumanity. In so doing it will abolish all the inhuman conditions of life summed up in its own situation. Marx here introduces the notion of *necessity* to characterize the proletarian revolt, and henceforth this addition remains part of his view. The proletariat will be forced to revolt not because of what it considers its aim, but because of what it is. While the "critical philosophers" merely reconceive reality in different ways, the workers know the difference between thinking and reality and find themselves unable to think away their practical debasement.

Marx also defends Proudhon's *What is Property?* against distortions by the Bauers, criticizes both Eugene Sue's *The Mysteries of Paris* for its dehumanizing aspects and the critically critical interpretation of it, and unfavorably compares Bauer to Hegel.

In his presentation of the history of French materialism Marx distinguishes two trends. One traces its origin to Descartes and is mechanical materialism which merges with natural science. The other goes back to Locke and leads to socialism, which in the practical field represents materialism. The two are united and since they emphasize man and matter they lead to humanism. Since interest is the principle of all morality, man's private interests must be made to coincide with public interests and the antisocial sources of crime must be destroyed. To the extent that this is what communism aims at, it is a humanism which finds its logical basis in materialism. The themes both of humanism and of the coincidence of individual and social interests have in recent years been revived and emphasized in the Soviet Union.

Marx's "Theses on Feuerbach" (1845) make explicit Marx's criticism of Feuerbach's abstract notion of man already evident in this joint venture with Engels.[14]

The German Ideology

In *The German Ideology*, written by Marx and Engels and completed by the summer of 1846, we find the first clear and positive statement of *the materialist interpretation of history* and of the interrelationship among man's economic, political, and intellectual activities. It also represents the final effort on the part of Marx and Engels to free themselves from the influence of Feuerbach, Stirner, and the so-called true socialists. The work is divided into three parts: I, Feuerbach; II, the Leipzig Concilium (concerning Bauer and Stirner); and III, True Socialism.

Part II consists of a critique of Bauer and Stirner, referred to as the "saints" who judge Feuerbach a heretic. Both Bauer and Stirner are satirized, the latter being referred to as "Sancho Panza" and "Jacques Le Bonhomme." The critique in this section parallels that of *The Holy Family*. Part III analyzes the tenets of the "True Socialists"—Hess, Grün, and Kuhlmann, among others—and their idealistic solutions come up for special criticism. Part I, despite its title is not primarily a critique of Feuerbach but a positive presentation of Marx and Engels' approach to the analysis of the history of human society, and it is on this that we shall concentrate.

Marx and Engels begin *The German Ideology* by pointing out that man creates false conceptions of himself and of what he thinks he ought to be and that he arranges these conceptions in the form of God, the normal man, and so on. These ideas then become his masters, and the creators bow to their creatures. This is true of Feuerbach, Bauer, and Stirner, all of whom shadowbox with ideas and stop at uncloaking what they consider to be false ideas. German criticism as a whole, however, has never left the realm of philosophy and has never examined its premises. The Young Hegelians tried to free men of their illusions by reinterpreting reality, but none had thus far looked into the relation of German philosophy with Ger-

Young Marx 47

man material reality. This task Marx and Engels propose for themselves in this work.

The premises from which they begin, they tell us, "are not arbitrary ones, not dogmas, but real premises from which abstraction can only be made in the imagination. They are the real individuals, their activity and the material conditions under which they live, both those which they find already existing and those produced by their activity. These premises can thus be verified in a purely empirical way."[15] Their realistic and materialistic orientation is clear. Since things, however, cannot be premises, Marx and Engels state the first premise of all human history, namely, that living human individuals exist. What they wish to examine is the physical organization of these individuals and their consequent relation to the rest of nature.

Man distinguishes himself from other animals when he begins to produce his means of sustenance. The way men do this depends on their physical organization and the materials that they find. "As individuals express their life, so they are."[16] This is to say that what men are depends on what and how they produce—on the conditions determining their production.

One of the facts about man is that he interacts with other men; according to Marx the form of this interaction is determined by production. This is likewise true of nations; in examining a nation's internal structure we see that it depends upon the stage of development which that nation has reached. In turn the stage of development is indicated by the degree of division of labor. This division consists in the separation of industrial and commercial enterprises from agricultural labor and eventually the separation of the commercial from industrial labor. There are, in addition, divisions within these branches.

The different stages of development in the division of labor, moreover, are correlative to different forms of ownership, the earliest of which is tribal ownership. This is characteristic of an undeveloped stage of production in which hunting, fishing, and later, agriculture predominate. In this first form of ownership social structure is an extension of the family and the type of government is a patriarchy. The second form of ownership is ancient communal and state ownership. This results when several tribes join to form a union. Private property develops, though it is still subordinate to communal ownership. In this stage, power is exercised over slaves communally; there exists an antagonism of town and country, later developing into an antagonism between town-states and country-states, between industry and commerce. In the second type of ownership, Marx and Engels placed Rome, which in their eyes "never became more than a city." The third type is feudal or estate property. The Middle Ages started from the country. The sparse population was spread over a wide area, and an enserfed peasantry with a nobility in control characterized the period. Later, towns, corporate property, and guilds developed.

In all cases the social structure and the state evolve out of the life processes of individuals and are related to what they produce. Thinking, consciousness, and ideas are interwoven with the physical activity and life of individuals. Similarly, laws, morality, politics, religion, metaphysics, and the like are also interwoven with the physical activity and life of individuals and cannot properly be understood in separation from them. Consciousness "can never be anything else than conscious existence, and the existence of men is their actual life-process."[17] In order to understand ideas, one must start from real men and not from ideas. "Life is not determined by consciousness, but consciousness by life."[18]

With this basis, Marx and Engels are in a position to discuss history. History, they claim, is neither a collection of dead facts (as it seems to be in the hands of the empiricists) nor an imagined activity of the imagined subjects (as it seems to be in the hands of the idealists), but a process of development under definite conditions. Without attempting a complete enumeration of all the premises to be used in the development of history, they do point out four necessary premises. The first is "men must be in a position to live in order to be able to 'make history.' "[19] Men must have food, drink, shelter, clothing, and so on, and they must produce in order to satisfy these needs. Though the English and French had written histories of commerce and industry, such concerns were alien to German philosophers of history. The second premise is that as soon as needs are satisfied, new needs spring up. The third is that men beget other men. There are relationships of man and wife, parents and children. The family is the first social relationship, though it is later subordinated. The fourth and last premise is that a certain mode of production is always combined with a certain mode of cooperation (social stage) and that this mode of cooperation is a "productive force." Society is a result of the totality of productive forces available to man.

But what of the *ideas* of men and of the part that ideas have played in history? For Marx and Engels language is practical consciousness, and both language and consciousness arise from the need to communicate with other men. Consciousness is thus a relationship and a social product. At first consciousness is purely animal, consisting merely in awareness of alien nature. The initial consciousness is a herd consciousness; indeed, the only difference between man's instinct and that of a sheep is that man's instinct is conscious. Man's consciousness, however, developed with his increased needs and with the natural division of labor that took place as a result of varying dispositions among men, such as differences in strength and needs, accidental differences of time and place. In time consciousness emacipated itself from the world, and pure theories were formed which came to be called by such names as "philosophy" and "morality." From this "we get only the one inference that these three moments, the forces of production, the state of society, and consciousness, can and must come into contradiction with one another"[20] because the division of labor makes intellectual and physical activity fall on different individuals. Those more intellectually oriented express the limitations within which the modes of production of a given period and place move. Division of labor yields unequal distribution of labor and products, and as a result we have property. The division of labor and private property, Marx and Engels tell us, are identical.[21]

The division of labor implies a contradiction between private and social interests, and the latter takes independent form as the *state*. In actuality, struggles within the state (as for instance between democracy and aristocracy) are illusory forms of class struggles.

Individuals seek their own interest and the communal interest is "alien" to them. This estrangement of private and communal interest can be abolished, however, given certain practical premises. These are noteworthy as being the prerequisites for a communist revolution. First, conditions must become intolerable so as to demand a revolution against exist-

ing conditions by the mass of humanity. This is produced when
the mass of humanity is propertyless, although wealth and
culture are being produced in the world. The former is necessary for revolt, the latter to preserve humanity from want and
from the beginning of a new cycle. Second, the development of
productive forces must be such as to make man a world-historical being—actions in one part of the world, for instance
the invention of a machine in England, having worldwide
consequences, for instance the creation of a proletariat in
India. This world-historical condition is necessary if communism is to be a worldwide and not merely a local development,
with the resulting danger that each extension of action would
abolish local communism.

Communism is not considered simply an ideal, for Marx
and Engels "call communism the *real* movement which abolishes the present state of things."[22] Civil society, moreover,
is "the form of intercourse determined by the existing productive forces at all previous historical stages, and in its turn
determining these."[23]

This "materialist interpretation of history" asserts essentially that economic (Marx and Engels use the word "material") production and the interaction created thereby are the
basic determining forces of history. These forces are the foundation for the state, and on the basis of economic production
and interaction all theoretical forms of consciousness, religion,
philosophy, etc., are explained. Consequently, the products of
consciousness cannot themselves be dissolved by merely
mental criticism but require a change or the overthrow of the
social relations which give rise to them. A mistake of former
historians has been to describe history in terms of political
action on the part of princes, generals, or statesmen and to
concern themselves with these men and their actions and
times. If, however, history and commerce, production and
exchange of the necessities of life themselves determine distribution and consequently the structure of the different social
classes, then the view of former historians is erroneous. Marx
and Engels tell us:

> History is nothing but the succession of separate generations,
> each of which exploits the materials, the forms of capital,
> the productive forces handed down to it by all preceding
> ones, and thus on the one hand continues the traditional ac-

Young Marx 51

tivity in completely changed circumstances and, on the other, modifies the old circumstances with a completely changed activity.[24]

History becomes world history the more the isolation of nationalities is destroyed through the development of modes of production and intercourse. In any given age the ideas of the ruling class prevail, and these "are nothing more than the ideal expression of the dominant material relationships, the dominant material relationships grasped as ideas. . . ."[25] The existence of revolutionary ideas in any given society presupposes the existence of the revolutionary class. Each new class puts itself in the place of the old and represents its own interests as those of society. The mistake of the idealist historians has been to take every age at its word and to believe what it says about itself. It separates the ideas from the conditions of these ideas; it links the ideas and personifies them. The idealist historians are able to give a plausible interpretation of history because the ideas are in fact linked. The ideas are not results, the one of the other, but are the reflections of the economic conditions of the society, and these conditions change from period to period. Each successive change is reflected in a change of ideas. The idealist theories make out their case, therefore, by linking together that which is linked not necessarily but accidentally.

The theory that the economic condition of the society determines the society is then used by Marx and Engels in explaining actual history. The greatest division of labor was between town and country, a division which still exists as a result of private property. Next came the separation of production and commerce and the formation of the merchant class, which led to a division of production between individual towns. This was followed by the rise of associations, and common conditions led to class conditions and the battle of one class against another. As manufacturers next developed, the bourgeoisie was protected by tariffs and the like, eventually resulting in the development of the proletariat. "The State is the form in which the individuals of a ruling class assert their common interests, and in which the whole civil society of an epoch is epitomized."[26] As these institutions receive political form, civil law develops.

The conclusions drawn by Marx and Engels in this interpretation of history are: (1) In the development of productive forces there comes a stage when destructive forces are called in and with them a class from which emanates the consciousness of the necessity of the revolution. (2) The revolution is against the class which has been in power, that is, against the state. (3) The communist revolution will be the dissolution of all classes. And (4) the communist consciousness is possible only when an alteration of man takes place on a mass scale, that is, by a revolution.

It must be remembered that this is an early statement of the Marxist conception of history.[27] The details are not worked out and merely an outline is presented. This is not the proper place, therefore, to discuss the validity of the doctrine presented here. We merely point out that the argument is not closely knit, that the conclusions are not completely substantiated by the body of the work, that the premises, since they are not self-evident, require some justification; and that a certain vagueness and lack of precision marks the definition of some of the key terms.

Basic Patterns and Beliefs

With *The German Ideology* Marx had for all essential purposes completed the philosophical framework in which he was to work for the rest of his life. He had not formulated his position in a vacuum or out of nothing. Working within the intellectual world of his time he took what he considered true from his predecessors and contemporaries, especially from Hegel and Feuerbach. He developed his own position vis-a-vis both of these thinkers and reinforced his own position by criticizing what he considered their errors. He tempered the philosophical framework which he forged by using it to criticize—as well as to satirize—the Left-Hegelians, the true socialists, and other random opponents.

We can thus enunciate certain patterns of Marx's thought —categories used in framing problems, certain ways of approaching, facing, and solving problems, and certain beliefs which he held and never relinquished. These patterns, categories, and beliefs are for the most part still present and current in contemporary Soviet thought.

First and foremost Marx's philosophic framework is "materialistic" where this means (a) that objects exist outside of mind and are not dependent on it; (b) that consciousness depends on matter for its existence (consciousness is determined by life, not life by consciousness); (c) that therefore there can be no purely spiritual entities, such as God, angels, or disembodied spirits; and (d) that the only correct approach to practical problems is through an analysis of actually existing entities and conditions (ideas, institutions, etc., are the result of the given economic conditions of any given time). To materialism we then add dialectics, interpreted materialistically. This means that (a) man is active not passive in his knowing and doing; (b) he is dynamically interrelated with other men and with nature and that apart from them he has no real existence; and (c) human reality is permeated with antagonisms or contradictions which provide the motive force for change and progress.

To these basic notions several others can be added, such as, essentially, Marx's vision of man and the reality of his plight. Man, for Marx, is the aggregate of social relations. He can and should be free to develop his natural capabilities, but he is in fact unable to develop freely. He is dominated by goods instead of dominating them; he is alienated or separated from the products of his labor, from himself, from other men, and from nature. The mass of men are close to being reduced to things, to machines. A search for the explanation of these inhuman conditions and a practical approach to their solution yield additional categories.

Marx sees his contemporary society as divided into two antagonistic classes, the capitalist class and the class of the proletariat. The proletariat and its aims are moreover identified with humanity and the aims of humanity. Man's alienation, man's inhumanity to man, the plight of the proletariat, however, can be understood only by analyzing the actual conditions which give rise to them. The ultimately determining factors which Marx uncovers are the division of labor and private property, which are basically identified. The means of freeing man to be what he should be is to free the proletariat from an inhuman situation. This can only be done by changing the economic base of society—by doing away with private property, the division of labor, and alienation. This change can only come, according to Marx, through a revolution of the proletariat. In the resulting situation there will be no private property, no division of labor, no alienation, and consequently man will be free to develop as he should. To this resultant condition Marx gives the name "communism."

That these statements were believed by Marx and that they are believed by Marxist-Leninists is what is essential to remember if we are to understand how they think. That they are unproven in Marx's early works we should remember if we are to remain critical. That there are variations of interpretation with respect to almost each statement we should not forget if we are to follow the development of Marxism up to the present day.

Armed with this philosophical framework, Marx consistently turns to the study of political economy. If, as the Marxist conception of history asserts, the economic conditions of society determine ideas, then the criticism of ideas is less fruitful than changing the economic conditions of society. But to change conditions it is necessary to understand them. Marx consequently turns to the study of political economy in order to understand the movement and development of society and to uncover the laws which determine that development. Given these views it is also understandable that he would try to prove the necessity and inevitability of communism in terms of any laws he might uncover from an analysis of the conditions of the age in which he lived. Thus we turn briefly with Marx to political economy.

Chapter IV
Marx and Political Economy

The Poverty of Philosophy
The Poverty of Philosophy, written by Marx during the winter of 1846-47, was published in July 1847. The title is suggestive of Marx's attitude towards idealistic philosophy, though the book is actually a critique of Proudhon's *The Philosophy of Poverty*. Marx had admired Proudhon's earlier work *What is Property?* He had met Proudhon in Paris in 1844 and in the course of lengthy debates had "infected him to his great injury with Hegelianism."[1] As a result of their discussions Proudhon, shortly before publishing this second work, wrote to Marx about it saying, "I await the lash of your criticism." It fell upon him, Marx tells us, in a fashion which ended their friendship forever.[2]

The book is interesting for the light it throws on Marx's approach to economics. Proudhon's mistake, according to Marx, is that in his attempt to present economic categories dialectically he treats them as if they were eternal ideas. Proudhon, like Hegel, puts things upside down. Economic categories are theoretical expressions of the social relations of production. These relations are provided by men and are the result of productive forces. In acquiring new productive forces men change their mode of production. In so doing they change their social relations. However, though productive forces are developed by men historically, men are not free to choose their productive forces. For each generation takes over the productive relations of previous generations and can at best modify them before passing them on to the next generation. There is, however, continual movement and growth, for all that exists exists by movement.[8] The movement of history produces changing social relations, industrial movement yields industrial products, and so on.

According to Marx's analysis feudalistic production and bourgeois production are both based on antagonism. In bourgeois society the production of bourgeois wealth leads to the poverty of the proletariat. When this antagonism develops sufficiently, Marx claims, it will assume a political character. A theoretician who does not see the material conditions necessary for emancipating the proletariat is a utopian system-maker. One who sees what is happening and becomes its mouthpiece proclaims *science*.

The introduction of the notion of science is extremely important, for it is science in this sense that Marx pursues, and it is in this sense of science that the results of his study are accepted and propagated up to the present time. Because his writings are presented as scientific they are accepted by many, much as the results of physics or chemistry are accepted. But it should be noted that this use of the word "science" is not ordinary in English. "Science," as it is popularly used in English, refers to the physical sciences in which repeatable experiments are made under strict controls. Marx's use is not restricted in this way and requires neither repeatable experiments nor control, for it consists primarily in describing what is actually happening. Its meaning is closer to our use of the word "knowledge," when this is accurate and objective.

What is clear to Marx is that the antagonism of the bourgeoisie and of the proletariat is the struggle of class against class. The means of resolving the antagonism and of emancipating the proletariat is revolt. The study of history is the study of productive relations; the study of the class struggle is the study of productive relations; and the study of the means of emancipating the proletariat is the study of productive relations. The study of productive relations, however, is the science of economics. So armed, Marx is in a position to proclaim in the *Manifesto of the Communist Party* what he sees happening, and so to become the mouthpiece of reality. In so doing he does science. He then continues the scientific search into what is happening and reports it in his economic writings.

The Communist Manifesto

In December 1847, at the second general congress of an international association of workers called the Communist League, Marx and Engels were commissioned to draw up a detailed theoretical and practical program for it. The result was the Communist *Manifesto*, in which Marx and Engels set forth their views on the class struggle, the revolution of the proletariat, and the eventual triumph of communism. The basis from which they proceed is the materialist interpretation of history dialectically conceived. The first draft of the *Manifesto*, written by Engels in question and answer form, was revised by Marx in the form in which it was published. The German version appeared in February 1848 and was quickly followed by a French version; an English translation appeared in 1850 and a Russian translation by Bakunin in 1869.[4]

The *Manifesto* is the public proclamation of the aims and program of the working class movement of communism, which demanded a radical reconstruction of society. Its fundamental proposition, as summarized by Engels, is the following:

> That in every historical epoch, the prevailing mode of economic production and exchange and the social organization necessarily following from it, form the basis upon which is built up, and from which alone can be explained, the political and intellectual history of that epoch; that consequently the whole history of mankind (since the dissolution of primitive tribal society, holding land in common ownership) has been a history of class struggles, contests between exploiting and exploited, ruling and oppressed classes; that the history of these class struggles forms a series of evolutions in which, nowadays, a stage has been reached where the exploited and oppressed class—the proletariat—cannot attain its emancipation from the sway of the exploiting and ruling class—the bourgeoisie—without, at the same time, and once and for all, emancipating society at large from all exploitation, oppression, class distinctions, and class struggles.[5]

The document has as its basis the materialist interpretation of history, which is here, of course, but summarily stated. Marx and Engels envisage the triumph of communism as ensuing from the development of the working class, which would result from united action and discussion. The union and revolution of workers would follow once they had had pointed out to them their actual condition, the direction of history, and the concrete action they were to take. The *Manifesto*, which attempts to do this, is divided into four main headings: I. Bourgeois and Proletarians; II. Proletarians and Communists; III. Socialist and Communist Literature; and IV. Position of the Communists in Relation to the Various Existing Opposition Parties.

The Communist *Manifesto* repeats much that we have already seen, but it does clarify somewhat the notion of class struggle and especially the doctrine of the proletariat; it elucidates to some extent the meaning of "communism"; it makes explicit the relativistic aspect of the Marxist conception of history; and it emphasizes the revolutionary portion of Marxism. It is action and not words that are important, and as a call to revolution the *Manifesto* is a moving document which has a certain crescendo to it. It also raises certain questions which will be of interest to our discussion of communist thought.

In Section I we find the definitions of "bourgeoisie" and "proletariat." The bourgeoisie is "the class of modern Capitalists, owners of the means of social production and employers of wage-labor."[6] The proletariat is "the class of modern wage-laborers who, having no means of production of their own, are reduced to selling their labor-power in order to live."[7] The distinctive feature of the class struggle in Marx's epoch, we are told, is that class antagonisms have been simplified into two great camps—that of the bourgeoisie and the proletariat. The former exercise over the latter a naked, shameless, brutal exploitation. But in order to exist the bourgeoisie must revolutionize the instruments of production; it thereby revolutionizes the relations of production, and with these, all the relations of society. The bourgeoisie needs constantly expanding markets all over the globe and so it produces more goods than society (composed in great part of the proletariat) can purchase. It is thus led to enforced destruction, to the conquest of new markets, and to more thorough exploitation of old ones. All this leads to more extensive and destructive crises, and eventually to the downfall of the bourgeoisie itself. The weapons for its destruction will be wielded by the class it has called into existence—the proletariat or modern working class. The lowest strata of the middle class is constantly sinking to the level of the proletariat and being absorbed by it; but eventually the workers will form combinations or trade unions, and, in fact, there is already, Marx and Engels point out, an ever-expanding union of workers. "The proletarian movement is the self-conscious, independent movement of the immense majority, in the interests of the immense majority."[8] The bourgeoisie is, therefore, producing its own grave diggers; its fall is inevitable, and the victory of the proletariat is equally inevitable.

In Section II concerning the proletarians and the communists we find something of communism itself. The interests of the communists coincide with those of the proletariat as a whole. Communism is international, independent of nationality. Communists are the most advanced section of the working class parties of every country, and their immediate common aim is conquest of political power by the proletariat. Though their distinguishing feature is the abolition of bourgeois private property (which has already been done away with for the proletariat), this does not mean the abolition of the personal appropriation of the products of labor or of *personal* property as such.

The stated hope of communism is the abolition of bourgeois individuality, bourgeois independence, and bourgeois freedom (where freedom means freedom to buy and sell). Marx and Engels say: "But don't wrangle with us so long as you apply, to our intended abolition of bourgeois property, the standard of your bourgeois notions of freedom, culture, law, etc. Your very ideas are but the outgrowth of the conditions of your bourgeois production and bourgeois property, just as your jurisprudence is but the will of your class made into a law for all, a will, whose essential characteristic and direction are determined by the economic conditions of existence of your class."[9] The technique of analysis here is to view any counter claims and counter ideals as the expression of class interests resulting from the economic conditions of capitalism. The relativism inherent in the Marxist position becomes apparent here, for to the extent that ideas and ideals are the results of economic conditions they are relative to those conditions and lose their validity as the conditions change. The word "freedom" has no meaning apart from a given human context, and it is the meaning in context that Marx and Engels wish to consider. They wish to abolish the bourgeois family which entails exploitation of children by parents, to rescue education from the influence of the ruling class of the bourgeoisie, to do away with the status of women as mere instruments of production, to abolish prostitution, to abolish nationalities for the proletarians have none, to abolish the hostilities among nations, and to do away with bourgeois religion, philosophy, and morality. In general they wish to sweep away conditions which produce class antagonisms and to abolish all classes. On the positive side, they desire to centralize the instruments of production in the hands of the state —the "state" being the proletariat organized as the ruling class. They wish to increase the total productive forces as rapidly as possible and to establish an association in which "the free development of each is the condition for the free development of all."[10] They wish, finally, to support every revolutionary movement against the existing social and political order.

After discussing various forms of socialism, the *Manifesto* concludes: "The Communists disdain to conceal their views and aims. They openly declare that their ends can be attained only by the forcible overthrow of all existing social conditions. Let the ruling classes tremble at a Communistic revolution. The proletarians have nothing to lose but their chains. They have a world to win. WORKING MEN OF ALL COUNTRIES, UNITE!"[11]

The Communist *Manifesto* is without doubt a strong and revolutionary document. It contains, however, a number of hidden premises and presuppositions which it is well to bring to light, and it raises questions, some of which are dealt with in the development of Marxism-Leninism. It is clearly moral in tone in criticizing bourgeois society and in describing the truly pitiable plight of the factory worker in the middle of the nineteenth century. But its criticism and the ideals it presents presuppose a concept of man and of what he can be, as well as certain value judgments which indicate what he should be. We have already seen something of the concept of man and of what he should be in Marx's earlier works. These are presupposed in the *Manifesto*. The following question arises, however: If bourgeois values and bourgeois society are attacked as reflecting existing conditions and the ruling class, do not the values implied in the *Manifesto* likewise reflect existing conditions and another (perhaps the working) class? If this is so, why do proletarian values have more validity than bourgeois values? How are the proletarian values themselves justified? The answers to these questions are not given in the

Manifesto, but part of the reply implied is that Marx and communist leaders see how history will inevitably develop and their value judgments are based on insight into the newly developing conditions of society. Their judgments are consequently those of the future whereas bourgeois judgments are those of the dying past. It is thus that Marx and Engels serve as an instrument of self-consciousness for the proletariat, just as Hegel served as an instrument of self-consciousness for the Absolute Spirit. This line of interpretation in its turn presupposes (1) that insofar as ideas or ideals are the expression of developing reality they are to be accepted; (2) that any given set of ideals, insofar as it reflects existing conditions, is acceptable only to the extent that those conditions remain unchanged. On these grounds, however, the *Manifesto* itself, since it reflects the conditions in Europe in 1848, remains valid only as long as those conditions remain the same; but as these change, the values enunciated by the *Manifesto* also change. The extent to which Marx would be willing to accept the relativity of the *Manifesto* is open to speculation, though he could maintain his position consistently only by so doing.

Later Marxists seem to hold that the values expressed in the *Manifesto* are not relative but are such as will remain valid (1) because the values of the *Manifesto* are the values of the proletariat. Proletarian values, they claim, represent the aims of mankind and so represent the aims of all men in the future classless society. They therefore will remain valid as long as the classless society remains. (2) These values are the values of an economic situation characterized by an absence of antagonisms. Thus, while the future society will develop, it will not change essentially; and so the values enunciated by the *Manifesto* will not change essentially. Crucial to these arguments are: the justification of the equation of the aims of the proletariat with those of mankind, proof that a classless society will inevitably appear and remain, proof that a society characterized by an absence of antagonisms will develop, and proof that the values enunciated in the *Manifesto* will coincide with those which express the developing reality of the future nonantagonistic society.

The notion of man which is presupposed faces the same difficulty of interpretation, for it is also a product of the material conditions in which Marx lived and so relative to his time. It is noteworthy that the humanism implied in the *Manifesto* is a class humanism concerned with classes rather than individuals and that it requires a violent overthrow and abolition of a portion of humanity, namely, the class of the bourgeoisie. To be consistent it must be admitted either that it is a humanism inhumanely arrived at with respect to the bourgeoisie or else that humanism becomes humanism only when man becomes man, that is, only in the future when a worldwide communistic system is established.

In the Soviet period these questions have to some extent been left open to limited discussion and interpretation. Soviet thinkers reject any bourgeois criticism of Marx as unfounded because all such criticism is merely a reflection of the vested interests of the bourgeoisie. But, as we shall see, the Soviets have not yet satisfactorily solved the dilemma of the relative and nonrelative facets of value judgments and of the place of ideals in a world of facts.

If value judgments are all relative, then Marx's are also; if some value judgments are not relative, if some exceptions are allowed, then one can ask what sort of check or what sort of proof one has that any stated judgment is not relative. The secret of proving that any particular judgment is insight into the necessary development of history as opposed to mere reflection of one's class prejudices must be disclosed. Undoubtedly, the best retreat is to claim that criticism in philosophy does not really make any difference, but only action does. The only difficulty is that this, too, is a claim.

Before leaving the *Manifesto* it is interesting to note that in the Preface to the Russian edition of 1882 Marx and Engels answer the question of whether Russia, where more than half the land was owned in common by the peasants, could pass directly to communism or whether it would have to pass through the intermediate bourgeois forms: "The only answer to that possible today is this: If the Russian Revolution becomes the signal for a proletarian revolution in the West, so that both complement each other, the present Russian common ownership of land may serve as the starting-point for a communist development."[12] Since the revolution took place in Russia but not in the West, either Marx and Engels were mistaken, or the Russian revolution will not lead to communism in Marx and Engels' sense, or the simultaneity of the Russian and Western revolutions must be interpreted as being within the same hundred or two hundred or more years. The

Marx and Political Economy 63

claimed necessity for continuing revolutionary activity in the West seems to support the third interpretation.

The Critique of Political Economy

Marx's mature writings and his major work, *Capital*, have to do with political economy—with the theoretical analysis of modern bourgeois society.[13] We are now in a position to inquire into his analysis. Our aim in this section will not be to present Marx's notions of political economy, but to seek the method behind his analysis and to see the role dialectics plays in it.

Though *Capital* presents the fullest and most complete of Marx's analyses of political economy, it is not his only nor his first work on the subject. In April 1849 Marx published a series of articles based on lectures he had given at the German Workers' Society in Brussels in December 1847. They appeared later in pamphlet form under the title *Wage, Labor and Capital*. In 1859 Marx published *A Contribution to the Critique of Political Economy* which presented the first portion of his economic analysis, the substance of which he summarized in the first three chapters of *Capital*. The first and only volume of *Capital* published in his lifetime appeared in 1867. In it Marx analyzes the capitalist mode of production, and its conditions of production and exchange. Though England is used as the chief illustration, the analysis, Marx claims, applies to capitalist production as such, and to "natural laws" —those "tendencies working with iron necessity towards inevitable results."[14] Marx presented a popular summary of his research in an address to the General Council of the International Working Men's Association in June 1865. It is known under the title *Wages, Price and Profit*.[15]

In the Afterword to the second German edition of the first volume of *Capital*, Marx states that the method employed in *Capital* had been little understood and that the various conceptions formed of it had often been contradictory. This is not surprising, for the method employed in *Capital* and the other politico-economic writings of Marx is not always easy to grasp in reading the works themselves. Lenin's comment that one cannot understand *Capital* without having read all of Hegel's *Logic* is to the point. In the Afterword Marx himself tells us something about his method. He emphasizes that it is dialectical, but as it is materialistic and not idealistic it is directly opposed to Hegel's method. The dialectical method nevertheless consists essentially in recognizing the negation and inevitable breaking up of the existing state of things. Its use implies that in analyzing a given state of affairs one should look for the contradictions within it, the direction in which the dynamic of the situation is developing, and the resolution toward which it is going. In applying the dialectic to economics, Marx says:

> The contradictions inherent in the movement of capitalist society impress themselves upon the practical bourgeois most strikingly in changes of the periodic cycle, through which modern industry runs, and whose crowning point is the universal crisis. That crisis is once again approaching, although as yet but in its preliminary stages; and by the universality of its theatre and the intensity of its action it will drum dialectics even into the heads of the mushroom-upstarts of the new, holy Prusso-German empire.[16]

In the periodic cyclical changes, evident in capitalistic societies, Marx sees the working of the dialectic in history. His task as a political economist is to uncover the contradictions causing these changes and to chart the laws of their activity. Thus, in the Preface to *Capital* Marx tells us: "It is the ultimate aim of this work to lay bare the economic law of motion of modern society."[17]

The first volume of *Capital* is the continuation of *A Contribution to the Critique of Political Economy* and in the Preface to this work Marx outlines the basic position which he carries over into *Capital*. It is a summary statement of the materialist interpretation of history. Legal relations and forms of the state have their root in economic conditions of life. The study of the economic conditions of life therefore serve as the guiding thread of Marx's study. In the social production of their life, men enter into various relations and the relations of production correspond to a definite stage of development of their productive forces. These forces constitute the economic *base* or foundation of society, and on this base or foundation the *superstructure*—the legal and political, philosophical, religious, and similar areas of social life—arises. The mode of production of material life influences the superstructure since it is not the consciousness of men that determines their being, but rather it is their social being that determines their con-

Marx and Political Economy 65

sciousness. Eventually, productive forces come into conflict with the existing relations of production and there begins an epoch of social revolution. With the change of the economic foundation, there is a resulting change in the superstructure.

Since the relationship of base to superstructure is central some light can be thrown on the exact relationship by turning to the letter of Engels to J. Bloch of September 21-22, 1890. In this letter, as well as in others, Engels insists that "according to the materialist conception of history, the *ultimately* determining element in history is the production and the reproduction of real life. More than this neither Marx nor I have ever asserted. Hence if somebody twists this into saying that the economic element is the *only* determining one, he transforms that proposition into a meaningless, abstract, senseless phrase. The economic situation is the basis, but the various elements of the superstructure: political forms of the class struggle and its results . . . also exercise their influence upon the course of the historical struggles and in many cases preponderate in determining their *form*. There is an interaction of all these elements in which, amid all the endless host of accidents . . . the economic movement finally asserts itself as necessary."[18] The economic conditions are the ultimate decisive and ultimately determining ones, and it is these conditions of society which Marx analyzes.

A brief quotation from the first volume of *Capital* shows how the terminology of dialectics is applied in economic analysis:

> The capitalist mode of appropriation, the result of the capitalist mode of production, produces capitalist private property. This is the first negation of individual private property, as founded on the labor of the proprietor. But capitalist production begets, with the inexorability of a law of Nature, its own negation. It is the negation of negation. This does not re-establish private property for the producer, but gives him individual property based on the acquisitions of the capitalist era: i.e., on co-operation and the possession in common of the land and of the means of production.[19]

Individual private property which produces its negation or antithesis, capitalist private property, is here given as a thesis. This negation is in turn negated, necessarily producing individual property based on the acquisitions of the capitalist era.

This is the resulting synthesis. The use of dialectics comes out clearly in the terms "negation of the negation," "contradiction," etc., which abound in Marx's politico-economic analysis. Both dialectics and the materialist interpretation of history are presupposed and employed throughout Marx's economic writings.

Engels in an article on Marx's *A Contribution to the Critique of Political Economy* quite accurately outlines the method of Marx's analysis. It is possible to carry on a criticism or an analysis of economics in two ways: either logically or historically. History provides a guiding thread in a continuous process, but history zigzags. Therefore, for clarity, the logical method (which is an historical method divested of historical form and disturbing fortuities) is somewhat preferable. This method must of necessity begin with the same things with which history begins, and its course must be a reflection of the historical course in an abstract and theoretically consistent form. In this method, one proceeds from the first and simplest relation which historically confronts us. Since what we begin with is an economic relation, this implies two sides which are related to each other, which in turn lead to a consideration of their interaction and so to the contradictions between them. These demand a solution. Since the method is historical, history has already provided the solution, and we know the new relation established as a result of the solution. This, in turn, develops its opposite and so on.

Political economy begins with commodities. This means that it begins from the moment products are exchanged for one another. An object is a commodity precisely because it is a relation between two persons, a producer and a consumer. Whereas former economists, especially the bourgeois economist, dealt not with persons but only with things, Marx's analysis shows that economics should really deal with the relation between persons and ultimately between classes. However, these relations, which are attached to things, appear as things. Marx, we are told, was the first to make this discovery and apply it to all economics. With respect to commodities, we can consider them from various aspects, and two points of view from which they present themselves to us are "use value" and "exchange value." Commodities are presented as the immediate unity of both in the form in which they enter the process of exchange. A number of contradictions arise here, and their solution is that the property representing the ex-

Marx and Political Economy 67

change value of all commodities is transferred to one special commodity—money. Money can be considered as a measure of value or price and as a means of circulation. The unity of both of these is found in real money. In its turn, money passes into capital. From this brief summary, one sees the dialectical movement, the antagonisms or contradictions inherent at each stage of economic analysis and the resulting syntheses or solutions. Though the method is logical in its development, it requires historical illustration and constant contact with reality. For these relations are not merely abstract but are claimed to have developed historically. Engels claims that these historical illustration are "proofs" of the correctness of Marx's economic theory, and that these proofs are introduced in great variety.

Marx brought to his economic analysis great sympathy for the truly wretched plight of the factory worker in his day and a vision—which we have seen—of what man can and should be. Part of Marx's method includes the documentation of the level to which the laborer had been reduced. Marx makes no explicit ethical judgment about these conditions. But anyone with any sensitivity could not help but be appalled at the conditions he reports and feel the moral overtones which infuse his descriptions. Marx's moral presuppositions and his view of man color and influence the presentation of his material and thus should also be mentioned in discussing his method.

Capital

In *Capital* Marx aimed at laying bare the economic law of motion of modern society. Without attempting a complete presentation of what takes place in *Capital*, we may summarize the main categories of volume I to help us understand the Marxian condemnation of capitalism. Marx starts from the notion of a commodity, which is any object outside of us which satisfies human wants. The common property of all commodities is that they are products of labor. If commodities are to be exchanged there must be some way of comparing their value, and this can only be done in terms of that which they all have in common, namely, labor. The labor-time required to produce a commodity must be homogeneous if commodities are to be compared. Each unit must be the same. This is achieved by considering as the basic unit the average, socially necessary time required to produce a commodity under normal conditions and with average skill. Furthermore, for comparison, skilled labor must be reduced in varying proportions to a common standard of unskilled, simple labor. A commodity has value, then, according to Marx, because it is a crystallization of social labor. The value of a commodity is determined by the amount of simple social labor time fixed in it. For instance, oil in the ground is valueless until someone finds it, brings it to the surface, and processes it for use. The amount of labor that goes into finding it, drilling for it, refining it, etc., is what determines its value. Moreover, the value of any given commodity is represented directly by the time of labor employed in its production and is inversely proportional to the productive powers of the labor employed. Machines, for instance, are capable of producing a great many products very much more quickly than they could be produced by hand. Consequently, the products so produced can be sold cheaper and are worth less than products produced by hand. The material used for the expression of the value of commodities which becomes the universal measure of value is *money*.[20] The *price* of any commodity is the monetary expression of its value or of the labor realized in it.[21] Men appropriate the products of other men's labor by alienating the products of their own labor.

Money which begets money is capital. Starting from the fact that capitalists increase the value of their capital through exchange, Marx inquires how this is possible. In general, he claims, profit must come from selling commodities at their real value. We cannot say that profit is made by overcharging or by deceiving the buyer, for if this were the case, what one would gain as a seller one would lose as a buyer. Where then does the capitalist's profit, or the surplus value of the commodity, come from?

Marx's solution is that one commodity is not sold at its real value. This commodity is labor power. As with all other commodities, the value of labor power is determined by the labor time needed for its production. In this case it is equal to the labor time necessary to produce the means of subsistence for the laborer and his family. The means of subsistence for the laborer consists of what is necessary and sufficient to keep him alive and to enable him to raise his children, who will be future laborers. The means of subsistence required by the laborer for one day might embody only half a day's labor; but this does not prevent the worker from working the whole day. Consequently, if he is paid a subsistence wage (equal to one half day's labor) but actually works a full day (and so produces value equal to a full day's labor), he produces more value than he receives in wages. The difference, according to Marx, is the source of surplus value or of the capitalist's profit. Likewise, if a laborer is hired by the week he may produce the equivalent of his means of subsistence by three days of work. But the capitalist has bought a whole week's work. The three extra days labor represents surplus labor on the part of the worker and surplus value for the capitalist. This surplus labor is unpaid labor, and the value produced by it is the source of the share of the capitalist class. Marx tells us that the oppressed class always performed unpaid labor whether they were slaves, serfs, or laborers. Clearly, a moral element arises here for one man, a capitalist, is taking something from another man, the worker, without paying him for it.[22] This is basically the inherent evil of capitalism.

Capitalists obviously are interested in as long a working day as possible in order that they may get a maximum of surplus value. The workers, however, fight for rest and time for themselves—for fewer hours. One of the fundamental struggles between capital and labor is over the determination of the length of the working day; another concerns the amount of wages. Marx describes this struggle at length, illustrating "the greed for surplus labor," examining the legal (and very low) limits to exploitation existing in England at that time, and so on. His presentation is a documental account of atrocious conditions which he often depicts in moral tones:

> The capitalistic mode of production (essentially the production of surplus-value, the absorption of surplus-labor) produces thus, with the extension of the working-day, not only the deterioration of human labor-power by robbing it of its normal, moral and physical, conditions of development and function. It produces also the premature exhaustion and death of this labor-power itself. It extends the laborer's time of production during a given period by shortening his actual lifetime.[23]

Since women can be hired for less than men, whenever possible this is done by the capitalist, for it increases his profit. In like manner child labor is used to replace woman labor wherever possible, for it is cheaper still. Thus, to the initial crime of robbery we have increasing exploitation and inhumanity toward labor fostered by the very nature of capitalism.

The use of women and children became possible when machinery dispensed with the need for muscle power. Moreover, in a family where all are employed the amount necessary to keep the family alive remains the same as when only the father was working; but an employer can get the labor of all the members of the family and pay them all at rates such that the total of their wages is but little more than the wage paid to the father alone in previous times. The workingman in a sense, is forced to become a slave dealer, selling his wife and children.[24] As machines are perfected, more and more workers are displaced by them, greatly increasing the ranks of the proletariat. Eventually, because of growing number of reserves in labor pools, the capitalist is able to obtain laborers at a rate even below the amount necessary for them to obtain the minimum means of subsistence. The greater the social wealth produced, the greater the industrial reserve army. But the greater this army in proportion to the active labor army, the greater is the mass of surplus population existing in misery. With the increase in misery there is also the growth of the revolt of the working class, which sounds the knell of capitalist private property.

Capital is not only an economic study but also a social protest. It decries the evils of the conditions of the working man and condemns capitalism as immoral in its very essence. Its moral condemnation, however, stands or falls with the labor theory of value, which has been rejected as inadequate by most Western economists, though still followed—with modifications—in Soviet analyses of capitalism. *Capital* is not itself an overtly revolutionary work; yet for all but the deaf it sounds the call to revolution. It is ironic that the call was heard and followed not in the capitalist countries of the West, such as England or Germany, concerning whose conditions Marx wrote, but in the comparatively backward, primarily agrarian country of Russia where Marx did not foresee the possibility of successful independent revolution. The very success of the Russian revolution tends to disprove the Marxist laws governing the development of capitalism and the rise of communism. Either this, or the revolution Marx predicted is still to come, and the Russian revolution is only incorrectly called Marxist and will not lead to a Marxian kind of communism.

Critique of the Gotha Program

In 1875 the two German workers' organizations, the Social-Democratic Workers' Party and the General Association of German Workers joined to form the German Socialist Worker's Party. The union was marked by a joint Program, published in February and adopted with only minor changes in May 1875. Prior to the Unity Congress at Gotha in May, Marx commented on the Program and dissociated himself from it. His remarks are extremely illuminating and important, especially his distinction between socialism and communism and the role of the proletariat in the transitional period following capitalism.

Marx's comments begin with a clarification of his position on the source of wealth. He underlines his view that not only labor but nature also is a source of wealth. This is consistent with his position in *Capital*. Consequently, he goes on, someone who has no property other than his labor power is forced to sell it because, without raw material on which to work, his labor power is useless. He is dependent upon the owners of the material conditions of labor—the capitalists—for work. He can work only with their permission, and so can live only with their permission—a slave, a wage slave, of the capitalists. In Marx's eyes this is another reason why capitalism is inherently immoral. And here also is the basis for the insistent Soviet claim that in the USSR the right to work is guaranteed to all and unemployment is nonexistent. If the means of production are owned by all, then everyone possesses not only his own labor power but also (at least in some sense and theoretically) the means of production. He is thus not dependent on any individual owner of the means of production for work and for his life. That he remains a slave of the state in conditions in which the state is the owner of the means of production seems equally clear from Marx's position, however, and should be kept in mind in analyzing present-day existing conditions.

In his "Critique of the Gotha Program" Marx turns his attention briefly to the actual emergence of communism from capitalism. His brief but seminal remarks are the basis for Lenin's elaboration and for the present-day position with respect to the development of socialism and communism. In emerging from a capitalist society Marx points out that the new communist society *a fortiori* carries with it the stamp of its predecessor. Its economic, moral, and intellectual birthmarks cannot disappear immediately following the revolution, but will fade away only gradually.

There are, consequently, two phases in the development of communism from capitalism. The first is a transitionary period, more correctly termed "socialism." The second is a higher phase correctly called "communism" as such. In the first phase the remnants of capitalism still exist and society will function according to the principle: *from each according to his ability, to each according to his work.* There will be inequality and some will have more, others less. But such inequality is a result of the inherited economic conditions. In this stage the division of labor remains, as does the antithesis between mental and physical labor. This transition period will also be marked by a politically transitional period in which the state will still exist though it will be *the revolutionary dictatorship of the proletariat.* An explanation of this is unfortunately not given by Marx, and it is left to be interpreted by those who came after him. The Soviet Union at present claims to be in the first or socialistic phase of development.

The second, the truly communistic phase, of communism will arrive when the economic structure of society has developed sufficiently to do away completely with the division of labor and the antithesis between physical and mental labor. Labor will have become not only a means of life but a prime want, wealth will flow more abundantly, and the productive forces as well as the all-round development of the individual will have been increased. The remnants of bourgeois society will have vanished, and society will operate according to the principle: *From each according to his ability, to each according to his need.*

This is the communist ideal, sketched by Marx in one paragraph of his "Critique." He had painted the evils of capitalism in great detail. One can only wish that he had used more paint in describing communism.

Mature Marxism

The most important and influential writings of the mature Marx were economic and not philosophical. *Capital* had the greatest impact, and Marx's reputation stands significantly on this work, the importance of which can scarcely be overestimated. He voiced a carefully documented protest against the pitiable situation of the working class, and his works were a

Marx and Political Economy 73

force in producing the ameliorations which later took place. He emphasized empirical historical studies, set the example for writing economic histories, and was a leader of the labor movement. He claimed to have uncovered the laws of capitalism and of its necessary development.

Marx's followers accepted his writings to various degrees. Some took the spirit of his work, some adopted certain parts and adapted or rejected others, still others accepted everything written by Marx as true and proven. It is worthwhile, before leaving Marx's writings, to inquire briefly into what Marx did prove in his writings. This is not to deny Marx's originality or importance, attested by his contributions to Western thought, economics, philosophy of history, and the labor movement. But because of claims made by his followers we should see what is proven in mature Marxism, those works published by Marx after 1847, which were known and influential during the second half of the nineteenth as well as during the twentieth century.

1) Dialectics, the concept of man and what he ought to be, the materialistic interpretation of history, the equation of the aims of the proletariat with those of humanity were all presupposed by Marx before he began *Capital* and his other economic works. We saw that they were not proved in his earlier works. Marx's economic analysis cannot prove these basic claims precisely because they are the presuppositions of his analysis. At best his later works which utilize them show that his presuppositions are descriptively useful.

2) The truth of the statement that the superstructure of society is ultimately determined by the economic conditions of that society is, as it stands, not strictly speaking provable. First, it is not clear precisely what it means. How are "economic" conditions determined and how are they intelligibly kept separate from labor laws, ethical concepts, and the like, with which Marx seems to admit they interact? That the superstructure changes as the base changes is something of a tautology, for society as a whole seems to change and develop. But that the one determines the other is something else. For instance, labor laws in the United States often have been passed under the influence of lobbying on the part of labor unions. Marx would be hard pressed to explain such legislation, which represents and safeguards labor, since according to his

thesis laws should represent the interests of the ruling class. These laws, moreover, certainly affect the economic base.

Second, if the above argument is rejected, then it seems the thesis that the base determines the superstructure is not open to verification, for if any instances which tend to disprove it are dismissed as being irrelevant, then its truth or falsehood cannot be tested. But if it cannot be tested it is strictly speaking neither true nor false. Furthermore, since it purports to be descriptive of actual empirical life it follows that if it cannot be tested empirically it is meaningless or unintelligible on the empirical level. The law of gravity, for instance, can be tested in the sense that we know that if it is true then bodies fall at the rate of $\frac{1}{2} gt^2$. We can then drop something and see if it does fall at that rate. Its meaning is given in the test. But if there were no way of verifying it, even in principle, we could not claim it to be true or false or even meaningful. If the theory of the relationship between superstructure and base does have meaning, then it can be shown to be wanting, for similar economic conditions result in different types of government, laws, and philosophy—as the histories of Europe and of America clearly illustrate.

3) The laws of capitalism which Marx uncovers must be falsifiable, if they are meaningful. But capitalism has not developed according to the supposed laws which Marx describes. The lot of the working class has not become worse but very significantly better; the standard of living in capitalist countries has risen, not fallen; abuses such as child labor have been done away with by law; progressive income tax has controlled the profit of the owners of production, and so on. If it is claimed that these are only temporary measures and that the laws will eventually work out, then the laws are neither falsifiable nor verifiable at the present time, and one may have to wait an eternity to see if they hold. Yet Marx certainly attempted to describe the direction in which capitalism was developing. He did uncover certain tendencies and may even be said to have described the capitalism of his time. But he failed to see that capitalism could be changed and modified in ways other than by the revolution of the proletariat. It was in fact changed by these other ways; and in part the very changes were due to Marx's graphic presentation of the intolerable conditions of the capitalism of his era. Thus, the inevitable revolt of the proletariat did not take place in Eng-

land, Germany, or the United States, where it should have occurred according to Marx. So-called communist revolutions have taken place in the USSR and China, primarily agricultural economies where, according to Marx, they could not be successful.

4) Marx pays insufficient attention to certain factors which altered the capitalism he describes. Armed with dialectics he interprets all economic interests antagonistically and fails to realize the role of cooperation in the development of society. Compromise, collective bargaining, and the like are not considered by him at all, and yet since Marx's time it is by these means that the antagonisms between capital and labor have often been resolved. In like manner he considers the state only as a repressive instrument wielded by the ruling class for its own interest and does not see that the state can also represent the interests of labor and protect its interest by laws. He never considers a truly representative government because of his preconception that the state is a tool of the ruling class and because he sees dialectical opposition everywhere. His picture of society in terms of black and white may have been an accurate portrayal of conditions at his time, but the rise of the middle classes has turned much of the area he describes into a gray which he did not foresee might be the synthesis of these opposites of black and white.

5) Finally, it seems fitting to remark that Marx considered himself more of a scientist than a prophet, yet his work is interpreted prophetically by many of his followers. He presupposes that private property is the basis of man's alienation and that once this is removed man will live in a society in which all will develop freely. However, he nowhere demonstrates that private property is the only nor even the essential source of man's alienation, nor does he prove that if it is done away with all men will be able to develop freely. The free development of all is certainly an appealing ideal toward which many people would strive. But that it automatically follows the abolition of private property can certainly be challenged and is challenged with respect to conditions in the Soviet Union, for instance, where private ownership of the means of production has been done away with but where many, if not most, men, according to Western standards, do not enjoy full freedom of self-development. As to the future state of communism, Marx, not being a prophet, says very

little indeed. He talks of it primarily in negative terms of "lack of private property" and the "absence of antagonism," but he enunciates very little about its positive content.

As a result, though Marx's importance is not to be underestimated, claims of his having proved any given proposition should be carefully scrutinized. Too often such claims are equivalent to the simple statement that Marx said or believed the proposition in question.

Chapter V
Engels and Marxist Theory

The Place of Engels

Engels' role in the development of Marxism is central, for he was Marx's closest friend, his collaborator on many works, and the most important expounder of Marx's thought. He edited the second and third volumes of *Capital*, and he wrote a great many prefaces to and summaries of Marx's works. He wrote his own major works well after the publication of *Capital*, and he claims very little credit for the Marxian approach to history and philosophy. In *Ludwig Feuerbach* he says:

> I cannot deny that both before and during my forty years' collaboration with Marx I had a certain independent share in laying the foundations, and more particularly in elaborating the theory. But the greater part of its leading basic principles, particularly in the realm of economics and history, and, above all, its final, clear formulation, belong to Marx. What I contributed—at any rate with the exception of a few special studies—Marx could very well have done without me. What Marx accomplished I would not have achieved. Marx stood higher, saw further, and took a wider and quicker view than all the rest of us. Marx was a genius; we others were at best talented.[1]

Likewise in *Anti-Dühring*, the most systematic presentation of the Marxist views in philosophy, political economy, and socialism, Engels assures us that his own contribution to the theory presented is insignificant.

Whether Engels is to be taken at his word is debatable. It seems quite certain that Engels describes his role accurately with respect to the basic tenets of the Marxist conception of history, to the main elements of the critique of political economy, and to the major portion of scientific socialism. Engels, however, presents scientific socialism in more detail than Marx did, and the question has been raised whether Marx did agree or would have agreed with Engels' presentation in its entirety. More importantly still, while Marx never presented any developed position with respect to the philosophy of nature, Engels does; while Marx concerned himself with history, economics, and society, Engels attempted to present a total world view in which all of reality was interpreted from a dialectical perspective. He thus developed what has become known as dialectical materialism. There is ground for holding Marx believed that everything—nature and thought, as well as history and society—developed dialectically. But whether his interpretation and presentation of how the dialectic develops in nature and how it is exemplified in the natural sciences, in mathematics, and in thought, would have coincided with that of Engels cannot be definitely determined. If, indeed, Marx was a genius and Engels at best talented, perhaps Marx's presentation would have been less controversial than that of Engels.

In any event Lenin and the Soviets following him have accepted all of the works of Engels as completely authoritative statements of Marxism. Lenin claims that "it is impossible to understand Marxism and to propound it fully without taking into account all the works of Engels."[2]

It is important to realize that in present day Soviet thought Engels' works play at least as large a role as do Marx's. Moreover, since Marx's early writings in philosophy were not known until after the Russian revolution, it is the writings of Engels which most profoundly influenced Lenin and the Soviets in philosophical questions. It is not surprising, therefore, that in the Soviet Union today Engels is more often quoted than Marx and that Engels' writings are more often referred to with respect to philosophical questions.

Life and Writings

Frederick Engels (1820-95) was born in Barmen, Prussia. He studied at the gymnasium, but before finishing he was forced to enter a commercial house as a clerk. Interested in studies, he educated himself and became a follower of Hegel. Like Marx, however, he studied the writings of Hegel only later to reject idealism and under the influence of Feuerbach to embrace materialism. In 1842 he settled in Manchester, where he entered a commercial house of which his father, a manufacturer, was a shareholder. Here he acquired first-hand contact with the pitiable conditions of the working class. Moved toward socialism by his experience, he was led to study and expose the plight of the workers in his book *The Condition of the Working Class in England* (1845).

In 1844 on his way back to Germany, Engels met Marx in Paris. As we have seen, an immediate, close, and lasting friendship developed. Together they coauthored *The Holy Family, The German Ideology,* and the *Manifesto of the Communist Party*. Like Marx, Engels was exiled from Brussels. He went to Cologne, fled to London via Switzerland, and finally became a clerk again in Manchester. He helped support Marx (who then lived in London) and corresponded almost daily with him. In 1870 Engels himself moved to London.

After his retirement Engels turned to the study of mathematics and natural science. He was prevailed upon by friends to answer the writings of Eugene Dühring, a reformer of socialism who threatened to split the German Social-Democratic Party. Engels' reply to Dühring appeared in the form of articles under the title *Herr Eugen Dühring's Revolution in Science,* known popularly, as *Anti-Dühring*. Published in a complete edition in 1878, the book is composed of three parts, dealing in turn with philosophy (including discussions of the natural sciences and of dialectics), political economy, and socialism. It contains not only an answer to Dühring, but presents the fullest and most systematic exposition of Marxism which we have from the pens of Marx and Engels.

During the years 1878-82 Engels worked on a book, *Dialectics of Nature,* which he never finished and which was first published in 1925. In it Engels devotes himself to expounding the three laws of dialectics and to applying them to the physical world and the physical sciences. He defends dialectics not only as a technique of description but also as a method to be employed in all scientific disciplines.

In 1886, three years after Marx's death, Engels was asked to review a book on Feuerbach. He seized the opportunity to present a "comprehensive, connected account" of his and of Marx's relation to Hegel, Feuerbach, and the Left Hegelians, as well as to present a concise statement of dialectics and the materialist interpretation of history. This short work is known by the title *Ludwig Feuerbach and the End of Classical German Philosophy*.

These three works contain Engels' major statements and contributions to philosophy. Also influential is a small work of his entitled *The Origin of the Family, Private Property and the State* (1884), in which he attempts to trace the origin and development of these institutions on the basis of a historical study of developing economic conditions. It unfortunately leans heavily on the writings of Lewis Morgan, whose work on the customs of the American Indian has not stood up to further research on the subject. The work thus exemplifies both the technique and the pitfalls of utilizing the Marxist approach to history in tracing the development of social institutions. Among his other numerous articles "The Housing Question" (1872-73—a defense of the claim that the evils of capitalism cannot be solved piecemeal and that for their solution capitalism must give way to communism) and "On Social Relations in Russia" (1875) can be singled out for their influence on Lenin and the Russian Marxists.

Throughout his life Engels subordinated his own interests to those of Marx. Likewise, after Marx's death Engels devoted an enormous amount of time preparing and publishing volumes II (1885) and III (1894) of *Capital*, which Marx had left in rough form. He also wrote prefaces to new editions of the Communist *Manifesto, Capital,* and other of Marx's works. Just as together with Marx he had been a leader in the International Working Men's Association, so after Marx's death he remained a leader and counselor of the international labor movement and of various European socialist parties. He was regarded as the most authoritative interpreter of Marx and, as noted, his influence on Soviet thought rivals, and in some fields surpasses, that of Marx himself.

Anti-Dühring

Anti-Dühring was originally written by Engels in 1877. Dühring, a teacher at Berlin University, propounded a reform of socialist doctrine. He had a substantial following in Germany which threatened to split the recently reunited socialist parties. He presented a complete system of philosophy, economics, and sociology, and Engels was called upon to reply to his system. After some time he agreed, and he tells us: "The systematic comprehensiveness of my opponent gave me the opportunity of developing, in opposition to him, and in a more connected form than had previously been done, the views held by Marx and myself on this great variety of subjects."[3] Engels claims to speak for both himself and Marx, who wrote one of the book's chapters on political economy and to whom Engels read the complete manuscript. The book is divided into an Introduction and three parts, entitled "Philosophy," "Political Economy," and "Socialism." Three chapters of this original work were made into a separate pamphlet in 1880, and a separate special introduction to the English edition was added in 1892. The separate pamphlet appeared under the title *Socialism: Utopian and Scientific*.[4]

In the Preface to the work, Engels tells us that after he retired from Manchester to London he spent the better part of eight years studying mathematics and natural science in order to convince himself that the same dialectical laws of motion in these areas maintained as those which in history govern the apparent fortuitousness of events. He claims that dialectics is derived from nature, that it is found there, and that the advance of theoretical natural science must bring the dialectical processes of nature even to the consciousness of the empiricists opposed to it. This application of dialectics to nature is worked out by Engels. Whether Marx would have said the same or substantially the same things if he had written on dialects in nature is a moot point. In *Capital* Marx did mention in passing that nature developed dialectically.[5] That the development of the dialectic in natural science is Engels', however, is fairly clear from his letter of May 30, 1873. In this he briefly outlines his ideas and ends with the request that, if Marx thinks there is something in his ideas, he refrain from talking about them lest some "Britisher" steal them.[6]

German philosophy culminated in Hegel. His basic insight, according to Engels, was that everything moves, changes, comes into being, and passes away. This actually was the return to an insight of the Greeks, for instance, of Heraclitus, but had been lost in the intervening centuries. Though the view of the whole was seen in a sense by Hegel, Engels tells us that the details of the whole must still be explained, and that this task can only be successfully filled by natural science and historical research.

For Engels, dialectics comprehends things in their essential connection and motion. "Nature is the proof of dialectics,"[7] and modern science furnishes this proof. Furthermore, if knowledge is the reflection of the universe, then, if the universe is in flux, true knowledge must be obtained by the dialectical method, which follows the motion actually taking place in nature.

Hegel found the method, Engels tells us, but he erred in claiming to have found the essence of absolute truth, for any system which claims to be absolutely true is final, complete, finished—and contradictory to the fundamental law of dialectical reasoning. Man's knowledge of the universe increases from age to age. Indeed, for Engels, modern materialism is dialectics and needs no philosophy standing above the sciences. The positive science of nature and history embraces all philosophy except the science of thought and its laws, namely, formal logic and dialectics.

I. *Philosophy.* Turning to Engels' analysis of Dühring's philosophy, we shall concern ourselves not with Dühring, a minor and forgotten figure, but with the positive statements Engels makes in answering the systematic statements of Herr Dühring.

Man is a product of nature, and man's thoughts and consciousness, since they are products of the human brain, are also products of nature. Not only can they not contradict nature, but they in fact reflect it. Consequently, the positive sciences, which make up our systematic knowledge, can never be complete. Moreover, "each mental image of the world system is and remains in actual fact limited, objectively by the historic conditions and subjectively by the physical and mental constitution of its originator."[8]

Engels' analysis begins with a study of mathematics in order to show that all knowledge is fundamentally empirical. It is his claim that while mathematics is independent of the particular experience of an individual it does not deal with an individual's own creations and imaginations. Rather, mathematics is basically derived from nature. The idea of number and the idea of figure are borrowed from the external world. The laws of mathematics eventually become divorced from the real world and seem to be something independent. (We have already seen this taking place in law and religion.) Because mathematics is originally derived from the external world, however, it can once again be applied to the real world. Lines, planes, angles are all taken from reality. In addition to what we receive from reality, there are two axioms, Engels tells us, borrowed from logic: (1) the whole is greater than the part (which is a tautology), and (2) if two quantities are equal to a third, they are equal to each other. Furthermore, just as mathematics begins with the actual world, so all the axioms of philosophy also begin with the actual world. Having established this principle, he is ready to show the defects of Dühring's system.

The technique of argument which Engels very frequently uses against Dühring consists of showing that Dühring's position leads necessarily to idealism, that is, to some notion of God or of creation. Since Engels feels that he has already shown that God does not exist and that creation is an impossibility (these are postulates of his materialism), once he has reduced Dühring to idealism he need go no further.

II. *World Schematism.* This section concerns the unity and being of the world. In opposition to Dühring's a priori method of dealing with the world and the unity of being, derived from the notion of being, Engels argues that one must start with what one is given. For Engels, the being of the world is certainly a necessary precondition for its unity; but its unity consists not in some notion such as being, but rather in its materiality, which he claims is proven "by a long and wearisome development of philosophy and natural science."[9] Likewise, we must go to experience to see how this unity expresses itself. When we are confronted with objects, we see that although they are all material, yet they exist separately. Some objects are white, others black. Some objects are animate, others inanimate, and so on. These differences must be found from experience. They cannot be deduced from any idea. Consequently, what we derive from an idea a priori does not necessarily pertain to the actual world, and the only way to find out about the actual world is to go to it and start from it.

III. *Natural Philosophy.* This consideration leads to a discussion of *natural philosophy, time, and space.* Dühring, from an analysis of the infinity of cause and effect claimed that the world must have had a beginning in time and that the number of bodies in the world must be finite. He says, "All

84   PATTERNS OF SOVIET THOUGHT

actual division has always a definite limit, and must have it if the contradiction of the counted uncountable is to be avoided."[10] At any given time in the universe there must be as many bodies as there are, and consequently, these bodies must be finite in number. Engels challenges this assertion, first, by attacking Dühring's notion of infinity as being the "uncounted uncountable." Second, Engels raises the question, "What was there before the beginning of time?" Dühring's answer is that the universe was in an unchanging state in some sense outside of time. Engels argues that this position is absurd, for certainly there is some notion of duration in which the universe must have been, even if it was in an unchanging state. More importantly, it raises the problem of how this unchanging state started changing. Clearly, Engels points out, some initial impulse is necessary, some prime mover, and, consequently, some notion of God. Since God, he has claimed, does not exist, and since the notion of God is necessitated by the notion of a finite universe, Engels holds that Dühring is wrong and that time and space must be infinite. This position is still defended in Soviet thought.

IV. *Cosmogony, Physics, and Chemistry.* There have been many theories about how the present world came into existence. The one that Engels opts for is the Kantian theory of the origin of all celestial bodies from rotating nebular masses. In this discussion we are led to raise the question of the relationship between matter and motion. Engels tells us, *"Motion is the mode of existence of matter."*[11] Matter and motion necessarily go together. Celestial bodies, molecules, atoms, organic life, all can be understood only when in motion; and without motion, there is no matter. Rest is only relative motion. "Matter without motion is just as inconceivable as motion without matter."[12] Both are, therefore, uncreatable and indestructible, and motion can only be transferred. In the appendix to *Anti-Dühring* a note concerning matter tells us that matter is an abstraction. We shall never find it if we look at individual things in a laboratory and try to isolate it. It is something all objects have, but it is not something in addition to the objects. If one asks to see being in addition to beings, one would be making the same type of category mistake as one would make if he asked to see fruit in addition to particular apples, pears, and bananas. Matter does not exist separate from existing objects. Dühring sees the self-equal state of matter, which he claims exists for a time as motionless. He answers the question of how it started in motion by saying that though it was motionless, it was loaded with force. To this Engels replies that once again what we need is a firer or mover or God, but since this has been rejected, the notion of a self-equal state of matter as motionless must likewise be rejected.

V. *The Organic World.* According to Engels the transition from one form of motion to another always remains a leap and a leap is a decisive change. This type of decisive change is clearest in the change from ordinary chemical action to life. Clearly, there is a leap, a new *kind* of being arising wherever we have life as opposed to inorganic matter. Dühring rejected Darwinian evolution, while Engels embraces Darwin as well as Haeckel's notion of the variation of species which results from mutual interactions of adaptations and heredity.

For Engels evolution is sufficient as far as it goes, but the line of descent ends or breaks off with the origin of life. To stop here once again implies a creator and deism. Life must be connected with inorganic matter and it must, therefore, be a result of chemical action. This leads to a brief discussion of organic life which Engels claims is cellular and which is something we find wherever we find albuminous bodies. He gives the following definition of life:

> Life, the mode of existence of an albuminous body, therefore consists primarily in the fact that every moment it is itself and at the same time something else; and this does not take place as the result of a process to which it is subjected from without, as is the way in which this can occur also in the case of inanimate bodies.[13]

He admits that this definition of life is in certain respects inadequate and says that from a scientific viewpoint one must go through all the forms in which it appears in order to gain an exhaustive knowledge of what life is. This is one of the ways in which philosophy would be replaced by science.

VI. *Eternal Truths.* Dühring presents laws which he claims are valid for all possible worlds and claims truths which are absolutely immutable. This is also true of the truths of ethics. For Engels this raises the question: is human thought sovereign? He argues that it can be sovereign only in the sense that man is able to know the world as it is, providing that by "man" we mean mankind, and providing that mankind lives long enough and that no limits are imposed on its knowledge by its perceptive organs or by the objects to be known. But, if the sovereignty of man's knowledge is only given in humanity, then certainly this should make us distrustful of our own knowledge, for the many generations which follow us will certainly put us right. With respect to individuals, moreover, there can be no sovereignty, for individual thought is necessarily limited and not absolute. There is something of a difficulty in Engels' position, however, which results from a lack of clarity and perception with respect to the notion of sovereign thought. He says that there are securely based truths, for instance that twice two make four, that Paris is in France, and the like. "Are there then nevertheless *eternal* truths, final and ultimate truths? Certainly there are."[14] But how we are to define these final and ultimate truths and separate them from the truths which are not final and ultimate are questions which Engels leaves unanswered.

Engels divides all knowledge into three great departments —first, knowledge of inanimate nature which is amenable to mathematical treatment. Here certain results are final and ultimate, and for this reason, these sciences are known as the exact sciences. But even with respect to these as we have progressed, for instance, into the notion of infinity in mathematics and calculus, we have introduced inexactness and controversy. This is all the more clear in astronomy and physics, where we need hypotheses. And, of course, hypotheses are not ultimate truths. The second broad general division of knowledge concerns living organisms. Here the only genuine immutable truths are such platitudes as all men are mortal, all female mammals have lacteal glands, which are in fact tautologies. Everything else is based on hypothesis, and, consequently, not on eternal truths. Third, we have the historical sciences and with these we have even less of a notion of eternal unchanging truth. He tells us that in the historical sciences we have only commonplaces of the sorriest kind, such as that Napoleon died on May 5, 1821. The difficulty of Engels' position consists in deciding, with respect to truth, what is trivial and what is not trivial. The truth of historical materialism, for example, serves as a premise from which deductions concerning the actions of the proletariat can be drawn. But the status of the truth of the materialist interpretation of history is ambiguous and seems to be either trivial or not absolutely true.

For Engels the notions of truth and error have validity only in an extremely limited field. Beyond this narrow field truth is relative. This is a result of the claim that knowledge reflects reality, which is constantly in motion and changing.

VII. *Morality and Law.* If what Engels has said is valid for truth in general, how much more so is it with respect to problems of good and evil. Engels points out that these conceptions have varied from nation to nation and from age to age and that even in the society in which he was living three ethical systems coexisted: the ethics of Christian feudalism, of the bourgeoisie, and of the proletariat. One conclusion can be drawn from this observation, he says: men ultimately derive their ethical ideas, which are part of the superstructure, from the practical economic relations of their class. Similarities in ethics, he says, stem from common historical background; for instance, as soon as movable private property is developed in any society, there appears the injunction "thou shalt not steal!"[15] But in a society in which all the motives for stealing have been done away with, the injunction "thou shalt not steal" would be meaningless, and hence could not be true. Since it would not be true, the statement could not be eternally true. Consequently, Engels declares, we must reject every attempt to impose eternal ultimate and immutable moral dogma or law, for morality has always been class morality and we have not yet passed beyond it. We shall pass beyond it only when all classes have been done away with and indeed when all recollection of antagonisms has been forgotten in practical life.

Engels next passes to the question of free will, which for him denotes the relationship of necessity and of freedom. The relation of these two is, for Engels, actually Hegelian. "Freedom is the awareness of necessity";[16] it is not independent of natural laws but consists in knowledge of these laws and in the possibility of utilizing them in achieving one's ends. A difficulty arises here which Engels does not discuss. It would seem that in some sense there is an implication that man with knowledge of the laws of nature or of history is able to use them as he wills. But if the laws really hold, it would seem that man's actions are also completely determined and controlled. For Engels:

Freedom of the will therefore means nothing but the capacity to make decisions with knowledge of the subject. Therefore the *freer* a man's judgment is in relation to a definite question, the greater is the *necessity* with which the content of this judgment will be determined; while the uncertainty, founded on ignorance, which seems to make an arbitrary choice among many different and conflicting possible decisions, shows precisely by this that it is not free, that it is controlled by the very object it should itself control. Freedom therefore consists in the control over ourselves and over external nature, a control founded on knowledge of natural necessity; it is therefore necessarily a product of historical development.[17]

The difficulty mentioned, which this notion of freedom involves, is shared by other systems, including Hegel's, Spinoza's, and those of many of the idealists.

It is interesting that Engels in the section on morality says:

But how young the whole of human history still is, and how ridiculous it would be to attempt to ascribe any absolute validity to our present views, is evident from the simple fact that all past history can be characterized as the history of the epoch from the practical discovery of the transformation of mechanical motion into heat up to that of the transformation of heat into mechanical motion.[18]

Engels is here saying that there are no absolutes and he includes his own view, admitting that it too does not have absolute validity. Many of the followers of Marx and Engels evidently ignore his statement that absolute validity cannot be ascribed to his views.

VIII. *Dialectics.* Having discussed ethics and morality, Engels then takes up dialectics. Dühring claimed that the principle of contradiction was valid and said that there are no contradictions in things. Engels says this is a partial view with which he would agree so long as things are considered in rest and side by side. However, when one tries to consider them in motion and interacting one with another, one sees that this view is absurd. Motion itself, Engel claims, is a contradiction. At the same time an object is both in one place and in another, and the resolution of this contradiction is precisely what motion is. Engels thus poses Zeno's paradox and accepts the claim that motion is contradictory. Since contradiction is true of all motion, and since all matter is in motion, it must likewise be true of all things. We have seen that contradiction is inherent in life as conceived by Engels, for a being that is alive is at each moment itself and something else. He brings the notion of contradiction into other realms. In mathematics, for instance, it is a contradiction that a negative quantity could be the square of anything, for every negative squared is a positive quantity. Yet in mathematics of any higher type we must necessarily use the concept of the square root of minus one.

We can formulate two additional laws of dialectics in addition to that of contradictions in everything: (1) the transition of quantity into quality and vice versa, and (2) the negation of the negation. These laws apply to all of reality, to nature, mathematics, history, society, thought.

The change of quantity into quality is taken, of course, from Hegel. Engel argues that at a certain point (called the "nodal" point) quantitative development suddenly changes into qualitative development. At this point there is a "leap" from one quality to another. For example, as we heat water we find that at 100°C. it changes from a liquid to a gaseous state. In chemistry carbon compounds, though their molecular structures differ only mathematically (and so quantitatively), exhibit different qualitative properties. Similarly, one can point to the differences between o_2 (oxygen) and o_3 (ozone), which exhibit different properties though composed of differing quantitative additions of oxygen atoms.

The law of negation of the negation likewise comes from Hegel, and in order to explain it Engels gives several examples. A grain of barley undergoes change and is negated when it becomes a plant. The plant in turn produces more grains of barley and then is again negated—the negation of the negation —when it dies. It has, however, produced ten or twenty or thirty fold as many grains as it originally started with. A similar dialectical development takes place with the development of a butterfly in animate nature. In mathematics we can posit A, the negation of which is minus A, and the negation of the negation is A^2 which contains both the square of A and the square of minus A. It is impossible to get rid of this negated negation and the negated negation is always so firmly entrenched in A^2 that the latter always has two square roots, plus A and minus A. In another realm we see that the negation of common property is private property and that the negation of the negation consists in a communistic type of common ownership of property. It is not a simple return to the original common property, for there has been a progressive development. Likewise, in philosophy we can take old materialism, see that it is negated by idealism, and see that this negation is in turn negated by the advent of modern materialism. What then is the negation of negation? Engels tells us it is "an extremely general—and for this reason, extremely far-reaching and important—law of development of nature, history, and thought; a law which, as we have seen, holds good in the animal and plant kingdoms, in geology, in mathematics, in history and in philosophy. . . . Dialectics, however, is nothing more than the science of the general laws of motion and development of nature, human society, and thought."[19] In order to understand the negation of negation, we must understand that negation does not merely mean saying "no" or denying that something exists or destroying what we start out with in any way we like. Every particular kind of entity is negated in its own way, and every idea is negated in its own way and gives rise to its own development. But on this view how can we know precisely in what way the thing is negated? Engels would undoubtedly tell us to look and see. However, how would we know, for instance, in mathematics that the negation of minus A is not minus minus A, which would give us what we originally started with; or, if we were to take the history of ideas, why could we not take realism and idealism and then take phenomenology as their synthesis? If the law of dialectics cannot tell what to expect in any given process, then at best the law of negation of the negation is reduced to a descriptive law and does not help to explain reality.

Engels' conclusion with respect to Dühring's revolution is that he has promised everything and has produced nothing. When we finish we are just as wise as when we began, and Dühring in Engels' eyes is thus refuted.

IX. *Socialism: Utopian and Scientific*. Engels states that modern socialism is the product of the recognition of the antagonism between capitalists and wage earners and of the anarchy existing in production. The early French socialists measured everything by reason, which was the idealized kingdom of the bourgeoisie. The sixteenth- and seventeenth-century utopians, such as More, drew pictures of an ideal society.

The government of reason of Rousseau's *Social Contract* led to the Reign of Terror. This, in turn, was followed by communistic theories (Morelly and Mably).

Three great socialists whom Engels treats in some detail are Saint-Simon, Fourier, and Owen. All three are utopian in their theories, however, for they all hoped to bring the kingdom of reason and justice to all humanity at once.

For Saint-Simon the class antagonism which followed the French Revolution was between workers and idlers. The time prior to the French Revolution had proved the idlers unable to rule, since their rule led to the Revolution. The proletariat, however, is also unable to rule, as was proved by the Reign of Terror. Consequently, Saint-Simon argued that the only ones left to rule are the scientists and industrialists (scholars, manufacturers, merchants, and bankers). He held that "all men ought to work," and he had the insight that economic conditions are the basis of political institutions. He also foreshadowed the abolition of the state by recommending control of things and processes instead of control of men.

Fourier attacked the hypocritical world of the bourgeoisie and applied dialectics to an analysis of society and to its historical development. He was one of the first to call for the removal of class distinctions.

The third of the great utopians, Robert Owen, claimed that man's character is a product of heredity and of environment. He directed a cotton mill of twenty-five hundred employees and ran it as a model colony, giving the workers conditions worthy of human beings. He used his profits for the benefit of all. Later, he embraced communism and came out against private property, religion, and marriage. Once he did this he was ostracized from society. He suffered financial ruin as a result of an unsuccessful communist experiment in America. He thereupon took up the cause of the workers, and largely through his instrumentality legislation was passed limiting the working hours for women and children in factories. He was also instrumental in setting up cooperative societies, labor bazaars, and the like.

All of these socialists were necessarily utopian, Engels tells us, because capitalist production had not developed sufficiently for them to be otherwise. Each had what he thought was absolute truth, but the difficulty was that the absolute truth of each contradicted the absolute truth of the others.

Socialism, Engels claims, had to be placed upon a real basis and for this the rediscovery of dialectics, known by the early Greeks, was necessary. If one realized that the economic structure of a society furnishes the basis for history, one could then explain the capitalist mode of production and point out its inevitable downfall by applying the theory of surplus value. Thus, armed with the materialist interpretation of history and the theory of surplus value, socialism became scientific. Previously, it was possible only to criticize the capitalist mode of production and its consequences and to reject them. It was not possible to explain them. With the materialist conception of history and the theory of surplus value, it became possible not only to explain them but also to point out their inevitable development.

Modern socialism is the reflection in thought of the conflict between productive forces and the mode of production, which is first reflected in the mind of the working class. The owners of the instruments of labor appropriate the product of the labor of others. This means that though production is socialized, that is, carried on by a number of people and not by a single individual, the results of labor are appropriated by individuals. This is the basis for the antagonism between the proletariat and the bourgeoisie. The perfecting of machinery, as we have seen, made human labor more and more superfluous and formed an industrial reserve army. The ability to expand because of machines led to the necessity of expansion. Unfortunately, expansion of markets cannot keep pace with the expanded production and periodic collisions are the result. These, Engels tells us, can be pointed to in cycles of depression, recovery, depression, recovery which had taken place over the last seventy years. The state cannot withstand such periodic depressions and will ultimately have to undertake the direction of production. The capitalist mode of production, therefore, which first forces out workers now forces out capitalists. The state is a capitalist machine, and, consequently, state ownership of productive forces is not a solution of the conflict, though within it can be found the elements of the solution.

The solution lies in harmonizing the mode of production, appropriation, and exchange, with the socialized character of the means of production. In essence, society as a whole must take over the productive forces. Once we understand these forces, we are in a position more and more to subject them to our will and ends. In this way social anarchy will give way to the social regulation of production according to the plan and the needs of the community.

The proletariat will seize political power and turn the means of production into state property. It will abolish class distinctions and antagonisms and do away with the state as state. The state is an instrument utilized by the ruling class to suppress the exploited classes. The state becomes unnecessary when there is no class to be held in subjection. State interference, consequently, in social relations becomes superfluous in one domain after another and withers away of itself. The government of persons is replaced by the administration of things and by the conduct of processes of production. "The state is not 'abolished.' *It withers away.*"[20]

This is possible, but it becomes a historical necessity only when the actual conditions for its realization are present. It presupposes a development of production in which monopoly and class leadership are not only superfluous but a hindrance to development. And, Engels claims, this point has been reached. It is time to replace the anarchy in social production by planning and by conscious organization. Man is now in the position to become master of his own social organization, and this will result in the "ascent of man from the kingdom of necessity to the kingdom of freedom."[21] This is scientific socialism. The accomplishment of these ends is the historical mission of the modern proletariat, and scientific socialism is the theoretical expression of the proletarian movement.

Ludwig Feuerbach and the End of Classical German Philosophy

In *The German Ideology* Marx and Engels settled their accounts with their philosophical conscience. Though the work was sent to a place of publication in Westphalia, circumstances prevented its printing, and Engels records that the manuscript was left to the gnawing of mice. Concern with Ludwig Feuerbach and Left Hegelians as such was put aside by Marx and Engels on the completion of *The German Ideology*. It is not until some forty years later that Engels took up the theme again. Because of the rebirth of German philosophy in England and Scandinavia Engels took advantage of a review of K. N. Starcke's book *Ludwig Feuerbach*, which he was asked to write for *Die neue Zeit*, in order to relate again how he and Marx separated themselves from Hegel and in order, he says, to give Feuerbach his due. Originally published in the fourth and fifth numbers of *Die neue Zeit* in 1886, the work was revised as a whole and brought out as a separate publication in 1888. In referring to *The German Ideology*, Engels writes: "The finished portion consists of an exposition of the materialist conception of history which proves how incomplete our knowledge of economic history still was at that time."[22]

Engels' *Ludwig Feuerbach and the End of Classical German Philosophy* is in four sections. The first deals with Hegel and the Young Hegelians, the second with the distinction between idealism and materialism, the third with a critique of Feuerbach, especially of his theory of religion and ethics, and the last is an exposition of what will later be called dialectical materialism.

Section I reviews the split between the Right and Left Hegelians over the statement "all that is real is rational; all that is rational is real." Most of what Engels relates here we have already seen, but it is interesting to study a few of the statements he makes. He claims that both history and truth are never finished and that as knowledge is always imperfect, so society also is imperfect. "A perfect society . . . can only exist in imagination."[23] The dialectics of history must continue; each stage of history is necessary and therefore justified, but each is destined to decay and must give way to a higher stage. This presumably applies to the stage of communism as well as to every other stage. In conjunction with the notion that nothing ever stops, Engels states that the revolutionary character of the dialectic is absolute and that this is the only absolute dialectical philosophy admits. The addition of this one absolute makes Engels' position consistent, but he does not show how this one absolute escapes the relativity to which all other truths are subject.

As we have seen, Left Hegelianism turned to criticism of religion and the existing state. Through Feuerbach materialism was placed on its throne again, and Engels tells us: "We all became at once Feuerbachians."[24] Both Hegel and Feuerbach, however, were thrust aside by the revolution of 1848.

Section II, dealing with materialism and idealism, is extremely important because the dichotomy between these terms and the meanings assigned them by Engels remain constant throughout the development of Soviet philosophy. He says that the great basic question of all philosophy concerns the relation of thinking and being. From the earliest times man came to believe thinking was not an activity of the body, but something else. Man was led eventually to the idea of immortality, since his ideas could well exist apart from his body. In a similar way natural forces were personified as God and were distilled until man finally arrived at a monotheistic religion. The origin, therefore, of the relation of thinking to being and of spirit to nature is a product of the ignorance of savages. Engels here gives the origin or the supposed origin of our notions of immortality and of God. It may be mentioned in passing that a critique of the origin of something is not a sufficient critique of its present value or validity. The claim that it is such is an instance of what is called the "genetic fallacy."

According to Engels the answer to the question "Did God create the world or has the world been in existence eternally?" divides all philosophers into two camps. Those who assert the primacy of spirit above nature and assume some sort of creation are called "idealists." The "materialists," on the other hand, regard nature as primary and consequently deny any notion of creation. The idea of creation is the dividing line between materialism and idealism for Engels; this is the way he uses the terms, and he considers any other use of them incorrect. These meanings, it should be noted, are not those ordinarily encountered in Western histories of philosophy and in Western thinking. Aristotle, for instance, according to this definition, might well be considered an idealist, for although he does not hold creation, he does hold the existence of a prime mover which is at least in some sense prior to and more important than matter. In general most of the thinkers generally classified as idealists are also considered idealists by Engels, but some—like Descartes—who are not generally classified as idealists are so considered by him.

Engels' materialism is rather naïve with respect to Kant and the idealists. He criticizes Kant's notion of the thing-in-itself and claims that

> if we are able to prove the correctness of our conception of a natural process by making it ourselves . . . then there is an end to the Kantian ungraspable "thing-in-itself." The chemical substances produced in the bodies of plants and animals re-

mained just such "things-in-themselves" until organic chemistry began to produce them one after another, whereupon the "thing-in-itself" became a thing for us....[25]

Such a statement shows a misunderstanding of the thing-in-itself. But here it is merely necessary to point out that for Engels knowing how to produce something and knowing how it acts is to understand all there is about that thing and all that is knowable.

Feuerbach claimed the material world was the only reality and that consciousness and thinking were products of the brain. "Mind itself is merely the highest product of matter." Engels quotes Feuerbach with approval, but neither analyzes Feuerbach's statements nor his premises. Materialism, Engels tells us, has a history and a development. French materialism was mechanical, antidialectical, and could not comprehend the universe as a process. It was unable, therefore, to explain history or to give a historical view of nature. The unhistorical view of nature with which it was bound, however, could be overcome once one was aware of three important discoveries, namely the cell, the transformation of energy, and the theory of evolution. Natural scientific materialism, moreover, was unable to explain knowledge. It could not reconstruct the historical and philosophical sciences on a materialistic foundation. These types of materialism were what Feuerbach was faced with, and he himself did not go beyond them.

Ideal aims, consequently, do not make an idealist, for all men are idealists in the sense that feelings, thoughts, impulses, and volitions are reflections of the external world in the brain and are ideal tendencies or powers. Engels does not explain how that which is a reflection of something else can in any sense have an ideal tendency built into it. This is a question which remains unanswered in his thought. The point he makes, however, is that a materialist as well as an idealist can believe in the progressive development of mankind.

The next section, dealing with religion and ethics, makes clear to what extent Feuerbach remained an idealist. For Engels, Feuerbach's idealism consists in his not accepting purely human relations but in his insistence that they "will attain their full value only when consecrated by the name of religion."[26] In other words, for Feuerbach, there was a relationship that was more real than that which actually took

Engels and Marxist Theory 97

place between real people. This notion of man, according to which there is some abstract Man more real or more important than existing men, constitutes Feuerbach's idealism in Engels' eyes. The ideal or other reality is more important than the concrete reality in which we live.

Feuerbach, Engels tells us, does not investigate historical man, historically determined; he makes the urge to happiness the basis of ethics without realizing that the urge to happiness thrives on material means. From the abstract man of Feuerbach, Engels claims, one can arrive at real living men only when one considers them as participants in history. The step of replacing abstract man by the science of real men and their historical development was started by Marx in *The Holy Family*.

Section IV is the most interesting and the most important of this book. It contains a statement, although an incomplete one, of the dialectic both in nature and in history, or of what is later known as dialectical and historical materialism. Dialectical materialism (the term was coined by Plekhanov) consists of a study of the general laws of dialectics and of their general application to nature and thought; historical materialism (Engels himself uses this term as the title of an article in *Die neue Zeit*) studies the specific development of dialectics in history or in the development of human society. Marx attempted to comprehend the world, history, and nature materialistically, and Engels claims that he carried this aim out consistently in all the domains of knowledge.

Marx adopted Hegel's dialectics but not, as we have seen, in its Hegelian form in which the dialectic consisted of the self-development of the absolute concept. For Hegel the dialectical progressive moment in history and nature was a copy of the self movement of the concept going on from eternity. This idealistic notion of the dialectic is done away with. What is substituted is:

> We comprehended the concepts in our heads once more materialistically—as images (*Abbilder*) of real things. . . . Thus dialectics reduced itself to the science of the general laws of motion, both of the external world and of human thought—two sets of laws which are identical in substance, but differ in their expression in so far as the human mind can apply them consciously, while in nature and also up to now

for the most part in human history, these laws assert themselves unconsciously, in the form of external necessity, in the midst of an endless series of seeming accidents. Thereby the dialectic of concepts itself became merely the conscious reflex of the dialectical motion of the real world and thus the dialectic of Hegel was placed upon its head; or rather, turned off its head, on which it was standing, and placed upon its feet.[27]

This statement of Engels gives both his and Marx's notion of the dialectic and of the relationship between knowledge and nature. Knowledge is dialectical insofar as it is a reflection of the dialectical movement present in nature. Engels adds at this point that the materialistic dialectic has been their sharpest weapon and best working tool. The claim is later repeated by Lenin and still later by Khrushchev.

The essential insight which Hegel had and which is appropriated by Marx and Engels is that the world is not made of things but of processes in which "a progressive development asserts itself in the end."[28] This insight allows Engels to explain not only the development of nature but also the development of man, which we term human history. What appears to be an accident is really a mask behind which necessity hides itself.

In applying to nature the notion that movement is basic to all things, Engels moves to a dialectical interpretation of natural science. Engels points to the three great previously mentioned discoveries which enable man to see the interconnection of natural processes. The first was the discovery of the cell, through which man was able to explain the development and change of individuals and species. The second was the law of the transformation of energy, which enabled him to see that all forces operative in organic nature are merely different forms of the manifestation of universal motion. All nature is thus a transformation from one form to another. The third, the Darwinian theory of evolution, enabled man to explain the development of one species from another. Armed with these three notions, Engels claims that we can now "form a comprehensive view of the interconnection in nature by means of the facts provided by empirical natural science itself."[29] In a very real sense, science will take the place of philosophy.

What is true in the realm of nature is also true in the

Engels and Marxist Theory 99

realm of history. Just as there is a necessary motion in nature, there is also a necessary motion in human history, although with a difference. In natural history forces are blind, whereas in explaining human history one must take cognizance of the fact that consciousness is involved. In the history of society the actors are conscious; they work toward goals. Despite this, however, the course of history is governed by laws, for although men have consciously desired aims, what is willed rarely happens. The *ends* of actions are consciously willed or intended, but all the results which actually follow are not. History is indeed made by men consciously following their own desired ends. But history is precisely the resultant of the many wills that operate in different directions and their manifold effect on the outer world. Motives are of only secondary importance. Yet since they seem to be, at least in one sense, the reason why men do things, a materialist interpretation must also be given of motives. What are the driving forces behind them? To answer this question, Engels states, we should realize that what we are really looking for are the motives of the masses, for it is the masses that change the world, not individuals. Individuals may be leaders; but without followers, nothing significant would happen. With respect to motives, that which sets men in motion must go through their minds, but it is ultimately determined by circumstances. For example, says Engels, in 1830 there were three classes—the aristocracy, the bourgeoisie, and the proletariat. What is the source of their development? For Engels it is purely economic. He briefly traces this development and claims that "in modern history at least it is, therefore, proved that all political struggles are class struggles, and all class struggles for emancipation, despite their necessarily political form—for every class struggle is a political struggle—turn ultimately on the question of *economic* emancipation."[30] (In passing let us just remark that a theory is not proved merely because one can explain certain phenomena by it.) Here follows a repetition of the doctrine of historical determinism. The dominant class of society uses the state to maintain its control over the suppressed classes. It passes laws in order to safeguard its interests. In time ideologies and religion are produced which likewise express the interests of the ruling class. All are determined by the economic basis, but the further removed from this basis the less obvious is the interconnection between them and the economic conditions of existence. Religion is the furthest removed from economic life and the most alien to it. An ideology is "occupation with thoughts as with independent entities, developing independently and subject only to their own laws."[31]

Engels concludes by saying that what he has presented is merely a sketch of the Marxist conception of history—"the proof must be derived from history itself; and in this regard I may be permitted to say that it has been sufficiently furnished in other writings."[32] Unfortunately, he does not say in which other writings the proof has been given nor in what way history can prove the Marxist conception of it. The fact that one can use the Marxist conception of history to interpret or describe history is insufficient to *prove* the theory, if by "prove" one means demonstrate that it is the only correct interpretation of history. Hegel's philosophy of history, for instance, can also be used to interpret or describe history, though it is hardly likely that Engels would admit that it is thereby proved.

Engels finally notes that the key to the understanding of history lies in the history of the development of labor and that the recognition of this insight found its response in the working class to which it was directed. "The German working-class movement is the inheritor of German classical philosophy."[33] Philosophy has thus become practical and removed from the sphere of pure thought. In a way this explains why, after *The German Ideology*, Marx was able to devote himself to practical concerns and paid little attention to technical philosophy. To be consistent in his thought he had necessarily to abandon abstract philosophy, and this is what he did. The claim that the working class and not the professional philosophers are the ones to whom Marxist works are addressed should not be taken lightly. For this is a key to Marxism as a philosophy of action as opposed to one of theory. It is because of the emphasis on practice as opposed to theory that Marxism has had its impact and that it is still so widely disseminated in the Soviet Union.

We see from this work that dialectics is the law of the motion of nature and of thought. It is used by Engels to explain nature as well as history, and thus he claims that the thoroughgoing materialistic explanation of the universe has been put forward and that this replaces philosophy.

Engels and Marxist Theory 101

We must keep in mind that this book is not so much a technical treatise as a popular one, directed toward the working class. Yet a number of questions can be raised. First, what is the validity of dialectics? Can it be validly understood apart from Hegel's method and what is the proof that it is correct? This question, which we raised earlier, is not answered by Engels and is passed on to the Soviet period. Second, Engels seems to hold that nature proves the truth of dialectics. But here we are faced with the same difficulty as with respect to the proof of the Marxist conception of history. Even if Engels is able to explain the workings of the universe by the application of dialectics—which is debatable —this does not necessarily entail that the universe works dialectically. It seems, rather, that this is merely another reconceptualization. And other, bourgeois, nondialectical theories have been at least equally successful in describing the laws of nature and in making significant advances in science and technology. Third, we saw that in Engels' writings there are certain ambiguities in terms, for instance, in the term "truth." These ambiguities are inherited by Lenin and Soviet philosophers, and we shall meet them again. Fourth, it is not at all clear why dialectics in Marx and Engels must proceed progressively or in a progressive direction rather than possibly in the reverse direction. In Hegel there was a good reason, namely, that the Absolute was developing toward itself. Since this is not the case in Marx and Engels, one can question the direction of the movement. Engels admits the existence of a retrogressive dialectic, but he still insists that history is necessarily developing toward a higher communistic stage. Nor is it clear in Engels' examples, for instance, in the qualitative change from water into steam that the later state can in any sense be considered an advance over the earlier. Fifth, Engels explains away such ideas as the "soul" and "God" by showing that they have humble origins in primitive thinking. That something originates in this way, however, does not invalidate the content of the ideas. We have already seen how such an argument is fallacious. Finally, some question can be raised as to qualitative leaps, for instance, the leap from inorganic to organic matter, the leap from unconscious to conscious matter. Though Engels claims to have given an explanation of how they happen, there is still the question of precisely what sort of change takes place in such leaps and also why such changes happen. Engels, however, has not yet had his last word on dialectics and for this we turn to his *Dialectics of Nature*.

Dialectics of Nature

There is some question as to the part Marx may have played in *Dialectics of Nature*, Engels' last book, and also some question as to whether Marx would have agreed with the ideas stated there. Engels started the work in 1875-76 and wrote it intermittently until he died in 1895. Unfinished, it was not published until 1925. He arranged the contents of the work into four folders—it consisted of ten articles or chapters and 169 notes and fragments—and also made two outlines planning what the book would be like. He corresponded with Marx while he was writing it and told him of some of the ideas it presented.

The three central ideas in the work are: (1) the union of matter and motion, (2) the qualitative difference between the forms of motion and the sciences which investigate them, and (3) the dialectical transition from one form to another, and so from one science to another.

The Introduction, often printed separately, traces the history of modern science from a dialectical point of view, and then the history of the development of man. Man is differentiated from the ape by his specialized hand and the concomitant development of his brain, consciousness, and speech. This development leads to the period when human history became possible and permits the interweaving of all of history, natural as well as human. Projecting into the future, Engels states that change will continue indefinitely, and hence he posits an eternal cycle of worlds in infinite time. The result is that nothing is eternal except eternally moving matter and the laws according to which it moves and changes. "We have the certainty that matter remains eternally the same in all its transformations, that none of its attributes can ever be lost, and therefore, also, that with the same iron necessity that it will exterminate on the earth its highest creation, the thinking mind, it must somewhere else and at another time again produce it."[34] In another of the famous chapters of this book, "The Part Played by Labor in the Transition from Ape to Man," labor is described (together with nature) as the source of all wealth, and it is claimed that labor created man himself. The development of man from the ape through the development of the hand is only sketched, but the origin of speech is outlined in some detail, and Engels relates how this leads to the formation of society. Human society, he says, is differentiated from animal society by labor, which begins with the making of tools. This leads to man's mastery of nature, made possible by his coming to know and to apply the laws of nature. The consequent development of society, as already seen, makes scientific socialism possible.

The most interesting section of the *Dialectics of Nature* deals with dialectics. The laws of dialectics, which are abstracted from the history of nature and from human society, are presented and stated clearly in this work. They are reducible to three: (1) the law of the transformation of quantity into quality and vice versa, (2) the law of the interpenetration of opposites, and (3) the law of the negation of negation. Engels assures us that these laws are *deduced* from nature and are not foisted on nature and history.

1) Something of the transformation of quantity into quality was shown in the examples given in *Anti-Dühring*, for instance in the change of water into ice or steam, in which a quantitative change of temperature brings about a qualitative change. The discussion in *Dialectics of Nature* is very similar to that in *Anti-Dühring*, the law of the transformation of quantity into quality being paraphrased in this way: "We can express this by saying that in nature, in a manner exactly fixed for each individual case, qualitative changes can only occur by the quantitative addition or quantitative subtraction of matter or motion (so-called energy)."[35] The qualitative changes are what separate the different sciences. It is the qualitative change, for instance, which separates mechanics, the science of heavenly masses, from physics, the mechanics of molecules, and both of them from chemistry, which is the physics of atoms. Where there are qualitative changes there must be different sciences. That there was a division of the sciences before Engels gave a dialectical basis for it merely shows that man had changed quantities to qualities without realizing it, just as Molière's Monsieur Jourdain spoke prose all his life without knowing it. Objective dialectics prevails throughout nature; subjective dialectics is dialectical thought, which consists in the reflection of the motion and opposi-

tion present in nature. The same laws apply to the development of nature, of society, and of thought. Yet because of differences of quality one science is not reducible to another.

Unfortunately, however, Engels gives no way of determining what he considers a qualitative as opposed to a quantitative change. The discussions of water and chemistry do not help much, for instance, for the change in the state of water from liquid to steam can be and is handled quantitatively in science in terms of pressure and the movement of molecules, and the difference between o_2 and o_3 does not affect the atoms which combine in different quantities.

2) The law of the interpenetration of opposites states that in dealing with reality we do not have a situation in which "either-or" predominates. In all of nature differences merge in intermediate steps. Metaphysics and the metaphysical outlook consider each thing as though it were distinct, as though it were separate, and in the metaphysical category one can speak of either/or. Such an outlook is valid for everyday life; however, it does not take into account the actual interpenetration and interrelationship of things, and in any particular thing it does not consider the differences of opposites contained in it. An example of opposites contained in a given entity is found in a magnet, which has a negative pole and a positive pole. No matter where we divide the magnet, we still find a negative and a positive pole. This law of dialectics does not concern itself with abstract identity, but deals with differences within identity. Every identity is exposed to mechanical, physical, and chemical influences, which are always changing and modifying its identity. Continual change is found in both organic and in inorganic nature.

The law of identity, $a=a$, whereby everything is permanent, is refuted by natural science, even though this type of thinking continues to dominate people's minds. Identity and difference are "one-sided poles which represent the truth only in their reciprocal action, in the inclusion of difference *within* identity."[36] Dialectics seizes identity and differences, necessity and chance, cause and effect, all linked and mingled together in any given individual entity, as well as in all of reality.

But in the statement of this law, too, there is no lack of confusion on Engels' part. Just what constitutes an "opposite" is never clearly stated. Sometimes it is a logical contradiction, sometimes a logical contrary, sometimes a "polar opposite," sometimes a difference of views or aims, and so on. Engels accepts Zeno's paradox as proof that motion is contradictory—though it certainly does not have to be accepted. Things admittedly develop and change, but this does not necessarily mean that they are contradictory; what is becoming can well be considered from two different though not contradictory points of view—from the point of view of what it is at any given time and from the point of view of what it is becoming. Indeed, if the object were always contradictory we could never know it, in the sense of understanding it or comprehending it, at all.

3) The law of the negation of the negation. The development of this law in *Dialectics of Nature* adds nothing that we have not already seen. We are told, however, that dialectical logic follows from dialectics in nature. Together with animals, man uses induction, deduction, abstraction, analysis, experiment, and synthesis, but it is only man who has dialectical thought.

As we have seen, however, the negation of the negation cannot be known from experience. Even in Engels' own examples there is no clear way of knowing what the negation of the negation is. When a seed develops into a plant it is negated. The plant then bears more seeds and dies. Both the additional seeds and the dying seem to be part of the negation of the negation. But if the plant died without bearing seeds, or if it bore seeds and did not die, then the negation of the negation would be different. The concept becomes so elastic that no matter what happens it can be described by means of the "law," and thus no light is thrown on the process of development analyzed. Dialectics becomes at best a technique of description, not of explanation or prediction. Nor is it clear how the dying or the multiplication of seeds would "elevate" the preceding dialectical stages of development. Deleterious mutations would pose an even more blatant counter example to the supposed law.

Before leaving the laws of dialectics we should also consider the emphasis Engels places on the notion of causality. He states that the idea of causality becomes established by the activity of human beings and by the observation that one human motion produces or determines another, the activity of man thus forming the test of causality. Regular sequences of phenomena may give rise to the notion of causality, but they afford no proof without man's testing. Man can produce motion which does not occur in nature, for example, in industry, and he can give the motion a certain direction. He then checks his causality by seeing if he has effected what he had intended. Man's ability to change nature is the most important basis of human thought. Knowing the forms of the motion of matter, we know matter itself, and from universal reciprocal action we finally get at the real notion of the causal relation. He continues: "For one who denies causality every natural law is a hypothesis, among others also the chemical analysis of heavenly bodies by means of the prismatic spectrum. What shallowness of thought to remain at such a viewpoint!"[87]

But despite Engels' emphasis on causality he seems oblivious to the implications of his claim. In the laws of dialectics we find more complex entities coming from less complex entities, we find leaps from one quality to another, we find the continual emergence of higher forms of being. The laws of dialectics describe these phenomena. With Engels' emphasis on causality it becomes incumbent upon him to explain how the higher comes from the lower, how the more complex comes from the less complex, and so on. Nothing can give what it does not have. The emergence of consciousness from unconscious matter requires, for example, a causal explanation in Engels' scheme which it nowhere receives. Nor does he even seem aware that the problem exists.

After a discussion of the laws of dialectics he proceeds to a detailed classification of the sciences based on the forms of motion. The subject matter of all the natural sciences is matter in motion. The simplest form of motion is mechanical. The motion of separated bodies is studied in astronomy; the motion of bodies in contact, in relation to one another, is handled by statics, hydrostatics, and gases. Physics deals with forces, and certain qualitative changes lead to chemistry, which leads to organic life, etc. Engels tells us, "*Classification of the sciences*, each of which analyzes a single form of motion, or a series of forms of motion that belong together and pass into one another, is therefore the classification, the arrangement, of these forms of motion themselves according to their inherent sequence, and herein lies its importance."[88] Mechanics has to do with the movement of masses; chemistry with the movement of molecules; organics with the movement of bodies in which the two are inseparable. Chapters on mathematics, mechanics, and astronomy, physics, chemistry, and biology then follow. Thus, he completes his sketch of dialectics in nature.

With Engels' death the original corpus of Marxism is closed.

Engels' Contribution to Soviet Thought
The contribution of Engels to Soviet philosophical thought is more far ranging than that of Marx himself. While Marx was the originator of the materialist interpretation of history and laid the foundation for scientific socialism he left large areas of philosophical inquiry essentially untouched. Engels, in his endeavor to continue Marx's work, filled in so many large gaps that it is only in his writings that Marxism approaches anything like a world view. That Marx may have held the same views as Engels is somewhat beside the point, for it is only in the later writings of Engels that a comprehensive view of the world emerges. Paradoxically, though Engels insisted that philosophy, except for dialectics and logic, would be replaced by the positive sciences, he laid the foundation for the development of Soviet philosophy.

Engels and not Marx is in fact the father of what is known as dialectical materialism. Though Marx emphasized both materialism and dialectics and though he sought the dialectical laws operating in history, economics, and social development, he did not specifically generalize his views or formulate the laws of dialectics in such a way that they applied to all of reality. Engels did precisely this. With Engels dialectics is applied to all reality—to nature in general, to the particular sciences, to thought, to history, to society, to mathematics, and so on. He attempted to specify the nature of matter, so central to a materialism. He set down certain doctrines concerning the universe, such as the claim that it is infinite, which have become frozen into dogma. He enunciated and developed the laws of dialectics and applied dialectics to the sciences and mathematics and used the notion of dialectics to classify the sciences. He stressed the notion of dialectical logic and emphasized the dialectical character of thought more than Marx had, while, paradoxically, placing less emphasis than Marx had on man's active role in the knowing process.

In historical materialism and scientific socialism Engels' contributions were not original, but he did develop Marx's position. His presentation of scientific socialism is more systematic than Marx's, and the concept of the state "withering away," though consistent with Marx's position, was first explicitly stated by Engels. His work on the origin of the state, private property, and the family, based on an application of the method of historical materialism, was likewise original. Engels also gives a much fuller discussion of ethics, though based for the most part on Marxian premises, than can be found explicitly in Marx's writings.

When one considers the broad scope of Engels' writings, that they were often hurriedly written while he was attending to the international labor movement and the editing of Marx's works, and that they were admittedly both polemical and often addressed to the mass of working men, it is not surprising that what emerges is frequently vaguely or ambiguously stated and often characterized by philosophical or scientific naïveté, lack of precision, and over generalization. What *is* surprising is that his works, despite these characteristics, have been raised to the level of dogma by his Soviet followers. Moreover, though Engels dealt with many areas which Marx had not discussed, he too left some questions in philosophy untouched and so quite open; he too left much unsaid, and so left much for the people who came after him to wrestle with.

Marxism and Revisionism

By 1895, the year Engels died, Marxism had become the official doctrine of the German Social-Democratic Party—an active, growing, influential, and legal political party. While the Communist *Manifesto* could proclaim in 1848 that the workers had nothing to lose but their chains, by the end of the century this was no longer the situation. With the help of the labor union movement, with increased European prosperity, and with social legislation of various types the lot of the German worker had not grown worse, as Marx had predicted, but had vastly improved. The middle class was not sinking, but rising and growing. The entrepreneurs were not exploiting the workers more and more viciously, but were helping them better their working and living conditions, and class hostility had not grown more and more acute, but had abated. The workers thus found their interests bound up with the existing social order, which they had hopes of continually, if gradually, changing to their own benefit by legal means.

These developments, as well as the ambiguities and lacunae in the theories of Marx and Engels, led to reinterpretations of and attacks on Marxism from within, which in turn provoked vigorous defenses. The situation was complicated with different positions advocated by different figures, and with controversies raging on the level of theory and on the level of practical applications of the theory. In general, however, we can divide the Marxists who engaged in these disputes into two broad groups: the "revisionists" and the "orthodox Marxists." The term "revisionist" was first applied to Eduard Bernstein (1850-1932), an influential German Social-Democrat. Bernstein, considering Marxism a living and so a changing doctrine, first tried to interpret and modify it in accordance with changing conditions. But when his interpretations were vigorously attacked as distortions of Marxism, he chose to defend his position as true independently of any claims to its being Marxist. Where Marx was wrong, Bernstein claimed, his doctrine had to be revised. And to his mind, it was wrong in many places.

Basically, Bernstein claimed that communism was a utopian ideal, unattainable for a long time to come. As a result he emphasized not the utopian and far-distant end, but the necessity of working for the constant, present improvement of the lot of the working class. He rejected economic determinism, arguing that economic factors were only one of the determining factors of history, among others. Therefore, he challenged the inevitability of the supposed laws based on the economic interpretation of history. As he saw that the conditions of the workers had the best chance for improvement if peaceful, legal means were used, he opposed violent class warfare and revolution and opted for using the labor union movement and socialist parties as agencies of reform from within the state, thus utilizing and eventually dominating the existing state apparatus. In philosophy he rejected dialectics, tended towards neo-Kantianism, and argued for the acknowledgment of universally valid ethical principles which, he claimed, could alone justify the socialist movement. Revisionism, as the doctrine of Bernstein and his followers came to be known, was condemned by Party conventions in 1899 and in 1903. But Bernstein's views remained influential both in Germany and in other parts of Europe, including Russia.

The term "revisionism" came eventually to be applied not

only to Bernstein and his followers but to any Marxist who made similar attempts to correct Marx and Engels by rejecting some of their doctrine. Exactly what constitutes rejection and what constitutes valid interpretation, however, is often a debatable and debated issue. "Revisionism" in Marxist circles has become a term of abuse often hurled by one Marxist at another who disagrees with him.

Among the "orthodox" defenders of Marxism who opposed Bernstein's revisionism the most prominent was Karl Kautsky (1854-1938), who edited the fourth volume of *Capital*, helped popularize Marx's economic doctrines, and, with respect to theory, remained the leader of the Social Democrats. He was, however, later joined by Bernstein in his opposition to the Bolsheviks, and in many instances his doctrine come close to that of Bernstein. He is considered an "orthodox" Marxist because all of his reinterpretations of Marx and Engels are reinterpretations in their defense and are attempts to preserve the purity of their doctrine. In 1883 he founded the socialist monthly, *Die neue Zeit*, which became the leading theoretical organ of Marxism. In opposition to Bernstein he defended the necessity for a radical change in the class structure and the probable necessity of a political upheaval. Though Engels had late in his life admitted that more was being accomplished by lawful than by unlawful means, Kautsky pointed out that Engels had never spoken against revolution as such and had never said that only legal means should be used. Kautsky accepted Marx's economic doctrine and the inevitability of socialism as a result of the class struggle. In his opposition to Bernstein he is clearly closer to Marx than is his opponent. But the ambiguity of the label "orthodox" becomes apparent when we look at one of Kautsky's last works, *The Materialist Conception of History* (1927-28), which, at least by Soviet standards, is in many ways unorthodox. Kautsky opposed the October Revolution in Russia, feeling that conditions were still not ripe for socialism. He stressed the claim that until a revolution occurred spontaneously, as it had not in Russia, it was not the best means for achieving socialism. Moreover, he distinguished between socialism and nationalization. The latter, he warned, is not the same as the former: the essence of nationalization is state ownership of the means of production; the essence of socialism is the improvement of the conditions of the working class. Where nationalization coincides

Engels and Marxist Theory 111

with this aim, it is well and good; where it does not coincide, it should be fought.

The fact remains, however, that Marxism finally triumphed not in Germany but in Russia. The twentieth-century German worker had much to lose by revolt and little to gain; the same was not necessarily true of the Russian peasant and the budding Russian proletariat. As Lenin was the successful leader of the October Revolution, his interpretation of Marxism, according to contemporary Soviet theory, is the touchstone of Marxist orthodoxy.

Part 2: Leninism

Chapter VI
The Russian Background

Russian Philosophy in the Nineteenth Century

Soviet thought is based not simply on the writings of Marx and Engels, but also, and especially, on the writings of Lenin—on his interpretations of "the founders of Marxism" and on his original doctrines. Lenin leaned heavily on the writings of Marx and Engels, but his thought was also influenced by nineteenth-century Russian revolutionary tendencies and by the economic and physical conditions of the Russia of his time. Russian thought in the last decades of the nineteenth century in many ways prepared the intellectual soil for the reception of Marxism in Russia; and Leninism is the product not only of the Marxist seed but also of the Russian soil. Within the Russian tradition can be found a Russian messianic consciousness with emphasis on the future and with the dream of Moscow as the "Third Rome" uniting East and West, a keen moral sense of the evils of capitalism and of bourgeois philistinism with a concomitant emphasis on communal life and ownership, and an emphasis on social and ethical problems rather than on purely speculative philosophical issues. The parallels with Marxist thought are clear, though the details of the development of these and similar themes are often strikingly different in Marxist and in Russian thought and are variously developed within the latter as well. Lenin, an heir of both Marxist and Russian thought, produced his own synthesis, often different from, though continuous with, the thought of his predecessors.

The Slavophiles and Westernizers

Among the intellectual tendencies present in Russia in the nineteenth century, Slavophilism was one of the earliest, flourishing especially in the 1840's. As the name implies, the Slavophiles were lovers of things Slavic and clearly preferred Russia with its Orthodox faith to the West with its rationalism and individualism. They stressed the unique aspects of Russian history and of the Russian path to a future, ideal society. The early Slavophiles, among whom Ivan V. Kireyevsky (1806-56) and Alexis S. Khomyakov (1804-60) are the most important, emphasized religion and the religious rather than the material aspects of man. They were defenders of freedom of the person, freedom of conscience, freedom of speech; they saw the Russian village commune as the haven of these freedoms and as the ideal type of social organization within which the individual person could develop in a community based on love. They were opposed to the state, to Western secularism, and to capitalist civilization in general, and they hoped to build a new, vital culture on the basis of religious faith. As a movement Slavophilism was truly Russian, but its weakness lay both in its one-sided appraisal of the West and in its idealization of Russian reality.

Partly in reaction to Slavophilism and partly as a result of contact with the West, a countermovement, known as "Westernism," arose. The Westernizers loved Russia no less than the Slavophiles, but they saw that Russia's future lay in the ways of the West. They tended to emulate Western European at the expense of Slavic culture. Among the major early Westernizers dominating the scene in the 1840's and 1850's were V. G. Belinski (1811-48) and A. I. Herzen (1812-70). They took their inspiration from Hegel, Feuerbach, and the French socialists. Like the Slavophiles they championed human freedom, but unlike them they were antiecclesiastical, defending a more secular humanism and a humanistic socialism. The anarchist Bakunin, whom we saw among the Left-Hegelians, is also often included among the Westernizers.

From the Westernizers in the 1860's came the "nihilists" (as Turgenev dubbed them in *Fathers and Sons*), the new generation to whom even such men as Herzen and Belinsky were too idealistic. N. G. Chernyshevski (1828-89) was the leading figure of this movement; N. A. Dobrolyubov (1836-61) and D. I. Pisarev (1840-68) were prominent names connected with it. The nihilists rejected sentimentalism, authority, and the traditional standards of culture and morality. They championed the freedom of the masses from oppression and envisaged a "new society" of "new men." For the most part they adopted a materialistic outlook. Science became something of an object of faith, political economy a subject of study. Chernyshevski, a Russian Feuerbachian, is probably best known as the author of the novel *What Is to Be Done?*, which became a catechism for revolutionaries. In this book Chernyshevski argues for the development of society from agrarianism to a type of cooperative socialism without going through the stage of capitalism. He considers the capitalist wage system immoral but, unlike Marx, he believes that a just and equitable system of distribution is more important for the new, socialist society than increase in production. For him, as for Marx, the interests of humanity as a whole coincide with the interests of the people, and for the sake of these interests he advocates the subordination of personal to social values. He inspired those who came after him both by his writings and by his example. Lenin was among those well acquainted with *What Is to Be Done?*, and he called one of his own works by the same title. Like Chernyshevski Lenin is an ascetic who sees the necessity of strengthening character by enduring pain. Unlike Chernyshevski Lenin attacks the peasant commune.

Narodnichestvo

Nihilism, despite its opposition to the romanticism of the earlier Westernizers, was itself still infected with utopianism. It spoke of a new society but offered no workable program for its achievement; yet it paved the way first for a movement known as "narodnichestvo" in the 1870's and finally for the advent of Russian Marxism. The term "narodnichestvo," used in various ways by writers, is elastic enough to include Herzen as the "father" of the movement according to some and such later Slavophiles as Dostoevski and Tolstoi according to others, such as Berdyaev. The quality common to all seems to be a genuine concern and feeling for the *narod*, or the common people. For "religious narodniks" such as Dostoevski and Tolstoi, the people were the guardians and protectors of a hidden religious truth; for the "social narodniks" the people were the guardians and protectors of the social truths lost by the cultured, sophisticated, ruling class.

The narodnichestvo of the 1870's and 1880's, which both led to Marxism and came to clash with it, can conveniently be called "populism." It was a movement of intellectuals who saw the common people, especially the peasantry, as the bearers and protectors of truth. These intellectuals, realizing that their culture was built at the expense of the people, saw themselves as indebted to them. The chief spokesmen of the movement were P. L. Lavrov (1823-1900) and N. K. Mikhailovski (1842-1904). Like the Marxists they were opposed to capitalism and to the bourgeois conception of property. Unlike the Marxists they insisted on the importance of the individual person; they saw history as determined not by economic forces but by individuals acting on the basis of subjective choice and for moral ideals; and they supported a type of agrarian, ethical, cooperative socialism. Mikhailovski rejected the application of Marx's analysis to Russia, claiming that Russia must find its own path to socialism by educating and preparing the people for it. In 1874 a mass "movement to the people," involving several thousand intellectuals took place. But the intellectuals were generally resented, mistrusted, misunderstood, and often denounced by the peasants. The failure of the movement led to a split among the populists, some advocating gradual preparation for a slow social transformation of society and others defending violence and revolution.

Among the early Russian advocates of revolution two deserve special mention: P. N. Tkachev (1844-86) and S. G. Nechaev (1847-82). The former, in many ways a convinced follower of Marx, argued that since Russia was about to enter the capitalist stage of development which would lead to a more stable government, a small revolutionary minority should seize power while it still had the chance. He hoped that socialism could be achieved in Russia in this way without going through the stage of bourgeois capitalism. Nechaev, who founded a revolutionary society called "The Axe" or "The People's Justice," was a forerunner of Lenin. With Bakunin he wrote a work called the *Revolutionary Catechism,* which preached an atheistic revolutionary asceticism, rigid discipline, and great self-control—all qualities which Lenin later both exemplified and defended. Nechaev, like Lenin, advocated

The Russian Background 117

small revolutionary cells, which were to bring about a revolution; he also broke with traditional morality, holding that what helps the revolution is moral, what hinders it is immoral—a dictum which Lenin both lived and made the cornerstone of communist morality.

Russian Marxism

In the 1880's, finally, we find Marxism entering significantly into Russian thought. Herzen and Bakunin had earlier attacked Marx in their writings (and so had helped to make him known in Russia), and Bakunin had translated the Communist *Manifesto* into Russian. In 1871 N. I. Zieber (1844-88), a professor at the University of Kiev, had written on Marx's economic doctrine, and in 1872 the first volume of *Capital* appeared in Russian. Marx's intellectual sources were the same as those which had influenced the Russian Westernizers, and his materialism, socialism, opposition to the evils of capitalism, and anti-individualism were all compatible with the developing Russian thought. After the assassination of Alexander II in 1881 failed to arouse the peasants to action, many felt that populism had had its day, and Marxism was championed as a more viable alternative.

Marxism provided a more comprehensive theoretical framework than the revolutionary intelligentsia had had up to that time. The Marxists in opposition to the populists, whom they considered utopian socialists, generally favored the industrialization of Russia. Narodnichestvo had paved the way for the acceptance of the notion of the proletariat, and the people were looked to as the creators of history and as those who would inherit the earth. Scientific socialism gave structure to this belief, which became an article of faith for the revolutionaries. Russian Marxism, however, was not homogeneous, and a number of different groups arose. The most important in spreading Marxism was the Russian exile group, "Liberation of Labor," of which Georgi Plekhanov (1856-1918) was the leader. In general, Plekhanov fought for orthodoxy against the various types of revisionism.

The so-called legal Marxists included P. B. Struve (1870-1944), N. A. Berdyaev (1874-1948), and S. N. Bulgakov (1871-1944). They were known as legal Marxists because they published in legal journals. In general, these men were intellectuals and as such were dissatisfied with most of the philosophy found in Marx. From Marx they went to Hegel, and thence to Kant, becoming neo-Kantian and assuming something of an idealist point of view. They were opposed to the determinism of the superstructure and the fatalism which they saw implied therein. Those, who like Berdyaev and Bulgakov sought God while holding some aspects of the Marxian theory, came to be known as "God-seekers." Others, like A. V. Lunacharski (1875-1933) and M. Gorki (1868-1936), rejected God but tried to find some sort of a God-substitute and so were dubbed "God-builders." For these latter, mankind as a whole and the collective achievements thereof were deified.

Another Marxist movement, known as "economism" was in general composed of those concerned exclusively with the economic (and not at all with the political) struggle of the working class. The economists strongly supported the labor union movement and were to a large extent nonrevolutionary. They were defeated by the writings of Plekhanov and especially by Lenin's *What Is to Be Done?* Empiriomonism was advocated by Bogdanov (a pseudonym of A. A. Malinovski, 1873-1928), who until 1910 had been a Bolshevik. He was influenced by Mach, the Austrian philosopher-scientist, and claimed that objects as such did not exist apart from experience. Bogdanov's position is one of the primary targets of Lenin's *Materialism and Empirio-Criticism.*

Early in the twentieth century the Russian Marxist party (the Russian Social Democratic Workers' Party) itself split into two groups, the Mensheviks (minority) and the Bolsheviks (majority). In general, the Mensheviks were in favor of the gradual development of socialism in Russia and of a diffuse, decentralized party organization with a large membership, while the Bolsheviks championed immediate revolution and a small, highly disciplined party. The Bolsheviks, led by Lenin, thus united revolutionary Russian tendencies with Marxian doctrine. The idea of the proletariat replaced the actual proletariat, and it was believed that a small minority, if well organized, could bring about the necessary revolution. Though the actual split of the Russian Social Democratic Workers' Party into the Bolsheviks and the Mensheviks occurred at the Second Congress of the Party in 1903, it was not until 1912 that the Bolsheviks formed an independent party. In the October Revolution of 1917 the Bolsheviks triumphed. They identified the Russian people with the proletariat and at-

The Russian Background 119

tempted to join the Russian search for universal social justice and the Russian method of coercion with many of the ideas of Marx. In Lenin, the revolutionist, we have an absolutist: in him we find totalitarian Marxism united with a characteristically Russian belief in absolute truth.

Plekhanov

Life and Works

Georgi Valentinovich Plekhanov (1856-1918), whose father was a landowner, was one of the most important Russian Marxists and one of the stoutest defenders of Marxism against the various Russian revisionists. He explained and defended dialectical and historical materialism as well as scientific socialism and contributed to Marxist literature in the philosophy of history, aesthetics, logic, and psychology. Lenin called his works on philosophy the finest in the international Marxist literature and claimed one could not really understand Marxism without studying all of Plekhanov's works.[1]

Late in 1875 Plekhanov joined the revolutionary movement of narodniks and by 1880 had become so involved that he had to emigrate to Switzerland to escape arrest by the czarist police. In Switzerland he studied the works of Marx and Engels and accepted them completely. One of the founders of the first Russian Marxist group, "The Emancipation of Labor" organized in 1883, he translated much of the Marxian literature into Russian and gave many lectures on Marxism. Having once been a populist he understood what they held. After his conversion to Marxism he attacked the populists, who wanted to turn the land over to the peasants and who held that it was possible to reach socialism directly from the peasant stage without going through the stage of capitalism. Plekhanov also argued against the populist view that individual heroes made history. In a pamphlet entitled *Socialism and the Political Struggle* he said the proletariat and not the peasantry is the driving force of the revolution. In 1884 he wrote a work called *Our Differences* in which he called for the formation of a working-class party in Russia. He also claimed in it that capitalism had already begun in Russia. He wrote voluminously against the populists, as well as against Bernstein, Struve, Bogdanov, and others. In *The Development of the Monist View* of History (1895), called by Lenin a book "which had helped to educate a whole generation of Russian Marxists,"[2] Plekhanov continued his attack on the populists and presented a defense and explanation of dialectical and historical materialism. In 1896 he wrote *Essays in the History of Materialism*, in 1897 *Essays in Historical Materialism*, and in 1898 *The Role of the Individual in History*. After 1900, with Lenin, he edited the two journals *Iskra* and *Zarya*. At the Second Congress of the Russian Social Democratic Party in 1903 Plekhanov voted with the Bolsheviks, though he was opposed to Lenin's desire to start the revolution immediately. In later life he straddled the Menshevik and Bolshevik positions on numerous issues. In the *Fundamental Problems of Marxism* (1910) he considers Marxism a logical development of the writings of Feuerbach. In 1917 Plekhanov returned to Russia and lent his support to the provisional government. He opposed the October Revolution, because he could see no possibility of establishing socialism at that time, and died in 1918.

Monistic View of History

Plekhanov's *The Development of the Monist View of History*, written in 1894 and published in 1895, is a polemic against the populist N. K. Mikhailovski. In this work Plekhanov criticizes the view of the populists, defends and explains dialectical and historical materialism, and attempts to demonstrate that Marxism is applicable to Russia, which had already entered the stage of capitalist development. It was consequently necessary to establish a class consciousness among the proletariat, since they—and not the populist "heroes"—would bring about the revolution.

The book is in six chapters: French Materialism of the 18th Century, French Historians of the Restoration, The Utopian Socialists, Idealist German Philosophy, Modern Materialism, and Conclusion.

As is still done in Soviet expositions of Marxism today, Plekhanov begins by drawing a distinction between materialism and idealism, both of which, he points out, are monisms in that they seek to explain all phenomena in terms of a single principle. Marxism not only explains everything in terms of matter, but finds therein the historical factor which produces society and its ideas. The French materialists mistakenly emphasized environment to the exclusion of ideas; idealists em-

The Russian Background 121

phasized ideas to the exclusion of everything else. The Marxist solution admits the importance of both environment and ideas. It admits that opinions govern the world, but sees that opinions themselves as well as the social environment must be explained, and seeks to uncover the factor in history which determines both.

The French historians of the Restoration sought the answers to all legal, moral, political, and economic questions in "human nature,"[3] though not all of them had the same conception of human nature. It was assumed that human nature was invariable, fixed once and for all. But how one could explain social *development* on this basis remained unclear. Social needs were explained by human nature and human nature by social needs. Thus, neither was explained and the French historians were caught in a vicious circle.[4]

The utopian socialists accepted the notion of human nature and deduced from it an ideal social order. But as with their predecessors, they were unable to agree on what man's nature was. They too argued in a circle, explaining man by history and history by man. The utopians focused not on society as it is, but on society as it ought to be.

Idealist German philosophy was the first to view all phenomena dialectically, from the point of view of evolution.[5] Hegel showed that leaps occur in both nature and society, that quantity develops into quality, that every phenomenon is transformed into its opposite. Thus, man, as everything else, was at last seen not as static but as developing. Hegel saw that every necessary process takes place in conformity to law and that man's activities were governed by laws. Man's freedom, consequently, consists of his discovery of the laws which govern his development. Hegel saw that instead of studying man's nature, one should study the nature of social relations. But in looking for what determines social relations, Hegel, the idealist, stopped at the "Concept" or "Idea."[6]

According to Plekhanov modern materialism, or "dialectical materialism" as he called the Marxist kind of materialism, gives the correct answer to the question of the real basis of social relations. The answer is not in ideas nor in human nature but in the external nature which surrounds man, in the material conditions in which he lives and works, in his means of production and his productive forces. Man changes his nature by acting on and changing the external world. Plekhanov then presents historical materialism as the basis for explaining the development of society. In several instances he also extends historical materialism to areas never specifically developed by Marx or Engels. He says for instance,"*the influence of the literature of one country on the literature of another is directly proportional to the similarity of the social relations of these countries.*"[7] He also considers interaction in international life and the formation of social psychologies. With respect to social ideas, he says a genius is a person who grasps the meaning of emerging social relations significantly in advance of his contemporaries; in art a genius gives the best expression to the prevailing aesthetic tendencies. The genius is thus not an individual standing outside of society but merely one who sees or expresses more clearly the tendencies of society.

The upshot is that the Marxian ideal is "the subordination of *necessity* to *freedom*, of blind *economic forces* to the *power of human reason.*"[8] It is a true ideal for it corresponds to economic reality. Moreover, Russia had entered on the path of capitalist development with the emancipation of the peasantry in 1861 and has continued along that path. The laws of capitalism which Marx uncovered are therefore at work in Russia and the harmful consequences of capitalist development can be weakened only if the self-consciousness of the Russian worker grows. Plekhanov concludes by pledging himself to strive for the Marxian ideal.

The Individual and History

In *The Role of the Individual in History* Plekhanov again attacks the populist view of the hero. The opponents of Marxism claimed that Marx and Engels had ignored the role of the individual, abandoning him to fatalism. The populists argued that heroes make history by leading the inert masses. Plekhanov took pains to argue against this position. If this view were followed consistently it would make senseless any attempt to organize the proletariat. There would be no need to organize them, for they would be led by the heroes.

Plekhanov asserts that the conception of the human will in Marxism is perfectly consistent with practical activity, because, according to Marx, the individual would see that it is impossible for him to act other than the way he does act. Plekhanov claims that this knowledge helps action, since freedom consists in being conscious of necessity. Consciousness of

The Russian Background 123

the necessity of one's actions increases the energy of the actor. One identifies with the stream of history and sees oneself as one of the forces calling it into being. Plekhanov tells us, *"men make history, and, therefore, the activities of individuals cannot help being important in history."*[9] Despite this, however, the course of history is not determined solely by the conscious actions of men, since the results produced are not always those intended. There is in history a hidden necessity operating according to immutable laws, though the activities of individuals have a certain particularity of their own within the given social conditions. Individual acts are not determined, but the choices available to an individual, as well as the pattern of historical development as a whole, are determined. Madame Pompadour and Louis XV, for example, had a peculiar and deplorable influence on France which was possible because of social forces in France at the time. Their actions had a certain particularity and peculiarity of their own, but their actions were possible because of the given social conditions. "The character of an individual is a 'factor' in social development only where, when, and to the extent that social relations permit it to be such."[10] As a result, at any given period in history, it is the form of organization present that determines both what is possible and the significance of the actions of particular talented or incompetent individuals. The fate of a nation thus may depend on accidents of the second degree, for instance, on the sudden death of a leader (or, it seems reasonable for us to add, on the appearance of a Lenin).

The causes of the French Revolution lay in the social relations and ultimately in the productive forces of France at the given time. The personal qualities of particular individuals made one person rather than another more fit to satisfy the social needs. If that individual had died, however, his place would have been taken by someone else. "Owing to the specific qualities of their minds and characters, influential individuals can change the *individual features of events and some of their particular consequences,* but they cannot change their general *trend,* which is determined by other forces."[11] Plekhanov tells us that what would have happened if A had died before solving problem X is that C, D, or E might have solved it. The crux of the matter, however, lies in the "might." There is no way of proving that individuals C, D, or E necessarily would have solved it.

A man of talent is a product of his social relations. Talented men are the products of a trend and do not create it. The trend produces the artist, not the artist the trend. The trend is determined by the productive forces and mutual relations existing between men in the socio-economic processes of production, though individual features reflect the personal qualities of the leading people.

Plekhanov concludes, therefore, that the development of productive forces must be regarded as the "general cause" of the historical progress of mankind, since these forces determine the social relations of men. These set the limits to man's effective action. Within this framework a person's actions are further limited by his particular historical situation, which we can call "particular causes," and which are themselves created by the productive forces. Finally, owing to the personal qualities of individual men and "other similar accidents," events take on their distinctive individual features. But neither such individual causes, nor the broader particular causes bring about fundamental changes or determine fundamental trends. They operate only within the limits of the ultimately determining general causes. Thus, if a public figure knows the direction that social relations are taking, he is able to know how the social mentality is changing and, consequently, is able to influence it. But in this sense, and in this sense only, it is possible for individuals to make history.

Plekhanov, unfortunately, does not and could not prove his claim that history would have been the same if some particular individual—an Alexander, Caesar, Napoleon, Lenin —had not appeared on the scene. Furthermore, when Plekhanov introduces his theory of multiple causality, he fails to analyze sufficiently the relationship of the major cause with the secondary and accidental causes; for it might well be argued that the major cause is made up of the totality of the so-called accidents of history, without presupposing any basic trend that is *inevitably* unfolding on the part of history.

With respect to freedom Plekhanov discusses the notion of an individual being free *to* act within certain limits determined by his socio-economic conditions providing that he is free *from* external impediments and that he has insight into the laws applicable in the given circumstances. An individual's freedom in history thus parallels his freedom in science. A scientist is free *to* change water into oxygen and hydrogen providing he has the proper equipment and the proper knowledge. And if he doesn't, someone else can just as well. But this explanation of history fails to answer the question of why a given individual does what he does in given circumstances. The conditions of freedom outlined by Plekhanov are necessary but not sufficient conditions for human action. The question of whether an individual does act freely is yet to be answered, and consequently so is the question of the true influence of the individual on history. Is an individual determined to act or is he free to act or not act? If he is free, and if his action is effective, then he is not determined by productive forces and can both act in opposition to them and use them for his own purposes. Finally, what is the mechanism of his action and how, if at all, can it be explained? These crucial questions remain unanswered by Plekhanov. There seems to be implied the thesis that *if* we knew enough we would see that individual accidents and choices are truly determined. But in the absence of any proof for this claim Plekhanov settles for the general determination of history by economic conditions and for the theory of causality in history outlined above. Marx uncovered the laws determining history's development in terms of classes, not of individuals; Plekhanov's attempt to handle the individual flounders on the rock of insufficient evidence and knowledge to prove his view. The Soviet philosophers have not made any significant advance beyond Plekhanov on the question of freedom.

Geography, Art, and Knowledge

In *Fundamental Problems of Marxism*, Plekhanov repeats much of the Marxist notion of history. However, he emphasizes the importance of geography in determining the forces of production. He states, for example: "Thus the peculiarities of the geographical environment determine the evolution of the forces of production, and this, in its turn, determines the development of economic forces and, therefore, the development of all the other social relations."[12] Likewise, he asserts: "We now know that the development of the forces of production (which for its part, in the last resort, determines the development of all social relations) itself primarily depends upon the peculiarities of the geographical environment."[13] And, "Thanks to the influence of the geographical environment, when a given development of the forces of production had occurred, there resulted a specific aggregate of the relations of production, differing in the two cases because the geographical environment was different."[14] Stalin, in his *Dialectical and Historical Materialism*, cited this notion of the importance of geography in Plekhanov's thinking as a "geographical deviation." The Soviets continue to hold Stalin's view on this question.

In the short work *Sudden Changes in Nature and in History*, Plekhanov explains how revolutions, political catastrophes, and the like do not come about suddenly but are the result of a process of development. The situation in history is similar to that in nature. An eclipse may be sudden for one who is ignorant of the causes of the eclipse, but an astronomer who has predicted it may have waited a long time for it. Sudden changes in history are prepared by social evolution and are an example of a change from quantity to quality. A revolution may produce a different type of regime, but the revolution itself is not sudden; it could have been predicted if one had seen the build-up or the changes in quantity which preceded it.

With respect to art and culture Plekhanov is the first Marxist to develop the correlation, at least on the whole, between art forms and the history of economic development. This was implicit in Marx's materialist interpretation of history, but not worked out in detail by either Marx or Engels. Plekhanov's main argument is that though psychological, religious, and other factors influence art, all of these are ultimately determined by economic factors. Though there is a relative independence of development, any stream of art which has any force at all is determined by the economic conditions of the time.[15]

Plekhanov's theory of knowledge[16] is more controversial than his presentation of historical materialism, and it was attacked by Lenin in *Materialism and Empirio-Criticism*. Plekhanov held a "hieroglyphic" theory of knowledge, being in this respect a follower of Helmholtz and Sechenov. He held, with them, that sensations are not *copies* of reality, but are *hieroglyphs*. Thought is not like reality, but makes us aware of reality. Consider a cube and a cylinder, for example. The shadow the cube casts on the cylinder is not like the cube, for the flat surfaces are curved; but any change in the cube yields a corresponding change in the shadow. Likewise, knowledge is not like an object, but any change that takes place in an object brings about a corresponding change in knowledge. This is sufficient to know and deal with the world. This position, he claims, as opposed to that of Bogdanov, preserves the distinction between appearance and reality, preserves the objective independence of the world, makes possible a doctrine of error, and avoids idealism and the Kantian unknowable thing-in-itself. But to Lenin, Plekhanov's theory of knowledge was a form of scepticism, if not of idealism, for knowledge is limited to appearances; only the hieroglyphs are known directly, and so reality remains both unknown and unknowable. We need scarcely add that Soviet theory of knowledge is based on Lenin's and not on Plekhanov's position.

Contribution to Marxism-Leninism

Plekhanov was a central figure in the development of Russian Marxism. In this respect his importance should not be underestimated. His original contributions consist mainly of interpreting Marx and Engels. He draws out some of the implications of historical materialism and applies Marxist theses to Russian conditions. As a defender of Marxism against change and revision he can be considered an orthodox interpreter—and is generally so considered by the Soviets, at least as far as his pre-1903 works are concerned. His contributions to dialectical materialism, as differentiated from historical materialism, are negligible. He could be characterized as a follower of Marx, interested in the problems that Marx was interested in rather than in those handled by Engels later in his life. He was a Russian as much as a Marxist, however, and was primarily concerned with the development of conditions in Russia and with the eventual revolution in Russia. As a good Marxist he was not only an armchair philosopher but he also engaged in the labor movement; yet in sum, Plekhanov was more of a philosopher than a revolutionary, more a man of thought than of action. He served as a teacher for a generation of Marxists, among whom one can number Lenin. It was not Plekhanov, however, but Lenin who was the decisive factor in the Russian revolution and the one whose stamp remains most clearly on Soviet thought.

Chapter VII
Lenin and the Party

V. I. Ulianov (Lenin): Life and Works

Vladimir Ilyich Ulianov (1870-1924) was born in the small town of Simbirsk. His father, a school inspector, had moved his family there shortly before Lenin was born. The second of six children, Lenin seems from all reports to have had a very happy childhood. As a youth he was extremely methodical in his studies and was an exemplary student. He was sixteen when his father died. Within a year his older brother, Alexander, became involved in a plot to kill Czar Alexander III; he was caught, tried, and hanged. The event seems to have sparked Lenin's desire for revolutionary activity and reform.

Soon after his brother's execution, Lenin was graduated from secondary school at the head of his class and went to the University of Kazan to study law. He was soon expelled, however, for being involved in a student disturbance and lived under police surveillance at a Kokushkino estate with his mother. The following year, at the age of eighteen, he started reading Marx. His family moved to the town of Samara, where he organized a Marxist group. After a period of studying on his own, he took his examinations and in 1891 received his law degree from the University of Saint Petersburg.

Lenin worked at law for a very short while and in 1893 left Samara for St. Petersburg. There he joined the "Elders," an underground Social-Democratic group. Early in the year 1895 he went abroad for medical treatment and met Plekhanov and Paul Axelrod (another of the founders of the Emancipation of Labor group) in Geneva. In September 1895 he returned to Russia, and in December he was arrested with proofs of the first issue of a clandestine newspaper. Though imprisoned for fourteen months, he led the "League for the Liberation of Labor" by means of a dot-dash code system placed in the books which his sister was allowed to bring him. Upon his release from prison he was banished to Siberia for three years. There he met and married Nadezhda Krupskaya, who worked devotedly and faithfully as his secretary throughout his life.

Lenin utilized his period of banishment to study, discuss, and write. In 1899 he published *The Development of Capitalism in Russia*. *The Aims of Russian Social Democrats*, which he had also finished in exile, appeared in March 1900, after he had left Siberia. This work is signed "N. Lenin," a pseudonym by which V. I. Ulianov was henceforth to be known. He chose "Lenin" because the Lena River flowed through Siberia near the place of his exile.

In May 1900 Lenin was one of the small group that decided to publish a paper *Iskra* ("The Spark") abroad. Lenin crossed into Germany and edited the paper, the first issue of which appeared on December 21, 1900. It was printed in small type on onion skin and smuggled into Russia by secret agents.

While in exile, Lenin had read Spinoza, Helvetius, Kant, Fichte, Schelling, Feuerbach, and Plekhanov, and was a convinced Marxist in philosophy. In 1902 his work *What Is to Be Done?* appeared. In it Lenin states his ideas concerning the party, calling for strong centralization and for a cell-type organization composed of dedicated revolutionaries. He also stresses the importance of the theory of political consciousness. In 1903 the break between the Bolsheviks and the Mensheviks, already mentioned, took place, and Lenin resigned from *Iskra*, which had become a Menshevik organ. In 1904 appeared Lenin's *One Step Forward, Two Steps Back*, in which he attacks the Menshevik position, defending the Party as an organization and a weapon of the proletariat. His *Two Tactics of Social Democracy in the Democratic Revolution* (1905) advocates an alliance of the proletariat and the peasantry, with the proletariat in the lead.

In October 1905 Lenin returned to Russia, where he campaigned for armed insurrection. He fled to Finland in 1906 to escape the police; the following year he was forced to leave Finland as well and went to Paris, from where he continued to direct the Bolshevik Party. He founded the weekly paper *Zvezda* ("The Star") in 1910 and the daily paper *Pravda* ("Truth") in 1912. After 1905 when Bogdanov and empirio-criticism began to grow in influence, Lenin turned to philosophy and together with Plekhanov defended dialectical materialism. His major philosophical work, *Materialism and Empirio-Criticism*, appeared in 1909 and deals with two main problems: the development of a materialist theory of knowledge and the clarification of the notion of matter. Both of these were made essential because the discovery of subatomic particles was lending support to idealism and to the claim that matter was "disappearing." Lenin presents a "copy-theory" of knowledge, according to which what is known is identical with the reality which exists independently of the knower.

When war broke out, Lenin led an unsuccessful movement to turn the imperialist war into civil war. He spent the early war years in Switzerland, where he again turned to philosophy. Here he composed his *Philosophical Notebooks*, which were eventually published in full in 1933. From these we can document his very great interest in dialectics. In 1913 he published "The Three Sources and Three Component Parts of Marxism," an article in which he briefly develops the theme that Marxism "is the lawful successor of the best that has been created by humanity in the nineteenth century—German philosophy, English political economy, and French socialism."[1] The following year he wrote a summary biographical sketch and exposition of Marxism for the *Granat Encyclopedia*.

From January to June 1916 Lenin wrote *Imperialism, the Highest Stage of Capitalism*, his most widely circulated work, in which he argues that imperialism, the last phase of capitalism, leads to imperialist wars and thus to the internal weakening and division of capitalist countries. He claims that socialism will triumph not in all countries simultaneously but successively in different countries. On the basis of this doctrine Stalin was to later develop the doctrine, still followed today, of the possibility of the success of socialism in one country. It is also from this doctrine that much of the peaceful coexistence line stems.

Lenin returned to Russia in April 1917 and presented his thesis on *The Tasks of the Proletariat and the Peasant Revolution*, rejecting the provisional government, demanding that power be placed in the hands of the proletariat, and calling for the nationalization of land and for the formation of the Third International. This plan, initially unpopular, was finally adopted by the Bolshevik Party. The Bolsheviks revolted in July in St. Petersburg, but their revolt was crushed. Lenin then fled to Finland, where he wrote *State and Revolution* (1917). Though directed mainly against the Mensheviks, it gives Lenin's view of the state and outlines the transition period from capitalism to socialism, claiming that this is the period of the dictatorship of the proletariat. It also sets forth the form of the Republic of the Soviets. In the autumn of 1917 Lenin returned illegally to St. Petersburg, where he was instrumental in bringing about the October Revolution. After its success, he became chairman of the Council of People's Commissars. Though in poor health he remained extremely active; in 1922 he suffered his first stroke. He remained interested in philosophy until his death, and we have indications that he read Hegel, among others, during his last period. He wrote to the editors of *Under the Banner of Marxism*, the Soviet philosophical periodical, to emphasize the importance of the study of dialectics and of philosophy in general. He suffered his third stroke on January 21, 1924, and died on that date.

What Is to Be Done?

One of Lenin's major contributions to Marxism is his development of a theory of the Party, its organization, and its role in the revolutionary struggle. The Party—Lenin's Party—spearheaded the Russian revolution, seized power, and has retained it until the present. The Party, as the self-appointed vanguard of the proletariat, is the guide and guardian of all aspects of Soviet life. Marxism-Leninism is the world-outlook of the Party and dialectical materialism is its philosophy, which it guards "like the apple of its eye."[2] The Party is the interpreter of Marx and so the custodian of the truth of Marxism; it is the arbiter of theoretical disputes; it unites theory and practice and fosters each by the other; it condemns heretics, deviationists, and revisionists. The Party is thus intimately linked with the development of Soviet thought and without understanding its theoretical basis the subserviance of Soviet philosophy and philosophers to the Party is almost incomprehensible. Yet it is a fact which must be understood if the patterns of Soviet thought are to be understood.

Though the Russian Social Democrats had been formed in 1898, they were composed of independent circles loosely linked together by neither plan nor discipline. This was a far cry from what Lenin thought was needed—a closely knit, highly disciplined Party composed of professional revolutionaries. He presented his theory of the Party in developed form in *What Is to Be Done?: Burning Questions of Our Movement* (1902). The work is noteworthy for its insistence on the importance of theory and on the interrelation of theory and practice.

The book begins with a discussion of "freedom of criticism." This cry had been raised by Bernstein and others. Bernstein denied the possibility of scientific socialism, he denied the existence of the contradictions inherent in capitalism which Marx claimed to have uncovered, he denied the necessity of the dictatorship of the proletariat, and he denied the theory of class struggle. He defended his position by claiming freedom of criticism with respect to the works of Marxism, for if they were wrong they deserved criticism. To Lenin, however, who considered Marx's works correct and in need of no criticism, this supposedly critical tendency appeared as nothing but opportunism. He accordingly interpreted freedom of criticism as meaning nothing but freedom for opportunism. "Those who are really convinced that they have advanced science, would demand, not freedom for the new views to continue side by side with the old, but the substitution of the old views by the new views."[3] Thus, in defense of Lenin's position it would seem that if someone were convinced of the truth of something, he would not generally tolerate the teaching of the opposite doctrine. There seems to be little reason to be tolerant, for instance, with respect to a teacher who wishes to teach that the earth is flat, for we are convinced it is round. The distinction between the *conviction* that one is right, however, and the *fact* of being right is the basis of the claim for tolerance; for people have often been convinced they were right while actually being mistaken. The possibility that Marxism is wrong is the point at issue, and

Lenin rejects this as a possibility. Moreover, though false criticism would eventually be shown to be false, Lenin argues that it might make some inroads on the minds of the noncritical thinker. For a revolutionary interested in achieving results, these inroads are to be avoided. Lenin thus claims that freedom of criticism should not be allowed, since it implies eclecticism and absence of principle. There can be no concessions in theory, he claims, for "without a revolutionary theory, there can be no revolutionary movement. . . . The *role of the vanguard can be fulfilled only by a party that is guided by an advanced theory.*"4 Without German philosophy, he adds, scientific socialism would have been impossible. The truth of Marxism must be kept free from the germ of criticism lest the revolutionary movement become infected and crippled.

Lenin then argues that though the strength of the revolutionary movement lies in the awakening of the masses, the masses need a consciousness and leadership which they can derive only from revolutionary leaders. Lenin's position is that Social Democratic consciousness does not arise spontaneously in the masses, but must be brought to them from without. The spontaneous awakening of the masses and the rise to consciousness of Social Democratic theories in the bourgeois intelligentsia took place simultaneously; but this consciousness must be brought to the masses and cannot arise from them. "To belittle Socialist ideology *in any way*, to *deviate from it in the slightest degree* means strengthening bourgeois ideology."5

To achieve its end Lenin claims that the Party needs a strong organization, systematic activity, and firm principles. The Party must educate the working class by "all-sided political exposure." It must "learn to apply practically the materialist analysis and the materialist estimate of *all* aspects of life and activity of *all* classes, strata, and groups of the population."6 Social Democrats must go to the people in all directions; they must go as theoreticians, as agitators, and as organizers. In order to accomplish this, the Social Democrats need training and organization so that they may best take advantage of the spontaneity of the masses. They must train themselves and be prepared to change their tactics, but not their doctrine, within twenty-four hours. The only way that this can be accomplished is by the presence of professional revolutionaries. This group, moreover, must be small and secret in order to be effective:

A small, compact corps, consisting of reliable, experienced and hardened workers, with responsible agents in the principal districts and connected by all the rules of strict secrecy with the organizations of revolutionists, can, with the wide support of the masses and without an elaborate set of rules, perform *all* the functions of a trade-union organization, and perform them, moreover, in the manner Social-Democrats desire. Only in this way can we secure the *consolidation* and development of a *Social-Democratic* trade-union movement, in spite of the gendarmes.[7]

Concerning professional revolutionists, he claims that: (1) they are necessary for the continuity of the movement, (2) they are the more needed, the more widely the masses are drawn into the movement, (3) they must be organized, (4) the more restricted they are in number the more difficult it will be for the police to catch the organization, and (5) a professional core will allow more workers to join in work under their direction. The professional revolutionist must be trained for years, and Lenin calls for "strict secrecy, strict selection of members, and the training of professional revolutionists."[8]

The concept of a well-organized secret Party composed of professional revolutionists was not original with Lenin, but he brought this notion into Marxism. For Marx the masses were to seize power openly and necessarily; for Lenin the Party was to direct the seizure of power by and for the masses. Marx disdained secrecy; for Lenin secrecy became a key factor in achieving the revolution. Moreover, for Lenin the Party assumed a quasi-infallible status and so rose above criticism, just as the Marxism upon which it was based also rose above criticism.

Finally, in this work, Lenin calls for the establishment of an illegal newspaper to unite the apparatus of the Party. It would be used to train, inform, unite, and establish contacts among the members of the party. He concludes by saying that this is what he is dreaming about and "we ought to dream!"[9] One must dream, he argues, if he is to run ahead and mentally conceive the working out of history. The differences between dreams and realities cause no harm providing the dreamer seriously believes in his dreams and is, at the same time, careful to observe the realities of life and to compare what he observes with the content of his dreams. As long as there is this realistic connection, all is well.

The Party and Partymindedness

Lenin continued to develop and implement his notions of the Party well beyond *What Is to Be Done?*. In *One Step Forward, Two Steps Back* (1904) he deals in detail with the differences between the Mensheviks and the Bolsheviks at the Second Party Congress and with the position taken by the new *Iskra* on questions of organization. Much of the work is a presentation of the minutes of the Second Party Congress with Lenin's commentary. The conclusion is that the Bolsheviks are revolutionary while the Mensheviks are the opportunist wing of the Party. The purpose of the Congress in Lenin's mind was to create the *real* Party of principles and organization. The basis of the party organization was two-fold: (1) centralism which "defined in principle the method of deciding all particular and detail questions of organization,"[10] and (2) a newspaper which would serve as the organ for ideological leadership of the Russian Social Democrats.

In this work Lenin sees the Party as the vanguard of the working class. The Party, he says, should be as organized as possible and should admit to its ranks no element which cannot be organized. He maintains that the stronger the organization, the harder the core, the more widely and richly it tends to influence the masses. For him the Party is the vanguard and should not be confused with the entire class.

Prior to the Second Party Congress, the Party consisted of unconnected circles, and its ties rested on friendship or confidence. The Party organized as Lenin intended would no longer be based on such ties. A Party member could, therefore, no longer refuse to work with another because of "lack of confidence" but must give reasons for such refusal based upon the principles of the program on tactics or upon Party moves.

In *Two Tactics of Social Democracy in the Democratic Revolution* Lenin argues that the outcome of the revolution is dependent upon the working class leading the people's revolution. The aims of the working class must be defined and an understanding of them must be spread. The Party is seen as being in advance of all others, and what places it in the front rank is that it has a precise program accepted by all. Details as to Party tactics and party congresses follow, with the conclusion that the Social Democrats are the representatives of the only advanced and revolutionary class and so must exert the initiative. "The workers . . . are striving to crush the reactionary forces without mercy, i.e., to set up a *revolutionary-democratic dictatorship of the proletariat and the peasantry.*"[11] It is significant that here Lenin calls for a union of the proletariat and the peasantry with the proletariat as the leaders. This, once again, is a change introduced by Lenin in the Marxian doctrine. In *The United States of Europe Slogan* (1915) Lenin characterizes the socialist revolution as an epoch of turbulent peoples and revolutions, and he emphasizes that the revolution must not be regarded as a single act. He argues for the possibility of the victory of socialism in only several or even in one capitalist country—another Leninist innovation in Marxism. The doctrine of the possibility of socialism in one country contradicts Marx's view that communism had to be world-wide to be successful. Since the Russian revolution was at best regional, either it was not a communist revolution or it was communist in a revised Leninist sense. Lenin argues that since the economic and political development of capitalism is uneven, one socialist country can stand up as a beacon attracting the oppressed classes of other countries to its cause. He argues similarly in *The War Program of the Proletarian Revolution* (1916, published in 1917) that since the development of capitalism is uneven in different countries, socialism cannot be victorious at the same time in all countries, but rather that it will win first in one or several countries while the rest will remain bourgeois or prebourgeois.

In the article "The Tasks of the Proletariat in the Present Revolution" Lenin finally calls for a change in the name of the Party from Social-Democrat to Communist. The workers, he claims, have no state; communism is actually the goal of the revolution, not socialism. Socialism, or the social ownership of the means of production and distribution according to the amount of work performed by an individual, is satisfactory as an intermediate step. But the ultimate goal is communism, which operates according to the principle: from each according to his ability, to each according to his need. He also points out that though democracy is a form of the state necessary for a transition period, in communism there is no state. Consequently, neither the label "socialist" nor "democrat" is appropriate as a Party label.

Lenin and the Party 137

The importance of the Party in Lenin's theory can scarcely be overemphasized. The Party is the vanguard of the proletariat and the proletariat is the most progressive element of the masses. The Party is thus in the forefront of all of humanity and the leader of the progressive elements. The Party sees most clearly what is needed by all of society, brings these needs to the consciousness of the people, and leads the way in social development. How the Party sees so clearly is never developed in detail. The closest one comes to an explanation is the claim that (1) the Party is armed with the laws of Marxism and operates according to them, and (2) the Party has the interests of humanity in mind and acts for these interests and not for personal gain or for the advantages of any particular group. If one challenges the so-called laws of Marxism, the first claim falls; if one questions whether the interests of humanity are really those enunciated by the Party, and if one remembers the Stalinist cult of personality, the second claim falls. But if one believes that the Party is indeed the most progressive element of mankind, then it does make sense to invest it with great power to bring about man's ultimate dreams. And it was in fact invested with extraordinary power once the October Revolution was successful.

The notion of *partiinost'* or of partisanship or of party-mindedness is one that follows as a direct result of the claim that the Party represents the interests of mankind. According to Marx, and to Lenin also, the superstructure of society always reflected the material base, and the state, law, morality, philosophy, religion, and the like were always expressive of the dominant class in any society. Their function was consequently to preserve the power of the ruling class and to justify it. The Party, however, represents no particular class but the workers, the masses, and eventually all of humanity. This means that the Party rises above the interests of particular classes and so in its laws, morality, philosophy, and so on, it reflects not class interests, but the interests of humanity. Moreover, the Party, in its function as the most advanced element of society, is in a position to determine, without class bias, what is true or false, right or wrong, better or worse for society.

With respect to philosophy Lenin defends the claim of partisanship and emphasizes that all philosophies other than Marxism reflect the opinions of the ruling classes of the societies they represent. Marxism represents the proletariat, and so in principle, humanity. Marx and Engels, Lenin claims, were admittedly partisan in philosophy. But because of this and because they saw their partisanship clearly, they were able to detect and combat deviations from materialism and concessions toward idealism.[12] Lenin, as the guardian of Marxism, saw himself as the opponent of revisionism and opportunism. And this role of guardian of the truth, preserver of orthodoxy, and representative of the proletarian—and so all human—interests continues to be an important part of the structure of Soviet thought.

The Party and Determinism

Lenin's emphasis on the Party and his conception of its role both in bringing about the revolution and in leading the proletariat to communism were central to his interpretation —or revision—of Marxism. Their introduction cuts deep into the heart of historical materialism, for if the proletarian revolution is the inevitable result of economic development and if, as Marx said, the proletariat would be forced to seize the means of production, then it would seem that a secret, professional, well-organized group of revolutionaries is not required to bring about a successful revolution. And conversely, if the Party is necessary, then it seems that the revolution is not inevitable. Likewise, if the superstructure is determined by the base, it becomes problematic why after the revolution the Party should be as important as Lenin claims. If changes in the economic base bring about corresponding changes in the superstructure there seems to be little need for the guidance of the Party.

The deterministic interpretation of history is repudiated by Lenin in fact, if not explicitly in theory, and a quasi-voluntaristic view emerges from his writings. In his view economic conditions continue to be basic to historical developments and set the limits of what is possible and of what man or society can achieve. A revolution consequently would fail if it were initiated before conditions were ripe for it or if it were poorly executed. To a very large extent the objective conditions of society determine when a successful revolution is possible. But these objective conditions in themselves do not necessarily produce a revolution, nor do they necessarily produce a particular type of revolution. To wait for a mass spontaneous proletarian revolution is, in Lenin's eyes, utopian. It will not come about by itself. It must be brought about, at the proper moment, by leaders: ". . . the spontaneous struggle of the proletariat will not become a genuine 'class struggle' until it is led by a strong organization of revolutionists."[18]

Economic conditions thus make possible a successful revolution and are a necessary condition for it. They are not, however, a sufficient condition. There must also be a group ready to carry out the revolution at the proper moment and ready to take over once the revolution is successful. This is why there must be trained professional revolutionists. Lenin then implicitly denies the *inevitability* of the proletarian revolution. He defends its *objective possibility* and its desirability, but he also emphasizes that it will not take place until—and unless—certain other conditions are fulfilled. According to Lenin the Party, armed with Marxist theory, is able scientifically to analyze the objective conditions of society and to determine both what is to be done and when to do it. But is is not forced to act. The advent of communism—like any other event—is not inevitable in the sense that it will come about no matter what happens or what men do, but it can be achieved *if and only if* men do what is necessary in the framework of the objective conditions of their society. The so-called Marxian laws of social development help one see what can and what should be done; they indicate, for instance, what will happen if men act in a certain way. But they do not necessitate men's acting in that way. This must certainly have been clear to Lenin, since the plight of the workingman was not becoming worse in his time—as Marx thought it would—but was becoming better.

This quasi-voluntaristic view of historical materialism also serves as a justification for the Party's power following the revolution. For communism will be achieved only if certain things are done. What these things are is determined by viewing the goal to be achieved in relation to the objective material conditions and the laws of social development. Objective conditions make only certain actions possible. But not all of these possible actions have the same result and consequently not all of them will lead to the desired goal. The Party, as the guardian of the ideal or goal to be achieved and as the custodian of the laws of social development, analyzes the alternative actions open to society, choses those means most conducive to achieving the end, and then directs society along those lines. That the Party may be mistaken in its choice seems a logical corollary, though one that is not stated by Lenin.

This Leninist interpretation of historical determinism is followed in the Soviet Union today. Likewise, the role of the Party in its determination of goals, both short range (such as in the Five-Year Plans) and ultimate (such as communism), continues to the present time. Such determination of the direction of development of the base by the decisions of the Party —and so by the superstructure—implies a new conception of the role and status of the superstructure. But this theoretical change is not made explicit until late in the reign of Stalin.

Marx, emphasizing dialectics in opposition to crass materialism, underlined the active role of man. Lenin clearly underscores man's active role in social development still more, in fact to such an extent that he implicitly repudiates economic determinism in any strong sense of determinism.

The State and Revolution

The first aim of the Party was to bring about a revolution, overthrow the existing state, and seize power in the name of the masses. Lenin put forth his theory of revolution and his ideas on the state in *The State and Revolution* (1917). For our purposes, this work is interesting not only for what it contains (especially concerning the withering away of the state), but also for the technique of argument used. For Lenin's interpretations of Marx and Engels have become the only ones accepted by the Soviets, and his method of accepting certain portions of Marx and Engels as true and proved is still a standard pattern of argumentation in the Soviet Union today.

Lenin tells us that his prime task in this work is to *"reestablish* what Marx really taught on the subject of the state."[14] Lenin's technique of argumentation consists first of all in accepting Marx and Engels as unimpeachable authorities and sources. He does not reexamine their arguments, but accepts both their arguments and conclusions. Thus, whenever he quotes them he considers the discussion closed. He quotes them both to refute opponents and to establish a base for discussion of a question that they did not deal with or did not develop in detail. His technique of using Marx and Engels as authorities is understandable in view of the fact that he was writing for a Marxist audience and was trying to combat what he saw as distortions of Marxism. He uses the technique of

Lenin and the Party 141

arguing by quoting in most of his other works as well. The technique remains characteristic of the writings of the Soviet philosophers, who quote Lenin with as much authority as he quotes Marx and Engels.

Argument by quotation, however, is a dangerous technique, for very often counterquotation can be marshaled in support of the opposite position. Lenin, for instance, argues for a tight, closely knit revolutionary group; yet one could turn to Marx and Engels and find ground for opposing such a revolutionary group and for seeking peaceful means of change. Engels' Introduction to Marx's *The Class Struggles in France 1848-1850*, for example, states:

> With this successful utilization of universal suffrage, however, an entirely new method of proletarian struggle came into operation, and this method quickly developed further. . . . And so it happened that the bourgeoisie and the government came to be much more afraid of the legal than of the illegal action of the workers' party, of the results of elections than of those of rebellion. For here, too, the conditions of the struggle had essentially changed. Rebellion in the old style, street fighting with barricades, which decided the issue everywhere up to 1848, was to a considerable extent obsolete.[15]

In the same Introduction, we find also:

> If conditions have changed in the case of war between nations, this is no less true in the case of the class struggle. The time of surprise attacks, of revolutions carried through by small conscious minorities at the head of unconscious masses, is past.[16]

What clearer refutation of Lenin's theory of the Party could one desire! And again:

> We, the "revolutionists," the "overthrowers"—we are thriving far better on legal methods than on illegal methods and overthrow.[17]

One might also quote statements of Marx and Engels with respect to the claim that the revolution will take place in capitalistic countries and not in agricultural countries such as Russia. Even the statement:

> If the Russian Revolution becomes the signal for a proletarian revolution in the West, so that both complement each other, the present Russian common ownership of land may serve as a starting-point for a communist development,[18]

does not support Lenin's position without considerable interpretation. One could—and many did—quote Marx and Engels to show that the means of production had to be sufficiently developed before communism would become possible.

The possibility of quoting Marx and Engels in opposition to Lenin's position necessitates taking into account counter-quotations if an argument is to be conclusive. Lenin does this only where an opponent has already used a quotation from Marx or Engels. Where this happens a second step of argumentation is required, for a bare quotation does not prove anything in the face of another seemingly contradictory quotation. In these cases Lenin—and the Soviets follow his example—attempts to show that the opposing quotation is (1) an early position adopted by Marx or Engels which they later changed, (2) taken out of context in such a way that its true meaning is distorted and that in context it is not contradictory, or (3) applicable only to the conditions in which Marx and Engels were writing and so is not pertinent. All three means are also open to the opposition. Where arguments limp, polemic is added. And where this too is indecisive, the decision of which interpretation is correct is decided by who triumphs in the field of action. Lenin, of course, led the Party to success, and his interpretations of Marx and Engels as well as his original philosophical contributions are held as sacrosanct in the Soviet Union today. Whenever theoretical disputes arise in the development of Soviet thought, the last court of appeal is not the validity of the arguments per se but the decision of the Party.

Utilizing these techniques of argumentation Lenin examines and develops the Marxian theory of the state. On a passage by Engels Lenin comments:

> The state is the product and the manifestation of the *irreconcilability* of class antagonisms. The state arises when, where, and to the extent that class antagonisms objectively *cannot* be reconciled. And, conversely, the existence of the state proves that the class antagonisms are irreconcilable.[19]

Lenin and the Party 143

Lenin uses this meaning of "state" throughout his discussion—and this special meaning should be kept in mind. The state is always for him a product and manifestation of class antagonisms. That the existence of the state proves that class antagonisms are irreconcilable is true, however, only if "state" is taken in this special repressive sense. By using the term in this sense it becomes contradictory to speak of a nonrepressive state, though possibly one can speak of nonrepressive governments.

Lenin then explains the rising of the state from the need to hold class antagonisms in check and its use by those in power to exploit the oppressed class. He also follows Engels in arguing that the state as a repressive force will wither away when there is no longer a subject class. A government of persons will be replaced by the administration of things.

For Lenin the proletariat is the leader of the toiling and exploited masses. The proletariat is not equivalent to the masses, as it was for Marx, but is the leader of the masses. When the bourgeoisie is overthrown, the proletariat will be a ruling class which will organize the masses for the new economic order. This departure from Marx's position is based on the consideration that Russia was primarily an agricultural country and the masses were largely peasants. This change of position ignores the fact that for Marx the revolution was to come in an industrial society.

Lenin says of Marx that "his teaching is the *summing up of experience*, illuminated by a profound philosophical conception of the world and a rich knowledge of history."[20] Lenin presumably considers his additional experience sufficient ground for modifying Marx. Since he is considering the revolution in an agricultural instead of an industrial society he adds to Marxism the claim that the transition from capitalism to communism will undoubtedly yield many different political forms but that the essence of all of them will necessarily be a dictatorship of the proletariat. The state will wither away when it is no longer necessary to oppress anyone, but the transition to a stateless society, Lenin is careful to point out, will necessarily be gradual. There can be no thought of abolishing bureaucracy all at once. State officials will, however, merely carry out instructions as modestly paid foremen and bookkeepers. All officials will receive workingmen's wages under the control of the armed proletariat. Although the democratic republic is the closest approach to the dictatorship of the proletariat, nonetheless, it must be remembered that a democracy is also a state and not the final goal of communism, in which the state will be abolished and there will be no subordination of one man to another. Lenin remarks that "clearly there can be no question of defining the exact moment of the *future* 'withering away'—the more so since it will obviously be a lengthy process."[21] In a capitalist democracy, he claims, the oppressed are allowed to choose from among the oppressors a representative who will actually oppress them in parliament. However, under the democracy to be established in the transition of the state to a communist society, the people will choose their own representatives, who will actually represent them, and, of course, there will be no need for opposition parties since there will not be an oppressed opposition. This is the theoretical basis for the one-party system of the Soviet Union today. Moreover, in the communist state, any excesses on the part of individual persons will be suppressed without special apparatus by the armed people itself. The causes of excess—exploitation, want, and poverty—will be removed, and excesses will wither away. The first phase of communism, which Marx called "socialism," gives to each according as he produces. In this stage the state still remains to safeguard the public ownership of the means of production as well as to safeguard the equal distribution of products in accordance with labor. Lenin states:

> Until the 'higher' phase of communism arrives, the Socialists demand the *strictest* control by society *and by the state* of the measure of labor and the measure of consumption; but this control must *start* with the expropriation of the capitalists, with the establishment of workers' control over the capitalists, and must be exercised not by a state of bureaucrats, but by a state of *armed workers*.[22]

In the first stage of communism, all citizens will become employees of the state, and the state will consist of armed workers. Accounting and control will be the main function of the state for this period. The revolution will consist in the proletariat destroying the whole state machine that exists in the capitalist countries and in replacing it with one of armed workers. The new class will command and govern with the aid of a new machine. All will govern, in turn, and thus the road will be paved for all being accustomed to no one governing. This is Lenin's theory. Actual practice, illustrated most dramatically by Stalin's reign of terror, gave the theory the lie. Nonetheless, the theory has not changed significantly to the present day.

Chapter VIII
Materialism and Empirio-Criticism

Materialism and Empirio-Criticism: Critical Comments on a Reactionary Philosophy (1908) is one of the major sources of Soviet philosophy. Though not Lenin's last word on philosophical issues, it is the fullest exposition of his position on theory of knowledge and of reality.

Since Marx and Engels had paid little attention to a systematic development of a theory of knowledge, some Marxists attempted to make up for this deficiency in neo-Kantianism of one type or another. Lenin considered that the neo-Kantian "Marxists" were threatening Marxism as radically as were the idealists and the Machian[1] philosophers of science. To preserve Marxism he felt compelled to refute all three attacks, to develop a theory of knowledge, and to clarify the status of "matter." The resulting polemical critique of his opponents[2] and presentation of his own position was hurriedly written in Geneva and the British Museum between February and May 1908. Lenin's insistence that its speedy publication was necessitated "not only by literary, but also by serious political considerations,"[3] indicates how closely he linked theory and practice, philosophy and politics. Being both polemical and hastily written, the book is not always clear and sometimes is seemingly contradictory, while subtle distinctions are sacrificed to scoring points against opponents. Yet its every word is held sacred by Soviet philosophers, who attempt to elaborate a viable theory of knowledge based on it.

Idealism, Realism, and Materialism

Lenin begins *Materialism and Empirio-Criticism* by considering and attempting to refute the idealistic arguments against materialism, which he traces back to George Berkeley, an eighteenth-century British philosopher. Berkeley, following Locke, held that the objects of knowledge are ideas or sensations. It is ideas which the mind knows. Objects of experience or perception are thus ideas of sensations and these—and the minds which perceive them—are what truly exist. Since all that we know directly are our perceptions, what could we possibly mean by "matter?" When I speak of a book, what I mean is something composed of certain qualities or sense data, that is, something which could be perceived. If I take away the book's weight, its shape, its color, and all its other qualities I will not find anything left over which I could call "matter." Consequently, matter is not only an unknown or unknowable something, but it is a fiction. As a result all that exists for Berkeley are ideas or sense perceptions and minds which perceive them. For him, to be is to be perceived or to perceive. However, things do not disappear when I or some other human is not perceiving them for what we consider to be things are constantly perceived by the mind of God, and it is this perception which gives them continuity. Since "matter" is thus an unnecessary and meaningless term, materialism is nonsense.

Lenin claims that all the idealist arguments are reducible to this argument of Berkeley's, and it is this which he tries to refute. Berkeley's position is generally termed "subjective idealism." It is idealism because it holds that everything that is real is mind or mind-dependent, and it is subjective because Berkeley believes there are a plurality of perceiving minds or subjects. It is usually distinguished from objective idealism such as Hegel's idealism, which claims that reality is a rational system or single totality, absolute mind, of which everything is a part. But Lenin treats both positions as equivalent. Insofar as either type of idealism is a statement about reality, claiming that what is ultimately real is mind or spirit, it is a metaphysical position. It can and should be distinguished from epistemological idealism, which is concerned not with reality but with our knowledge and which holds that our knowledge of objects is constitutive of them. Lenin does not distinguish the two, and his failure to do so leads to certain basic confusions, for the opposite of epistemological idealism is realism—the position which maintains that objects are essentially as they appear to us, that our knowledge of them is not constitutive of them but corresponds to what they are. And realism is compatible with a variety of metaphysical positions including materialism (or the claim that only matter exists), dualism (or the claim that both matter and mind or spirit exist), and neutral monism (or the claim that only one basic kind of stuff exists which may manifest itself as either matter or mind). Lenin argues against epistemological idealism. But he claims thereby to prove not realism but materialism.

Following Engels, Lenin claims that there are only two great camps in philosophy: the materialists, who hold that nature or matter is primary and mind secondary, and the idealists, who hold that the reverse is the case. Between these two he acknowledges that there have historically been various forms of "agnosticism" (or epistemological scepticism), exemplified, for instance, by Hume and Kant. The "agnostics" deny the possibility of knowing the world as it is and refuse to take a stand on the primacy of spirit or matter. But according to Lenin any such agnostic position leads either to solipsism (which claims that I am the only person who exists for I am the only one I know directly) or to idealism. Solipsism is obviously false. Hence Lenin claims that all the present-day arguments against the materialist position of Marx and Engels are either obviously false or are reducible to the idealistic position. Having dispensed with intermediate positions his simplified task is to refute idealism and defend materialism.

In opposition to idealism Lenin maintains that "materialism, in full agreement with natural science, takes matter as primary and regards consciousness, thought, sensation as secondary, because in its well-defined form sensation is associated only with the higher forms of matter (organic matter)...."[4] But what he actually defines here is not materialism in its usual sense but rather realism which he confuses with or equates—without justification—with materialism. He also appropriates the point of view of science for materialism without defending this appropriation, though Machians and idealists with equal justification can claim science as their own.

Sensation is defined by Lenin as "the direct connection

between consciousness and the external world; it is the transformation of the energy of external excitation into a state of consciousness."[5] It should be noted in this definition that consciousness is something different from energy and that the difference is qualitative. The mechanism of the leap from external excitation to consciousness is not explained, but the two parts of it, Lenin claims, are given in our experience. Sensation, we are told later, "depends on the brain, nerves, retina, etc., i.e., on matter organized in a definite way."[6] It is the result of the action of objects which exist outside and independently of our sense organs, and is thus the "subjective image of the objective world."[7] Sensations give information about objective reality, the only reality that there is. Consequently, it is via sensation that one is in touch with reality. "Sensation reveals objective truth to man."[8] "My sensation is subjective, but its foundation (or ground—*Grund*) is objective."[9]

Blurring the distinction between epistemology and metaphysics, Lenin uses the word "materialism" instead of "realism" because he holds that any realism that oscillates between idealism and materialism is a muddle. He never argues this against the claims of dualism or neutral monism, but merely asserts his position. Aristotle, for example, can be considered a realist because he holds that objects exist independently of the knower. Yet Aristotle also affirms the existence of an immaterial prime mover. On the ontological level it would seem that he holds spirit is primary and not matter. Following Engels, Lenin would claim that Aristotle could be correctly called a realist only if he gave up his prime mover and became a consistent materialist; otherwise he would be confusing incompatible positions. Consequently, Lenin uses the term "materialism" to identify what he would call a consistent realistic position. But he does not justify this reduction of realism to materialism, and the result is a confusion of ontological and epistemological categories. All the arguments which he uses to defend materialism are in fact arguments for realism, and since he does not justify his reduction of the one to the other, his appropriation of the arguments for materialism is indefensible. In a similar illegitimate manner he appropriates for materialism the viewpoint and arguments of common sense. He then goes on to enunciate a number of arguments against idealism:

1) He claims that the world and other people exist inde-

pendently of us, which as we saw, is the claim of realism. He argues that our sensations and our consciousness are an image of the external world; since the image cannot exist without the thing imaged, the external world must exist. This is the naive belief of mankind and the starting point of the materialist theory of knowledge. The only difficulty with the argument is that it presupposes what it is supposed to prove.

2) Lenin argues that the earth once existed without man or other organic matter. This is the testimony of science. Consequently, matter existed before man, sensations, or selves, and so matter must be primary. The idealist theory which holds that things depend upon the knowers must be wrong since there was a world before there were knowers. This argument also limps, however, because a follower of Berkeley could well admit that the world existed before human beings while claiming that God was always there to perceive the world. Similarly, the claim that for human knowledge to be possible there must be objects for us to know is at best an argument for epistemological realism. It by no means necessitates the ontological primacy of matter over spirit, and such a reduction is plausible for Lenin only because he excludes a priori the existence of an other-than-human mind or spirit.

3) Lenin's third argument against the idealists hinges on the difference between the unknowable and the unknown. Yesterday, he says, we did not know that coal tar contained alizarin; today we do. From this he draws three conclusions: (a) Things exist independently of our consciousness: since coal tar contained alizarin before we knew it, its properties are not dependent on our knowledge of them. (b) There is no difference in principle between phenomena or appearances and the Kantian thing-in-itself. There is only a difference in what is known and in what is not yet known. The distinction between phenomena and things-in-themselves is nonsense. (This argument misses Kant's point.) (c) We must think dialectically, for knowledge emerges from ignorance and inexact knowledge becomes more complete as we progress. From this, Lenin claims, "the sole and unavoidable deduction to be made . . . is that outside of us, and independently of us, there exist objects, things, bodies and that our perception are images of the external world."[10]

4) A fourth argument against the idealists consists in showing that the physical world existed when there was no

society and that consequently the physical world does not require man to organize it. Moreover, since the world existed independently of man, Lenin again claims that matter must be primary and not spirit.

5) The fifth argument against idealism is based on the notion of objective truth. Lenin claims that there must be objects which we reflect if there is to be any such thing as objective truth. If one denies objects, then objective truth is impossible. Consequently, only a materialist, and not an idealist or agnostic, can have objective truth.

Lenin's arguments against idealism are polemical and are stated with great vigor but with little precision. As a result, they are not conclusive. But even if they were conclusive they would at best prove epistemological realism. They would not, of themselves, either prove materialism or disprove metaphysical idealism. Yet Lenin claims that they do prove materialism, and his claim is echoed by his Soviet followers. Henceforward, consequently, idealism will be for them a term of abuse and reproach—a practice faithfully continued in Soviet philosophy.

The Copy Theory of Knowledge

One of Lenin's central endeavors in *Materialism and Empirio-Criticism* was to refute the theory of knowledge of empiriocriticism and to present his own "copy" theory of knowledge. His approach to the complicated issues involved is straightforward, naïve, and simplistic; he characteristically wastes no time on subtleties of analysis or argument. Knowledge for Lenin is essentially a reflection or copy of reality. Any views that tend to modify this central claim are rejected as idealist, Kantian, or obscurantist.

The basis and the starting point of his theory is the sum total of human practice—or all of human experience available to him. On this basis Lenin takes the commonsense realistic stance that the world exists independently of us. It exists independently of our sensations, of our consciousness, and of man in general. This is the data given to all healthy, normal people, unspoiled by philosophy; we have already seen his arguments against the idealist alternative. Lenin then affirms that there is a direct connection between consciousness and the external world, which, as we have seen, is sensation. Sensation is "the transformation of the energy of external excitation into a state of consciousness,"[11] but consciousness is not itself energy. There is some sort of a leap that takes place between the two, some sort of a qualitative transformation. Though this transformation requires an explanation, Lenin does not provide it, for science will eventually supply us with one, and there is no need for idle speculation. What is essential for Lenin is that we acknowledge the existence of the external world, sensation, and consciousness.

The nature and status of consciousness, which are central to his theory of knowledge, are unfortunately never clarified and remain to plague Soviet philosophers today.[12] Lenin, quoting Engels favorably, holds that thought and consciousness are the products of the brain and that mind is the highest product of matter. Mind, ideas, and the like are for Lenin functions of the brain. Both thought and matter are real in the sense that they exist, "but to say that thought is material is to make a false step, a step towards confusing materialism and idealism."[13] Mind is not matter, but a product of matter. One must maintain their contrast as well as their dialectical relationship. But how, then, does the immaterial come from matter? In answer to this question, Lenin quotes Boltzmann:

> The idealist compares the assertion that matter exists as well as our sensations with the child's opinion that a stone which is beaten experiences pain. The realist compares the assertion that one cannot conceive how the mental can be formed from the material, or even from the play of atoms, with the opinion of an uneducated person who asserts that the distance between the sun and the earth cannot be twenty million miles, for he cannot conceive it.[14]

That one cannot explain how the immaterial comes from matter by no means affects the fact that it does. A further statement that the unextended cannot act on the extended would likewise be rejected by Lenin as a false objection, for obviously mind does act on body and body on mind. In answer to a number of theoretical questions that may arise, Lenin tells us that the crowning structure of philosophical materialism is the materialist conception of history, not materialist epistemology. Just as social relations reflect social being, so consciousness in general reflects being.

According to Lenin consciousness is an image of the external world, and the image implies the thing imaged. Though sensation is admittedly subjective, its foundation is

Materialism and Empirio-Criticism 153

objective. The relationship of the subjective and the objective is one of correspondence; thus, our ideas, derived from sensation, correspond to real objects outside us. We know truly when we truly or correctly reflect objective reality, or when our ideas coincide with what is the case outside of us. Moreover, when we use our senses properly and within the prescribed limits of perception, we can be certain that our perceptions are objective and that they are true copies of the thing perceived. Images or copies coincide or correspond with objects.

Lenin is emphatic in his insistence on correspondence, and he denies any kind of a hieroglyphic theory. One of the major difficulties with a hieroglyphic theory is that we would somehow have to know that our sensations are not the same as what they represent. But, how could one possibly compare the world and hieroglyphics if one can never get beyond the hieroglyphics in order to carry on the comparison? In Lenin's eyes such a theory indicates a distrust of perception and introduces an element of agnosticism which he has already rejected as incompatible with materialism. Moreover, he argues for his own position from the fact that we do make progress in knowledge. That we can discover alizarin in coal tar shows, he claims, that there is no difference in principle between the phenomena and the thing itself. There is only a difference in what is presently known and what is unknown but knowable. What we know gives some insight into what the thing is, into its nature or essence. But such knowledge is always relative. It is never exhaustive because each atom, like all of nature, is inexhaustible.[15]

The next step in Lenin's theory of knowledge is the question of proof: how is his theory proven? His answer is that it is proven by practice, experiment, and industry. By the results of our action we prove that our perception of the external world is as we pictured it. If our perception of an object is incorrect our attempt to use it will be unsuccessful. Experience, taken in the widest sense to include not only what we perceive but also scientific theories, proves or disproves the truth or falsity of our knowledge. We know, for instance, that the earth goes around the sun, even though to ordinary perception it might seem that the sun goes around the earth.[16] Practice is sufficient to refute agnosticism and idealism, Lenin tells us, though it allows indefinite progress in knowledge and "can never, in the nature of things, either confirm or refute any human idea *completely*."[17] Such are the main tenets of Lenin's copy theory of knowledge. His view is basically naïve realism and suffers from its strengths and weaknesses. To it is added the Marxian notion of the interrelation of theory and practice, and the materialist conception of history according to which social consciousness reflects and is determined by social being. Lenin's theory is in fact presented only in embryonic form. He presupposes such things as the validity of the senses, correspondence, and realism instead of proving them. He fails to consider how we can account for ideals which go beyond what is given in sense experience, he does not justify or explain the derivation or status of the categories we employ, and he does not discuss how we can have knowledge of the past since it is no longer present for us to reflect or copy. These and other difficulties and omissions pose some of the problems which are inherited from Lenin by Soviet philosophers.

Truth
Closely related to Lenin's theory of knowledge is his treatment of the meaning and criterion of truth. Knowledge for Lenin consists of a subjective reflecting of objective reality. "Truth" is equivalent to "true knowledge" and consists of correctly reflecting reality. Objective truth, he holds, can be further subdivided into absolute truth and relative truth.

Insofar as truth pertains to propositions, it seems that Lenin holds a correspondence theory of the meaning of truth. This means that a proposition is true if it consists of a subject a and a predicate b which are related by some relationship R (expressible as aRb), providing that in the objective world (independently of the assertion of aRb) there exists something corresponding to a and something corresponding to b and that these two are related in the way the proposition states. Thus, the statement "The book is on the table" is true, if both the book and the table in question really exist and if the book is on the table. By extension Lenin also seems to hold that sensations, images, and concepts can also be said to be true if they are accurate copies of reality.

What Lenin means by *objective truth* can be equated with this extended notion of correspondence. Concerning the existence of objective truth Lenin quotes Marx's second thesis on Feuerbach to the effect that "the question whether objective

Materialism and Empirio-Criticism 155

truth can be attributed to human thinking is not a question of theory, but is a practical question."[18] Commenting on this he says, "The 'objective truth' . . . of thinking means *nothing else* than the *existence* of objects (i.e., 'things in themselves') *truly* reflected by thinking."[19] For objective truth there must be objects existing independent of us, which we reflect. If truth were only the organizing form of human existence (as idealism and "agnosticism" claim), then there would be no such thing as objective truth.

But Lenin does not stop here. To recognize objective truth, he claims, is to recognize also *absolute truth*. Lenin uses the term "absolute truth" in two different senses, which we should be careful to distinguish. In one sense it refers to the complete and adequate reflection of the sum total of reality. This is an ideal never to be fully attained, for no individual human being can reflect the totality of reality. Though mankind as a whole will jointly reflect a great deal more than an individual, obviously some aspects of reality will not be reflected, for instance, the geological activity which took place before the advent of man on earth. The second sense of "absolute truth" refers to the correct reflection of part of reality. Thus, the statement "Paris is in France" is both objectively true and absolutely true, for Paris is indeed in France. Absolute truths (in this second sense) tend toward absolute truth (in the sense of the totality) as their limit.

A particular partial reflection of reality is "relatively true" if it contains a core of truth but is not completely true. Boyle's law, for example, which states that the volume of a gas is inversely proportional to its pressure, is true under certain conditions. As knowledge advanced, it was found that Boyle's law is not universally true; it is only approximately true or only approximately reflects objective reality. Lenin therefore calls it a relative truth. Absolute truth and absolute truths are made up of relative truths. A scientific theory, for instance, may have a core of objective truth which is absolutely true; yet through new discoveries the core may well be expanded. In Lenin's words "the *limits* of approximation of our knowledge to objective, absolute truth are historically conditional, but the existence of such truth is *unconditional*, and the fact that we are approaching nearer to it is also unconditional."[20] The discovery of the atom is an historically conditioned truth, as are the discoveries of the various subatomic particles. But every such discovery of objective knowledge is an advance of absolute knowledge, marking a development from relative to absolute knowledge. The line between absolute and relative knowledge is indefinite, but the two are dialectically interrelated in an upward movement. For Lenin the path of truth is science.

Having thus defined truth, how do we know when we have truth? The answer, as we have already seen, is by practice, experiment, and industry. Lenin quotes Engels favorably: "The result of our action proves the conformity of our perceptions with the objective nature of the things perceived."[21] If our knowledge were not true, if we did not adequately reflect the object, then it would be impossible for us to use it successfully. Knowledge is useful when it reflects objective truths. Yet this does not make Lenin a pragmatist. For a pragmatist such as William James, the *meaning* of truth is pragmatic, that is, to say that something is true means that it works or succeeds. For Lenin the meaning of truth is correspondence, though the primary *test* of truth is pragmatic. We can tell whether some scientific theory is true by seeing whether we can act in accordance with it to produce certain results. But what we *mean* when we say that the theory is true is that it is a correct reflection of objective reality. Though Lenin holds correspondence as the meaning of truth and practice as the major test of truth, this does not preclude his also using coherence as a test for some truths, for example, for statements about the past, though he does not explicitly state this. The statement "Caesar crossed the Rubicon" means that there actually was a man called Caesar who did cross the Rubicon; but the way someone in the present would test the truth of the statement would be to see how well it cohered or formed one piece with the rest of what we know of the past and of the present. Finally, we should not forget that for Lenin the source of knowledge is the senses, and the direct evidence of the senses is thus also a test of truth.

Lenin's discussion of truth is climaxed by his claim that Marxism has revealed certain absolute truths:

> But inasmuch as the criterion of practice, i.e., the course of development of *all* capitalist countries in the last few decades, proves only the objective truth of Marx's *whole* social and economic theory in general, and not merely of one or other of its parts, formulations, etc., it is clear that to talk of the

"dogmatism" of the Marxists is to make an unpardonable concession to bourgeois economics. The sole conclusion to be drawn from the opinion of the Marxists that Marx's theory is an objective truth is that by following the *path* of Marxian theory we shall draw closer and closer to objective truth (without ever exhausting it); but by following *any other path* we shall arrive at nothing but confusion and lies.²²

Lenin thus claims that the whole of Marx's social and economic theory is an objective truth. And here, of course, is one of the crucial differences between Soviet and most Western philosophers, historians, and economists. Even if one were to accept Lenin's theory of truth, it would not follow that historical materialism is true in general; and the test of practice, many Westerners claim, has not verified it. But if one does accept both Lenin's notion of truth and the truth of historical materialism—as the Soviets do—then it is consistent to hold that it alone is true. It thus becomes understandable why Marxism-Leninism is the only philosophy that is taught in the Soviet Union.

Matter

In opposition to Hegel's idealism, Marxism, from the days of Marx, emphasized its total adherence to materialism. It had not, however, clearly defined what was meant by "matter." The discovery of subatomic particles made impossible the view that atoms were the ultimate components into which matter could be uniformly reduced. And as smaller and smaller particles were discovered matter itself seemed to be "disappearing." The view that science could make no statement about the ultimate nature of reality and that it should concern itself only with the world of appearance or phenomena grew in prominence. Such a view threatened the Marxist materialist claims that science, like ordinary perception, dealt directly with reality as it was and that reality was ultimately and totally material. Lenin attempted to resolve these difficulties in *Materialism and Empirio-Criticism.*

Lenin begins his discussion of matter by reiterating the basic distinction between idealism and materialism. Here he is concerned with the relation of matter and knowledge, and his approach to the meaning of "matter" is primarily epistemological. "Matter is a philosophical category denoting the objective reality which is given to man by his sensations, and which is copied, photographed, and reflected by our sensations, while existing independently of them."[23] This, according to Lenin, is a philosophical definition of matter. He also calls it "the objective reality given to us in sensation."[24] "Matter" is thus one of the most comprehensive and ultimate concepts of *epistemology*, though correlative with "sensation" and "thought," in conjunction with which it is defined. Lenin insists that "the *sole* 'property' of matter with whose recognition philosophical materialism is bound up is the property of *being an objective reality*, or existing outside our mind."[25] "Matter" from a philosophical point of view is for Lenin primarily an epistemological category.

But what of matter in itself from ontological and scientific points of view? From the former Lenin seems to equate "matter" with "being" or "reality." Everything that exists is material. We have seen, however, that Lenin insists that mind is not reducible to matter, though dependent on it. There thus arises a difficulty which Lenin does not satisfactorily resolve. Mind, Lenin admits, is certainly real, but if all that is real is matter, then mind must be material—a conclusion he explicitly denies. His position is that objects, things, substances are material. Mind, however, is not an object or substance but merely a *product* of matter and a derivative of it, though not reducible to it. This merely pushes the above difficulty back a step. The question then becomes: Are the products of matter material? If they are, then mind is material. If not, then mind is not material, and there really *is* something which is not material. Lenin cannot *consistently* hold that mind is not reducible to matter and also claim that whatever exists is material. Yet he makes both claims and is followed by the Soviets in holding both.

From a philosophical point of view the only necessary property of matter, Lenin says, is that of being an objective reality. From a scientific point of view, however, matter was considered to have other properties, such as impenetrability, inertia, and mass. The crisis of materialism was brought about because subatomic particles did not have the properties thought to belong to matter as such. If subatomic particles did not have the properties of matter, then they must be immaterial and "matter is disappearing." Lenin's solution is simply and rather obviously to deny that impenetrability and the like

Materialism and Empirio-Criticism 159

are properties of matter as such. They are rather properties only of certain states of matter. The question of the structure of matter and of atoms is not a question of philosophy but of science. Lenin seems to distinguish between the scientific and philosophical concepts of matter, disclaiming knowledge of the necessary properties of the former and claiming only one necessary property for the latter. This dichotomy of matter, however, as the Soviet philosophers later discovered, tended to separate the two concepts of matter and made it possible for Soviet scientists to adopt Kantian, agnostic, or idealistic positions in science—a state of affairs incompatible with the all-pervasive character of dialectical materialism. Lenin's distinction between the philosophical and scientific concepts of matter, though initially followed, was later dropped, and his position was reinterpreted.

The reason for this reinterpretation becomes clearer when we add to Lenin's treatment of matter certain other tenets which he inherited from Engels: matter is in motion,[26] space and time are both objectively real[27] and infinite, there are objective laws in nature, and objective causality is reflected with approximate fidelity by human ideas.[28] Are these claims ontological and true only of philosophical matter, or are they true of scientific matter also? If the distinction between the two notions of matter is allowed, the answer is ambiguous. But clearly Lenin thought the statements were objectively true, and thus no view of matter which denies them (as some interpretations of relativity theory do) is to be allowed. The Soviet—and more consistent—position is that philosophical and scientific matter are the same.

The status of motion, space, and time is also somewhat ambiguous in *Materialism and Empirio-Criticism*. It seems that matter in motion or matter and motion are eternal. But then is motion something in addition to matter? It would seem not, for matter is all there is. We are left, then, with the position that motion is a property of matter, yet whether it is a property of matter as such or only of certain states of matter is never made clear. If it is eternal but is not the property of matter as such, then there must always have been those states of matter of which it is a property. But this is a scientific, not a philosophical claim, and one for which there is still insufficient evidence. On the other hand, if motion is a property of matter as such, why does Lenin say that the sole property of matter is that of being an objective reality? Likewise, it is not clear whether space and time, which Lenin claims are objective, are something in addition to matter or again whether they are properties of matter. The same choices as were available to us with respect to motion apply here as well, and the same difficulties.

In holding the existence of objective laws of nature and objective causality Lenin reiterates Engels' position on freedom and necessity. Freedom consists in the capacity to make decisions with knowledge of natural laws. In explaining Engels' position, Lenin points out four facts which he considers essential: (1) there are laws of nature, (2) nature is primary, human will and mind are secondary and necessarily adapt themselves to nature, (3) there is a necessity unknown to man, though our collective knowledge is constantly growing, and (4) practice, our mastery of nature, provides the objective criterion of the truth of our knowledge.

Natural science, according to Lenin, unconsciously assumes his teaching concerning objective reality. Modern science not only assumes it, but is itself "giving birth to dialectical materialism."[29] The claim is repeated by Soviet philosophers today despite the fact that most Western scientists deny it and seem to use science at least as efficiently as—and often more efficiently than—their Soviet counterparts.

Chapter IX
Lenin's Philosophical Legacy

Materialism and Empirio-Criticism was a major excursion into philosophy, but it was in great part polemical and motivated more by practical necessity than by the desire for philosophical reflection. Throughout his life theory remained for Lenin an adjunct of practice—an adjunct, however, which he never considered as anything but essential. The period of 1914-16, when he again returned to philosophy, is no exception; yet it differs from his earlier excursion into philosophy, for he concentrates on philosophy—this time Hegel's—not for purposes of refutation, but evidently to develop and clarify his own thought. This period ends in no polemic. Rather he leaves behind a philosophical legacy, only part of which was claimed and used by his immediate followers, though it remained and remains a rich source for controversy and for possible future development.

The Essentials of Marxism
The background against which Lenin's foray into Hegelian philosophy can best be appreciated is provided by several of his shorter works of the 1913-14 period. In "The Three Sources and Three Component Parts of Marxism" (1913), "The Marx-Engels Correspondence" (1913), "The Historical Destiny of the Teaching of Karl Marx" (1913), and his article "Karl Marx"

(1914) for *Granat's Encyclopedia* Lenin summarizes and explains what he considers to be the fundamentals of Marx's teachings. It should be remembered that Marx's *Economic and Philosophic Manuscripts* and *The German Ideology*—the main sources of Marxian humanism—had not been published and were unknown to Lenin. The importance Lenin would have placed on them is therefore problematic, though in general any tendency toward humanism seems lacking in his works.

Marxism, for Lenin, is a complete and harmonious world view, which is all-powerful because true, and which continued and completed the best creations of the most advanced countries of humanity: classical German philosophy, classical English political economy, and French socialism and revolutionary doctrines.[1] Though its completeness as a world view can be questioned, Lenin sees Marxism as fulfilling this function. As an all-encompassing world view, according to him, it is incompatible with superstition, religion, or any view that stems from (and so defends) bourgeois society. As all-encompassing it brooks no divergent views; as true, it should not be compromised. Though not explicitly stated by Lenin, the Soviet line of "no peaceful coexistence of ideologies" follows as a corollary. It should be noted, however, that as the continuance and supposed completion of German, English, and French thought, the sources and inspiration of Marxism are obviously Western.

With respect to Marxian philosophical materialism Lenin claims that it alone is consistent and "true to all the teachings of natural science."[2] In his actual exposition of Marx's philosophy he relies on Engels, whom he quotes at length. He emphasizes both materialism and dialectics. The essence of Marx's materialism, as presented by Lenin, is made up of the claims that "the real unity of the world consists in its materiality," that motion is the mode of existence of matter, and that man is a product of nature and consciousness a product of the human brain.[3] He also points out that "freedom is the realization of necessity" and that Marx's materialism is distinguished from vulgar materialism by being dialectical (instead of mechanistic), historical, concrete, and revolutionary.[4]

Dialectics for Lenin is not only the science of the general laws of motion but "the doctrine of development in its fuller, deeper form, free from one-sidedness—the doctrine, also, of the relativity of human knowledge that provides us with a reflection of eternally developing matter."[5] He mentions the three laws of dialectics (the interpenetration of opposites, the transition from quantity to quality, and the negation of the negation), but emphasizes that materialist dialectics does not consist of "wooden trichotomies."[6] In "The Marx-Engels Correspondence" he says: "If one were to attempt to define in one word, so to say, the focus of the whole correspondence, the central point around which the entire network of the ideas, expressed and discussed, turns—that word would be: dialectics."[7] But Lenin's concern is not with abstract dialectics but with the *application* of dialectics to all fields.

Historical materialism, for Lenin, is the extension of philosophical materialism to human society; it is a *science* which shows how, in consequence of the growth of productive forces, one system of social life develops from another. He presents the doctrine of the superstructure as parallel to the copy theory of knowledge: "Just as the cognition of man reflects nature (i.e., developing matter) which exists independently of him, so also the *social cognition* of man (i.e., the various views and doctrines—philosophic, religious, political, etc.) reflects the *economic order* of society. Political institutions are a superstructure on the economic foundation."[8] This provides the means for studying the activities of the *masses* of the population and for studying the rise, development, and decline of social-economic formations.

But for Lenin the most important part of what Marx discovered and proved is that the history of mankind is the history of class struggles. In the present epoch Marx further showed that society is essentially splitting up into only two classes: the bourgeoisie, which dominates, and the proletariat, which is really a revolutionary class.

This leads Lenin to Marx's economic doctrine and to a brief summary of *Capital*. He outlines Marx's labor theory of value, the key notion of surplus value, and the exploitation which it involves. He calls the doctrine of surplus value "the cornerstone of the economic theory of Marx."[9] The development of capitalism leads to its own downfall.

Lenin begins his discussion of socialism by saying: "From the foregoing it is evident that Marx deduces the inevitability of the transformation of capitalist society into socialist society wholly and exclusively from the economic law of the movement of contemporary society."[10] The truth of scientific socialism thus stands or falls with the truth of the economic "laws" which Marx uncovered. The essence of scientific socialism lies in the struggle of the proletariat against the bourgeoisie and the ultimate seizures of power by the former, resulting in the *dictatorship of the proletariat*. In 1908 Lenin had called the doctrine of the class struggle "the foundation of Marxism"[11] but he later emphasized:

> To confine Marxism to the doctrine of the class struggle means curtailing Marxism, distorting it, reducing it to something which is acceptable to the bourgeoisie. Only he is a Marxist who *extends* the recognition of the class struggle to the recognition of the *dictatorship of the proletariat*.[12]

The consequence of this dictatorship will be the abolition of classes, of nations, and of the state.

These doctrines form for Lenin the heart of Marxism. It need hardly be pointed out that they are too fragmentary and incomplete to form a total world view; but each portion is vague and general enough so that it could be interpreted and applied by Lenin to his own needs. Marx's supporting details, specific arguments, and precise predictions all fall by the wayside and have no importance for Lenin. It is the general scheme that he needs and uses, for he is interested not in a dogma, but in a guide to action.[13] He looks on Marxism not as something final, but as a tool to be developed and used—specifically to be used in bringing about the dictatorship of the proletariat.[14]

Philosophical Notebooks

From a study of Lenin's writings on Marx two points stand out as fundamental in his view of Marxism: the dictatorship of the proletariat and dialectics. His aim is to achieve the former. But, convinced that action must be guided by theory, that reality and its laws must be correctly reflected and understood if action is to be successful, he feels the necessity of developing and deepening his theoretical framework. It is not at all surprising, then, that at a crucial time in European history and at a time when he is charting the action which will result in the 1917 Russian revolution, he turns to a study of Hegel. If it is true that successful action requires a theoretical base and that reality is dialectical—and Lenin was convinced of the

Lenin's Philosophical Legacy 165

truth of both these statements—then it is no waste of time for him to deepen his knowledge of dialectics. From his *Philosophical Notebooks* we find that during 1914-15 he engaged in a detailed study of Hegel, the original, though idealistic, master of dialectics.

Marx had moved from Hegel through Feuerbach to materialism, dialectically interpreted. Lenin moves from materialism through Marx to Hegel. And his study of Hegel seems to give him a new and keener insight not only into dialectics but also into the writings of Marx himself. While reading Hegel's *The Science of Logic* he notes: "It is impossible completely to understand Marx's *Capital*, and especially its first chapter, without having thoroughly studied and understood the *whole* of Hegel's *Logic*. Consequently, half a century later none of the Marxists understood Marx!"[15] This judgment applies also to Lenin's own earlier reading of Marx, and he notes, as if in a moment of new insight, that "Marx *applied* Hegel's dialectics in its rational form to political economy."[16] He also seems to learn from Hegel that the method Marxists had been using in criticizing Kantians, Humians, and idealists (and that he himself had used in *Materialism and Empirio-Criticism*) was unsatisfactory, for it consisted in merely rejecting the positions in question instead of correcting, deepening, and extending them.[17] After reading Hegel he sees idealism not as nonsense but merely as a one-sided doctrine, divorced from nature.[18] Not only is dialectical idealism closer to dialectical materialism than is crude materialism,[19] but in Hegel's *Logic* itself, the most idealistic of Hegel's works, Lenin claims "there is the *least* idealism and the *most* materialism."[20] The implications that this judgment has for the interpretation of Marxism are legion, but it is certainly clear that this period marks a change in Lenin's thinking, a change characterized by his emphasis on dialectics. This period can with some justification be termed Lenin's Hegelian period.

The volume called Lenin's *Philosophical Notebooks* is a collection of notebooks used by Lenin to record his philosophical readings. Not intended for publication, the ten notebooks—eight of which date from 1914-15 and were entitled by Lenin "Notebooks on Philosophy"—were first published in 1929-30 in *Lenin's Miscellanies* IX and XII. They were first published separately in 1933, and succeeding editions have included additional material. In general the *Notebooks* consist of summaries and excerpts of books in philosophy which Lenin read, as well as his marginal comments, underlinings, notes on his readings, and various fragments. *Philosophical Notebooks*, as presented in volume 38 of the fifth edition of Lenin's works, begins with a resume of *The Holy Family* made in 1895. In 1903 there are entries made in Switzerland of notes on Ueberweg's *History of Philosophy* and Paulsen's *Introduction to Philosophy*. Other entries made in 1904 and 1909 include a summary of Feuerbach's *Lectures on the Essence of Religion*. From 1908 we have remarks and underlinings which he made in Plekhanov's *Fundamental Questions of Marxism*, Abel Rey's *Modern Philosophy*, A. Deborin's *Dialectical Materialism*, and V. Shulyatikov's *The Justification of Capitalism in West-European Philosophy*. The period from 1914-15 makes up the bulk of the notebooks and is the most important. Lenin here returns to German classical philosophy (and to Hegel in particular), which he had underlined as the philosophical source of Marxism. In 1914 he outlined at length and commented on Hegel's *The Science of Logic* and made notes on a number of reviews of Hegel's *Logic*. In 1915 he worked through Hegel's *History of Philosophy* and his *Philosophy of History*, as well as through Aristotle's *Metaphysics*. It was in this year also that he wrote the essay "On The Question of Dialectics."

Lenin's *Philosophical Notebooks* are a storehouse of comments. Since they were not made for publication they should be used with care; since they are comments on books he was reading, made while reading, they are nonsystematic, sometimes ambiguous, and sometimes apparently contradictory. Yet certain of his central positions emerge with respect to dialectics, nature, logic, and theory of knowledge—positions which are definite advances over his thinking in *Materialism and Empirio-Criticism*.

He notes early in his reading of Hegel that, following Marx and Engels, he is trying to read Hegel materialistically or as materialism stood on its head. But for him this means only putting aside "God, the Absolute, the Pure Idea, etc.;"[21] for Hegel's dialectics, and indeed his *Logic*, when shorn of these and related more specifically to nature, seem to Lenin to be thus made materialistic.[22] The essence of Hegel's *Logic* is for Lenin his dialectical method, and the clarification of the notion of dialectics reflects Lenin's greatest debt to Hegel. For dialectics is Lenin's key both to reality and to theory of knowledge. The basic insight that everything is related, that there is a vital connection of each thing with everything else, and that this is reflected in flexible, mutually related concepts is Hegel's great contribution to "science," a contribution which was continued by Marx and must be carried further in the elaboration of knowledge.[23] According to Lenin, Marx and Engels made giant strides over Hegel not in dialectics but in the science of history[24] and in the application of Hegel's logic to political economy.[25]

Dialectics for Lenin "is the teaching which shows how *Opposites* can be and how they happen to be (how they become) *identical*—under what conditions they are identical, becoming transformed into one another—why the human mind should grasp these opposites not as dead, rigid, but as living, conditional, mobile, becoming transformed into one another."[26] The essence of dialectics for him is the doctrine of the unity and identity of opposites. He repeats this over and over again.[27] Though he lists sixteen elements of dialectics,[28] the heart of the matter is that everything that is is many sided, related to everything else, and developing. The source of development of each thing comes about because of its internally contradictory aspects and the struggle of these tendencies. This causes the transition of one thing into another, of quantity into quality, accompanied by leaps and often by a certain repetition at a higher stage, an apparent return to the old (negation of the negation).[29] Lenin does not list the laws of dialectics, as Engels did, but he emphasizes the relatedness and dynamics of all things. Negation is not so much a law as a "moment" or stage of connection, of development, which preserves the positive element of what is negated.[30] Evolution is the result of the struggle of opposites: this is the source of self-movement (motion itself "is a contradiction, a unity of contradictions"),[31] for the unity of opposites is necessarily conditioned and temporary. What distinguish dialectical from nondialectical transitions are *leaps*, contradictions, the interruption of gradualness; gradualness explains nothing without leaps.[32] Contradictions exist in things, but this means that "every concrete thing, every concrete something, stands in multifarious and often contradictory relations to everything else, ergo it is itself and some other."[33]

Since reality is dialectical, its reflection in knowledge must also be dialectical. But here Lenin goes far beyond the copy theory of knowledge he presented in *Materialism and Empirio-Criticism*. There knowledge was only dialectical to the extent that it reflected movement in the objective world. In the *Philosophical Notebooks* knowledge is a process which itself proceeds dialectically, and the mind is not merely a passively reflecting mirror but an *active* agent. Marx had previously pointed to the mind as active, and Lenin correctly says that "dialectics *is* the theory of knowledge of (Hegel and) Marxism. This is the 'aspect' of the matter (it is not 'an aspect' but the *essence* of the matter) to which Plekhanov, not to speak of other Marxists, paid no attention."[34] Indeed, Lenin himself had failed to see this prior to his reading of Hegel.

The difficulty with knowledge stems from the fact that in trying to reflect movement it necessarily fragments, stops, and so kills it. Concepts are static representations of what is essentially moving.[35] What one must do then to reflect reality is to make one's thoughts *flexible* so that they reflect the all-sidedness of the material process and of each individual thing[36] in order that the relations of each thing to everything else is grasped and in order that the sliding or shading or passing of one thought into another is seen. "Cognition is the *process* of the submersion (of the mind) in an inorganic nature for the sake of subordinating it to the power of the subject and for the sake of generalization (cognition of the universal in its phenomena)."[37] Here Lenin emphasizes the active role of the mind *subordinating* nature and the mental *process* of generalization. Cognition is an approximation of thought to the object,[38] but one in which the mind apprehends in its own way. He goes so far as to say "man's consciousness not only reflects the objective world, but creates it."[39]

Man perceives the world through his senses. Lenin had already observed this. However the thought process is itself dialectical. It is not simple but complex. Sensuous representation, for instance, cannot apprehend movement as such, the movement of an object at 300,000 km./sec. Yet thought does. Thought reflects reality, but between reality as sensuously reported and as represented in thought there is a leap. And this leap is called abstraction.[40]

In abstraction man reflects nature in universal concepts, categories, and laws. A universal concept which really reflects reality for Lenin comprises the wealth of the particular and singular.[41] In some sense the individual *is* the universal.[42] "The

Lenin's Philosophical Legacy 169

individual exists only in the connection that leads to the universal. The universal exists only in the individual and through the individual. Every individual is (in one way or another) a universal. Every universal is (a fragment, or an aspect, or the essence of) an individual. Every universal only approximately embraces all the individual objects."[43] There is an absolute within the relative.[44] Moreover, since it is mind which abstracts and produces the universal, human concepts represent nature in a distinctive way. It is possible for man to abstract incorrectly, to falsify, and to introduce freedom of thought or fancy.[45] Indeed, "even in the simplest generalization, in the most elementary general idea ('table' in general) *there is* a certain bit of FANTASY."[46] This is the source not only of error but also of fictions, and it is this, ultimately, which makes flights of fancy, false ideologies, and alienation possible. It also makes possible the *ideals* which men try to bring into actuality.[47]

From general concepts we pass to more inclusive categories which are focal points in man's attempt to know and master the world. They are stages in his process of knowledge and the tools which he uses to express laws.[48] A law is an essential expression by man of relations (causality being one among many), connections, and dependencies in the processes of nature.[49] It is always narrow, incomplete, and approximate, though it can be brought closer and closer to a correct reflection of nature. Science attempts systematically to represent moving, eternally developing nature in ever more adequate laws. Presumably, the approximate character of laws applies not only to the physical sciences but also to the so-called Marxian laws of social development.

Logic, for Lenin, in the true Hegelian spirit, is concerned not with external, empty forms of thought, but with "the development of the entire concrete content of the world and of its cognition," with the general laws of movement both of the world and of thought.[50] Thus, dialectics coincides with logic and both coincide with theory of knowledge. Logic is dialectics, and both are and mean the same as theory of knowledge.[51]

Logic, according to Lenin, is derived from the development of nature and reflects this development. Logic is ingredient in the world, and logical laws are the reflections of the way things are. The most common logical "figures," for instance the figures of the syllogism, are the most common relations of things in the world.[52] It is because man in his practical activity was led by the nature of reality to repeat in his actions thousands and millions of times the figures of logic that they came to acquire the significance of axioms and their self-evidence.[53] The laws of logic are valid because they reflect the structure of reality. (Unfortunately, Lenin ignores the fact that the logical law of contradiction has the status of self-evidence and that if it is a correct reflection of reality then reality cannot be contradictory.)

Man proves or verifies the validity of his logical forms and of their application in the various sciences by practice, that is, by applying these laws to achieve his ends. Man's activity proves the coincidence of logic and being. Man is himself a product of nature, and his actions are engendered by the objective world and presuppose it.[54] But by subjectively reflecting the laws of reality man can utilize them to achieve his ends, to realize his ideals, and to change the reality of which he is a part. Man's practical activity and the degree to which he achieves his end are the ultimate index of the accuracy with which he has understood reality, of the truth of his concepts and laws. Thus, nature is primary and man is its product. But man as a living entity perceives the world and is capable of progressing dialectically from sense perception to thought and from thought to action or practice, in which he not only checks the objective truth of his perceptions and thoughts but also changes nature itself. Finally, the purpose of thought is ultimately action and *"practice is higher than (theoretical) knowledge, for it has not only the dignity of universality, but also of immediate actuality."*[55]

In *Philosophical Notebooks* Lenin emphasizes—in the eyes of some of his followers *overemphasizes*—dialectics and goes far toward developing a more adequate theory of knowledge. His stress on the coincidence of dialectics, logic, and theory of knowledge, however, is far from clear and is replete with difficulties. He also seems unaware of the difficulties that his emphasis on dialectics poses for a truly materialistic philosophy; the other alternative is that he saw the difficulties but was willing to sacrifice materialism on the altar of dialectics, providing he could do so without introducing the notion of God or the Absolute. At all events, the emphasis on dialectics coincided well with Lenin's vision of man as an active being who

Lenin's Philosophical Legacy 171

could change reality and objectively realize his ideals. Activity and revolution were Lenin's primary goals—dialectics and theory of knowledge being necessary but subsidiary tools.

Ethics and Militant Materialism

In the busy years of the revolution and the period immediately following it Lenin was too busy a leader to pursue his interests in philosophy. Nonetheless, the interest seems to have remained alive, and two short but philosophically noteworthy pieces, written at the height of his political power, form part of his philosophical legacy and influence the patterns of Soviet thought. The first is his speech at the Third All-Russian Congress of the Russian Young Communist League (Oct. 2, 1920), known as "The Tasks of the Youth Leagues." The other, known as "On the Significance of Militant Materialism" (1922) is a letter he wrote to the periodical *Pod znamenem marksizma* (*Under the Banner of Marxism*).

In "The Tasks of the Youth Leagues" Lenin begins by saying it is the youth who will build the new communist society and that the youth must be taught and trained to do this. The foundation of this teaching, according to Lenin, must be the best of all accumulated human knowledge. Youth must take what is good from the old school, enrich its mind with the treasures of mankind, and utilize them in the development of society, in the electrification of the country, and in the development of industry and agriculture. This, he claims, is the foundation of communism and not slogans or conclusions learned by rote. "You are faced," he says, "with the task of construction, and you can cope with it only by mastering all modern knowledge, only if you are able to transform Communism from ready-made, memorized formulas, counsels, recipes, prescriptions, and programs into that living thing which unites your immediate work, and only if you are able to transform Communism into a guide for your practical work."[56] Lenin may well have been right. But we shall never know. For in the decades following his death communism was in fact reduced to memorized formulas, counsels, and recipes, at least as far as theory was concerned.

In asking what specific features should be emphasized in teaching communism, Lenin mentions ethics first of all: "The whole object of training, education, and teaching the youth of today should be to imbue them with communist ethics."[57] This is one of the few places in his writing in which he speaks about ethics, and his discussion in this speech makes up his longest statement on the subject.[58] What he says is all the more interesting when we remember that much of the original impetus for Marx's writings and research was moral indignation at the plight of man and of the worker in particular.

Lenin repudiates all bourgeois, religious, or supposedly eternal morality. Rather, he says, communist morality "is entirely subordinated to the interests of the class struggle of the proletariat. Our morality is derived from the interests of the class struggle of the proletariat."[59] And further, "morality is what serves to destroy the old exploiting society and to unite all the toilers around the proletariat, which is building up a new, communist society."[60] Before the revolution whatever helped bring about the revolution was moral. After the revolution, whatever helps develop society towards communism is moral. For, according to Lenin, the ultimate moral ideal, the ideal which should be realized by action, the absolute "moment" in the relativity of moral judgments, and the criterion by which all actions should be judged, is the ideal of communism. Unfortunately, the ideal itself has never been sufficiently defined to act as a concrete norm for morality. As a consequence everything desired or commanded by the leaders of the proletariat, by the leaders in fact of the Communist Party, became tinged with a moral glow—including the vast injustices and abuses perpetrated under Stalin, and now so acknowledged by the Soviets.

"On the Significance of Militant Materialism," written less than two years before his death, is a letter addressed by Lenin to *Under the Banner of Marxism*, a journal of philosophy and the social sciences founded for the defense of materialism and Marxism. Lenin emphasizes that the journal should be an organ of militant materialism and as such should be an organ of militant atheism,[61] which "must devote a lot of space to atheist propaganda."[62] This advice was heeded, and the spirit of militant atheism continues to receive official support up to the present time.

In addition to militant atheism, Lenin calls for an alliance with the representatives of modern natural science and for a systematic study of dialectics. Here his advice has been followed less religiously. He says:

Lenin's Philosophical Legacy 173

We must understand that without a solid philosophic grounding, no natural science and no materialism can hold its own in the struggle against the onrush of bourgeois ideas and against the restoration of the bourgeois conception of the universe. To hold its own in this struggle and to carry it through to the end with complete success, a naturalist must be a modern materialist, a conscious adherent of the materialism which is represented by Marx, i.e., he must be a dialectical materialist. To attain this aim, the contributors to the magazine *Under the Banner of Marxism* must organize a systematic study of Hegel's dialectics from a materialist point of view, i.e., the dialectics which Marx has applied practically in his *Capital* and in his historical and political works.[63]

He further advises the journal to print, interpret, and comment on excerpts from Hegel's principal works and to become "a kind of 'Society of Materialist Friends of Hegelian Dialectics.'"[64]

Lenin's admiration for Hegelian dialectics, which we saw in his *Philosophical Notebooks*, thus remained with him throughout the remaining years of his life. It forms part of his philosophical legacy. Yet it has still to be fully exploited in Soviet philosophy, and parts of it remain as latent fuel to which a match may yet be put.

In the period since Lenin's death *Materialism and Empirio-Criticism* has consistently formed a major building block of Soviet philosophy. It still remains one of the prime sources cited and studied by Soviet philosophers. His *Philosophical Notebooks* have fared less well. They were not published until 1929-30 and then circulated only in small numbers. During the 1930's and 1940's they were officially ignored, as we shall see, and dialectics was deemphasized. It is only after the condemnation of Stalin in 1956 that they emerge again. With them Hegel also has been exhumed to such an extent that in 1956 *Kommunist*, the theoretical and political organ of the Central Committee of the Communist Party of the Soviet Union, ran an article pointing out the importance of Hegel and the study of dialectics and said of Hegel's *Science of Logic* that "this work has not lost its significance even in our times."[65] Since then many Soviet philosophers have clearly been turning to Lenin's *Philosophical Notebooks* in their discussion of the categories, of theory of knowledge, of the status of logic, and of the coincidence of dialectics, theory of knowledge, and logic. It is cited extensively in the basic textbooks on Soviet philosophy, and in the *Philosophical Encyclopedia*. An English translation of it appeared for the first time in 1961, and though it is volume 38 of Lenin's *Collected Works* it was printed well in advance of most of the earlier volumes. The "Preface" to the work says: "The study of the great ideological content of *Philosophical Notebooks* is of tremendous importance for a thorough grasp of Marxist-Leninist philosophy, the theoretical foundation of scientific communism."[66] Thus, the *Philosophical Notebooks* have recently been coming into their own.

With the death of Lenin the classical corpus of Marxism-Leninism is closed.

Lenin's Contribution to Soviet Thought

It is virtually impossible to overemphasize the importance of Lenin's writings for Soviet thought. His authority is considered by the Soviets on a par with that of Marx and Engels, but his influence is greater than theirs because it is only Lenin's interpretation of Marxism that is considered orthodox; his corrections of and additions to Marxism remain the last word; and he, rather than Marx or Engels, is cited most often in doctrinal discussions within the Soviet Union and in ideological disputes among the communist countries of the world. It is with good reason, then, that current Soviet ideological and philosophical thought is not called "Marxism" by the Soviets, but "Marxism-Leninism." It was, after all, Lenin and not Marx or Engels who successfully carried through the first so-called communist revolution, and who "proved" the correctness of his thinking according to the theory of the interrelation of theory and practice.

Leninism has been called by some Western critics an extreme deviation from Marxism,[67] and much can be said in support of this view. The current and official Soviet view, however, was stated by Stalin in 1927 and has been consistently adhered to since then. In the words of Stalin, who played the largest role in the deification of Lenin:

> Lenin was, and remains, the most loyal and consistent pupil of Marx and Engels, and he wholly and entirely based himself on the principles of Marxism. But Lenin did not merely

Lenin's Philosophical Legacy 175

carry out the doctrines of Marx and Engels. He developed these doctrines . . . in accordance with the new conditions of development, with the new phase of capitalism, with imperialism.[68]

Whether Lenin's interpretation of and additions to Marxism be termed "deviation" or "creative development," it is clear that Marxism-Leninism is in some ways significantly different from the doctrine expressed in the writings of Marx and Engels.

In the sphere of economics Lenin was faced with the fact that capitalist society was not developing as Marx's *Capital* had predicted. Lenin remedied this not by denying the accuracy of *Capital* but by claiming that in its normal development monopoly capitalism had reached its last stage, a stage which had not been mentioned by Marx but which did not contradict any of his analyses—the stage of imperialism. But it became more and more difficult to hold this line as former colonies broke away from or were granted independence, apparently without serious consequences to the imperialist mother countries. Together with his doctrine of imperialism Lenin also placed such great emphasis on colonial revolution that often it seemed that colonial and not proletarian revolution was to bring about world communism.

Together with this doctrine came another, which Lenin justified by an appeal to changing times and conditions. This is the doctrine of socialism in one country. For Marx, as we have seen, the communist revolution had to be worldwide. For Lenin, though the revolution would eventually spread to all countries, it was possible for it to be successful in a single country. This country was Russia. Once Lenin's revolution was successful, he had all the more reason to emphasize the possibility of the victory of socialism in one country, especially when revolutions in other countries failed to materialize. This also gave him the opportunity—developed by his successors—to claim that communists everywhere should strengthen and support Russia, the one country in which the revolution had been successful. The international communist movement thus received a Russian national flavor, since Russia became the center and stronghold of the movement. Reciprocally, the Soviet Union became the center for the export of revolution and for the support of all attempts by the proletariat in bourgeois countries to overthrow their governments and gain control of power. Thereafter, Soviet thinking tended to equate the good of the Soviet Union with the good of communism and vice versa.

As a direct result of the building of communism in the Soviet Union the notion of the dictatorship of the proletariat became equated with the Soviet state form of dictatorship, and the vague notions concerning the period of transition from capitalism to socialism received concrete form according to what took place in the Soviet Union.

Lenin had emphasized the importance of the Marxian notion of the dictatorship of the proletariat, but he had given it an essentially new turn. For him the dictatorship of the proletariat became the dictatorship of the Communist Party, for the Party was the vanguard of the proletariat, just as the proletariat was the vanguard of the masses with whom (especially the peasants) they were to join forces. Marx envisaged a revolution of workers seizing power in an industrial country. Lenin brought about a revolution by professionals, members of the Party, in a largely agricultural country. The nature of the Party, moreover, was his creation, and certainly non-Marxian. The Party was first of all secret, not open, as the Communist *Manifesto* proclaimed. Second, it was composed of professional revolutionaries, ruled with iron discipline. Third, once in command it was totalitarian, all-powerful, and brooked no interference or opposition.

In the realm of theory the Party ruled, as it did everywhere else. This fact, referred to as *partiinost'* ("partisanship" or "party-mindedness"), henceforth shapes Soviet thought and is essential to its development. The patterns which emerge reflect Party needs, goals, and changes. Lenin's emphasis on dialectics, transferred to emphasis on action, gives Marxism a voluntarist slant. The triumph of communism is seen as inevitable, but only inevitable if the Party, armed with the laws of social development, sees to it that the necessary steps for its triumph are taken.

Lenin equates all the writings of Engels to the writings of Marx, endows them with equal authority, and calls both their writings "Marxism." He is followed by the Soviets in this, as well as in his tendency to lean more heavily on Engels than on Marx. His copy theory of knowledge, as presented in *Materialism and Empirio-Criticism* becomes dogma, as do all his writings. The only exception is his *Philosophical Notebooks*,

Lenin's Philosophical Legacy 177

in which he emphasizes dialectics and especially the unity of opposites, which he considers the essence of dialectics. It is only after Stalin's death that the *Philosophical Notebooks* exert a significant influence. Then, the doctrine of the coincidence of dialectics, theory of knowledge, and logic is taken up strongly, at least by many, and dialectics is raised again to a central position in the official theory, after having suffered a serious decline during Stalin's reign. Lenin's emphasis on the unity of opposites, however, remains muted, preference being given to Engels' exposition of the laws of dialectics, and though Lenin's quasi-eulogy of Hegel is acknowledged verbally it has not been very vigorously exploited.

In the developing pattern of Soviet thought Lenin adds much to the content of Marxism-Leninism, but his most significant contribution to the *pattern* of thought is that because of him Marxism (and Marxism-Leninism) is officially recognized as a body of truth which is developing and not static and which can be modified, at least in part and from above, by its custodians, the leaders of the Communist Party. Henceforth, the content of Marxism-Leninism is determined by the Party; its leader or leaders become the judges of orthodoxy.

Part 3: Soviet Philosophy and Ideology

Chapter X
The Development of Soviet Thought

Mechanism versus Deborinism

The success of the October Revolution in Russia marks the beginning of a new phase in Soviet thought. For the success of the revolution even in one country not only ratified in some sense the correctness of the revolutionary theories of Marx, Engels, and Lenin but also necessarily forced a change—at least in emphasis—in the role of philosophy. Once the revolution had been a success, the central concern of theory vis-à-vis developments in Russia could no longer be revolution; it became the construction of a communist society. Moreover, for the first time in the history of its development, Marxism moved into the university. Marx, Engels, and Lenin were revolutionaries, not academicians; they were concerned with theory for the sake of practice, not with theory for its own sake. After the revolution, however, Marxism came to replace all other philosophy: Marxists replaced the bourgeois philosphers in the universities, the philosophical journal *Pod znamenem marksizma* (*Under the Banner of Marxism*) was established, the Institute of Philosophy was founded, the technical work of producing textbooks was begun, and that of translating the works of Western philosophers was continued. Marxist philosophy became for some not a part-time enterprise but a full-time job, which they pursued as professionals.

The period of the 1920's in Russia was one of philosophical discussion and controversy. The Marxist-Leninist heritage was ambiguous, at least in part. A basic disagreement arose which, though ultimately settled by a political decree, was rooted in the heart of dialectical materialism; it continues to divide Soviet philosophers today just as truly though not as obviously as before. Both sides in the controversy being Marxist, both quoted Marx, Engels, and Lenin in their own behalf, and both insisted that their interpretation was the only correct interpretation of Marxism. This much of the pattern of Soviet thought was already firmly established. The method by which the controversy was resolved set the precedent for another and henceforth central aspect of the developing pattern.

The two main contenders in the philosophical debates of the 1920's came to be known as the "mechanists" and the "Deborinists." The one group emphasized the essentially materialist aspects of dialectical materialism; the other, the dialectical aspects.[1] The tendency to emphasize one or the other continues today.[2]

In 1922 S. Minin, generally considered a "vulgar materialist," wrote an article in *Under the Banner of Marxism* calling for the abolition of philosophy and for its replacement by the positive sciences.[3] He was joined by other philosophers, including Liubov Isaakovna Akselrod (1868-1946), who was also known as "Orthodox," and Ivan Ivanovich Skvortsov-Stepanov (1870-1928). Vulgar materialism soon gave way to mechanism, which was most adequately championed by Bogdanov and Nikolai Ivanovich Bukharin (1888-1937). Though the whole group was known as the "mechanists," there were differences in the particular positions espoused by the various members.

The primary bone of contention between the mechanists and their opponents, the Deborinists, was the meaning of "dialectics." The center of controversy revolved around the questions of whether there were contradictions in nature and whether there were dialectical, qualitative leaps. The answer to both questions for the mechanists was "no," since they claimed that all motion was external and all change reducible to and expressible in mechanistic terms. In general the mechanists held:

1) Philosophy is not a separate science. They supported

this positivist position by quotations from Engels in which he says that philosophy will ultimately be replaced by the positive sciences. For the mechanists, dialectics is not itself a science, but the method of all the sciences.

2) All motion is external. The mechanists denied that there are contradictions in nature and held that each thing is a unity, without internal contradictions. Contradictions for them, exist only in the mind; to maintain any other position is to espouse Hegelian mysticism. Yet an object might have the capacity for development in mutually exclusive (and so contradictory) ways and might be acted on by different forces tending to push it in different directions. This is dialectics made materialistic. But all motion comes from without, and is describable in mechanical terms. Bukharin and Bogdanov defended this position in what is known as the "equilibrium theory."

3) There are no leaps in nature and no qualitative changes. All higher phenomena can be described in terms adequate to describe lower phenomena and ultimately can be described in mechanical terms. This position is known as "reductionism." Thus, mental processes could be reduced to and adequately described in terms of psycho-neural processes; these in turn could be reduced to biological processes, these to chemical processes, and these to physical or mechanical processes. Even social phenomena could eventually be reduced to the laws of mechanics if sufficient information were available. Thus, qualitative differences and Hegel's dialectical leaps are done away with, and nature is seen as unified and developing only in complexity.

The mechanists also came to be identified with a strictly determinist (as opposed to a voluntarist) position in economics and social theory, according to which progress toward communism would be gradual, without leaps, and inevitable.

The Deborinists were so named because they were generally students or supporters of Abram Moiseevich Deborin (1881-1964), who defended the independent status of philosophy and argued that it was necessary to base science on philosophical principles. Moreover, not only could dialectics be used in describing natural phenomena but it could also be used as a guide in empirical research. As opposed to the mechanists the Deborinists held that nature was dialectical and that the unity and contradiction of opposites were the source of matter's motion. They contended that Engels had shown that any other position necessitated a prime mover. They likewise defended the law of the transition of quantity to quality and the necessity of dialectical leaps. As Engels and Lenin had made clear, they argued, one could reduce neither mind to matter nor living matter and its laws to inanimate matter and its laws. Finally, they claimed there were leaps in history as well as in nature, and though socialism was inevitable it could be attained only by taking the appropriate means.

The cause of the Deborinists was enhanced in 1925 by the publication of Engels' posthumous and incomplete work, *Dialectics of Nature,* and of Lenin's *Philosophical Notebooks,* first in excerpt and then more fully in 1929-30. Though both sides claimed support from these works they were more clearly in line with the Deborinist position.

By 1929 the Deborinists were the victors of the controversy. Deborin was by then the editor of *Under the Banner of Marxism,* director of the Institute of Philosophy, and had control of the philosophy section of the Soviet Encyclopedia; his followers had control of the philosophical section of the State Publishing House. The final page of the controversy between mechanists and the Deborinites was written by the Party, and this way of solving disputes became part of the pattern in the development of Soviet thought. In 1928 Stalin spoke of the presence of right and "left" deviations from the party line.[4] In February 1929 he dubbed "Bukharin's group" as "a group of Right deviators and capitulators who advocate not the elimination, but the free development of the capitalist elements in town and country."[5] Mechanism, it was claimed, was the philosophical basis for the rightist political deviation, and both the philosophical and political positions arose from the same social base. In April 1929 the Second All-Union Conference of Marxist-Leninist Scientific Institutions officially condemned mechanism as a "clear deviation from the Marxist-Leninist philosophical position."[6]

The Deborinist victory itself, however, was short-lived. On June 7, 1930, the Deborinists were attacked in *Pravda* by three party theoreticians for political neutrality in philosophy (for not being "party minded"), for separating theory from practice, thus ignoring the practical problems of building socialism in the U.S.S.R. and of promoting international revolutionary activity, for underestimating the importance of Lenin (while over-emphasizing Hegel and Plekhanov), and for failing to recognize the Lenininst stage as a new step in the development of Marxist philosophy.[7] In December Stalin called Deborinism "menshevizing idealism,"[8] and on January 25, 1931, the Central Committee of the CPSU officially condemned Deborinism.[9]

As mechanism had been linked with right deviationism, Deborinism was linked with "left" deviationism or Trotskyism.[10] V. V. Adoratsky (1878-1945), M. B. Mitin (1901–), and P. F. Judin (1899–) emerged as part of the new editorial board of *Under the Banner of Marxism* and as the new breed of philosopher, the party ideologist.[11] Henceforth, philosophy in the Soviet Union was not an autonomous monarch and queen of the sciences, as Deborin had envisaged, but an arm of the Party and subservient to it. Philosophical controversy had come to an end by political decree. In general, the Deborinist position, as corrected, became the official position reaffirmed after Stalin's death. However, for roughly the next two decades after the condemnation of 1931, the only significant voice to be heard in the realm of Soviet thought was that of Joseph Stalin.

Thus ends the first period of Soviet philosophy. Its imprint on Soviet thought is still written large. The tension between dialectics and materialism, positivism and philosophy, brought to light in the 1920's appears again in more subdued form after the death of Stalin. Likewise, the ambiguous relation of philosophy and science, never clearly defined during the mechanist-Deborinist controversy, continues and later reappears.[12] The emergence of technical Marxist-Leninist philosophy and professional Marxist-Leninist philosophers introduces professionals into Marxism whose task is not to foment revolution but to teach, write textbooks, translate philosophical works, conduct research in the history of philosophy, answer and fight against all non-Marxist-Leninist philosophy, attempt to resolve technical difficulties, omissions and contradictions in the classics, and develop technically defensible philosophical positions as required by the Party. The reliance on Marx and Engels, found in Lenin, is now extended to include reliance on Lenin as well, as interpreted first by Stalin, later by the Party. Most important of all, from this time on philosophy is subservient to the Party, and the Party is the arbiter of disputes and the ultimate judge of orthodoxy.

Stalin's Consolidation

Joseph Vissarionovich Dzhugashvili, better known as Stalin, was born on December 21, 1879, in the little town of Gori in Georgia.[13] His father was a peasant shoemaker. Stalin was educated at the elementary clerical school in Gori and then at the Tiflis Theological Seminary, from which he was expelled in 1899 for propagating Marxism. At the age of seventeen he joined a Social Democratic organization, and in 1901 he was sent to Baku to form a sister organization there. From then until the October Revolution of 1917 Stalin was continually engaged in revolutionary activity. He was repeatedly arrested and exiled, but each time managed to escape and carry on his work. He sided with Lenin and the Bolshevik position from the start and gradually worked his way up in the Party. In 1912 he became a member of the Bolshevik Central Committee. After the October Revolution in 1917 he was appointed People's Commissar for the Affairs of Nationalities. In 1922 he became General Secretary of the Party, and by appointing Party secretaries at the lower echelons established Party control. After Lenin's death he was one of a triumvirate (Kamenev and Zinoviev were the other members) to head both the Soviet government and the Communist Party. But in short order he became sole ruler and virtual dictator of the Soviet Union until his death on March 5, 1953. In February 1956 in a special report to the 20th Congress of the Communist Party of the Soviet Union, Nikita Khrushchev laid bare the crimes of the Stalin era and so ended the Stalinist "personality cult."

Unlike Marx and Lenin, Stalin was neither philosophically inclined nor trained. But he ruled the Soviet Union during its formative period and by virtue of necessity had to face and resolve the problems both of consolidating the gains made by the revolution and of building socialism. As head of the Party he developed—or revised—the Marxist-Leninist heritage in the light of concrete circumstances—by practice more than by theory. In dialectical materialism he remained always a neophyte, and though his scant writings on the subject dominated Soviet thought from 1938 until 1956, they had no lasting impact. Yet the fact that his writings dominated in this area during his reign underlines the importance of the Party leader in matters of theory, reinforces the doctrine of *partiinost'*, and indicates the extent of the subservience of philosophy to the Party in the Soviet Union. In the realm of historical materialism Stalin's theory was concretized in action. Though Soviet documents no longer mention Stalin or acknowledge his contributions to Soviet thought, his innovations in this realm have for the most part been preserved and are still followed.

There is no complete collection of Stalin's writings. A sixteen-volume edition was planned by the Marx-Engels-Lenin Institute, but only thirteen volumes, the last ending with his writings of January 1934, were published before the baring of his crimes by Khrushchev. The last three volumes never appeared. Of his early writings, many of which were written in Georgian, none are of great significance though a few are worthy of note. In his article "The Agrarian Question" (1906) Stalin spoke against socialization, nationalization, and municipalization of the land, holding that the peasants should confiscate the land and divide it among themselves. In this way peasant support for the revolution could be initially secured. Though not formally decreed in 1917, this is in large measure what happened after the revolution.

Stalin's articles "Anarchism or Socialism" of 1906-7 are interesting for their discussions of dialectical materialism. These foreshadow his later writings on the subject which were to be treated as dogma for almost two decades. Stalin's understanding of dialectics as evidenced in these articles was —and remained—confused. He speaks only of the dialectical method, and not of dialectics as such, though his exposition touches on all aspects of dialectics. Life, he says, is in continual motion and development and must be viewed as such, and not as static. But statements such as "all that which really exists, i.e., all that which grows day after day is rational, and all that which decays day after day is irrational and, consequently, cannot avoid defeat"[14] show his philosophical confusion. What is decaying, of course, also exists. The reference is obviously to Hegel's "what is real is rational"; but Stalin fails to see that though this statement makes sense in Hegel's idealistic framework it becomes unintelligible in his own framework. He equates the "new order" with "qualitative change,"[15] quotes Marx and Engels, emphasizes that the development of matter precedes the development of consciousness, confuses ideals and ideas, and holds that the development of content (the material side) precedes the development of form (the ideal side).[16] He is orthodox in applying this when he says "we must help to bring about a radical change in economic relations in order, with this change, to bring about a radical change in the habits and customs of the people, and in their political system,"[17] but he is less so when he emphasizes—as he will even more later—the importance of "human striving and will."[18]

The third early work worthy of note is Stalin's "Marxism and the National Question" (1913), originally published under the title "The National Question and Social-Democracy." In it he penned the solution to the nationalities problem which he later had the opportunity of putting into effect: allow regional (as opposed to national) autonomy for crystalized units while establishing unity from below among the workers of all nationalities.

Stalin's later works, however, have had lasting impact on Soviet thought. In April 1924 he delivered a series of lectures at Sverdlov University entitled *Foundations of Leninism* in which he outlined what he considered the essence of Leninism and in which he interpreted Lenin's doctrine. To this should be added *Concerning Questions of Leninism* (1926), in which he continues and adds to his previous work. Both of these, in addition to a number of other works, were collected and published under the title *Problems of Leninism*. This volume appeared in eleven editions, each of which varied in contents.

We have already seen the controversy in philosophy which took place in the 1920's. Stalin's intervention was noteworthy in condemning Bukharin, in dubbing Deborin a "menshevizing idealist," and in the official decree which condemned Deborinism as a deviation from Marxism.

From 1931 the Party was the final arbiter in philosophy, and during his rule the Party was Stalin. The primary task of the professional philosophers became the education of the masses and the training of the teachers in the new monolithic world view of the Party. The magnitude and importance of this task should not be underestimated. Professionally, they did little creative work and concerned themselves primarily with translations of and commentaries on various works in the history of philosophy, including those of Democritus, Aristotle, Descartes, Spinoza, Hegel, and some of the pre-Marxist Russian philosophers. Lenin became the recognized authority of Marxism. Contributors to *Under the Banner of Marxism* hacked out the official position, essentially that of Deborin. Controversy was significantly absent. Articles on Hegel appeared sporadically, and the journal was neither militantly atheistic nor a "society of materialist friends of Hegel." Its influence seems to have equaled its dullness. It also failed to concern itself seriously with the problems of building socialism or with practical problems generally until 1941, when it became an organ of antifascist propaganda, which it remained until its last issue, nos. 4-5 of 1944. The philosophers also engaged in writing articles for the large encyclopedia, preparing a dictionary of philosophy, and writing a few textbooks in the history of philosophy. Generally speaking, their output was small.

The only philosophically significant event during this period was the appearance of the *History of the Communist Party of the Soviet Union (Bolsheviks): Short Course*, which contained a section entitled "Dialectical and Historical Materialism", long attributed to the hand of Stalin. It is important primarily because it was slavishly followed and quoted in works of Soviet philosophy from its appearance until Stalin's death, and because the *History* was used as a basic text in Soviet and Party schools and became familiar to a generation of Soviet people still alive today.

In 1942 Mitin, reciting the accomplishments in the field of philosophy in the U.S.S.R. since the revolution, could name Stalin alone as having made any creative contribution, and as having uncovered new laws of the development of socialist society.[19] Besides outlining work done in the history of philosophy and in dialectical and historical materialism, Mitin noted the absence of work in logic and the need for a text. In December 1946 the Central Committee published a directive recognizing the importance of logic and psychology and ordering that appropriate texts be written, teachers trained, and courses taught in these subjects in secondary and eventually in elementary schools.[20] Once again the Central Committee had intervened.

The proclamation concerning logic and psychology was the first indication of official concern with either the level of stagnation to which philosophy had sunk or the lack of a medium for restless intellectuals to express themselves at all. In June 1947 the Central Committee of the Communist Party called a conference of philosophers and ideologists to discuss and criticize Professor G. Alexandrov's *History of West-European Philosophy*. Since Alexandrov's previous work on the history of Western philosophy[21] caused no such storm, since the book under discussion had been awarded a Stalin Prize and been adopted by the Ministry of Education as a university textbook, and since Alexandrov was himself made head of the Institute of Philosophy a few years after the conference, it seems that Alexandrov's book was merely the pretext for calling a conference of philosophers.

The main address was made by A. A. Zhdanov (1896-1948), a member of the Politburo, and a spokesman for Stalin. In his speech he first criticized Alexandrov's book, and then criticized the general situation in philosophy. He criticized Soviet philosophers generally for lack of productivity, isolation from the people, professional ignorance, cliquishness, failure to interpret Western philosophy in the Marxist manner and to recognize Marxism as a qualitatively different philosophy, cowardice with respect to applying Marxism to contemporary problems and to the contradictions still existing in Soviet society, and failure to keep up with and interpret developments in the natural sciences.[22]

The call to productivity was sounded, and the end of idleness on the part of Soviet philosophers and ideologists was demanded. A new philosophical journal, *Voprosy filosofii*, was founded, and the first issue contained the speeches made at the Alexandrov conference. The editor was B. M. Kedrov, though he was replaced before the end of his second year. The journal is still the leading philosophical organ in the Soviet Union. Thus, discussion and controversy were reintroduced into professional philosophical writings. But while reminiscent of the discussion of the 1920's in that there was debate, there was actually less essential divergence of opinion and scarcely any creative development. As in the 1920's a debate broke out over the relation of science to philosophy and another over the status of logic. Other disputes, for instance, concerned the relation of psychology and philosophy; but there was no questioning of the bases of Marxism-Leninism, and deviations from the party line were quickly criticized

The Development of Soviet Thought 189

either in the pages of the journal itself or in the pages of *Kommunist* (called *Bol'shevik* until September 1952) or *Pravda*. Stalin and the classics were still quoted ad nauseam. An increase of activity was noticeable, however, in the attempts of philosophers to disseminate the Marxist-Leninist world view more assiduously and widely and in their efforts to read and refute contemporary bourgeois philosophers. Criticism and self-criticism increased, and there were more combined efforts in writing books.

The most noteworthy development in Soviet philosophy of the period came from the pen of Stalin. In 1950 he wrote five letters on linguistics which appeared in *Pravda* and which were published under the title *Marxism and Linguistics*. Though the topic was ostensibly far removed from philosophy, Stalin dealt to a significant extent with the superstructure-base dichotomy and defined the active role of the superstructure in society. This is a change which has had wide repercussions, including new official interest in the function of morality, law, and social consciousness, an interest which augmented rather than diminished after 1956. Stalin's *Economic Problems of Socialism in the U.S.S.R.* (1952) was less influential, appearing shortly before his death. In it he examines the development of economic laws under socialism and cautions his readers against too drastic an interpretation of the active force of the superstructure.

Stalin's death in March 1953 marked the end of his dictatorship. The revelation of his crimes to the Soviet people in 1956 marked the end of the cult of the individual. But his influence on Soviet thought, though in part reversed and though not openly acknowledged, remains significant.

History of the CPSU (b): Short Course

The *History of the Communist Party of the Soviet Union (Bolsheviks): Short Course* first appeared in 1938. It was written by a commission of the Central Committee of the Party, though it was often attributed to Stalin's hand alone.[23] Widely used, for many years it supplied not only the basic instruction on Marxism-Leninism but also on party history, including information on the Narodnik movement, Plekhanov, Lenin's writings and activities until the revolution, and Soviet history from then until 1937. It mirrors the stature of both Lenin and Stalin, who is made at least his equal. Though it gives an admittedly distorted picture of many events and has been replaced,[24] it is important because (1) much of what it describes remains the official version of Soviet history and thought; (2) it was not only widely used, but the section on dialectical and historical materialism, attributed to Stalin, was eulogized as being a great creative step in the development of Marxist-Leninist philosophy and was repeated, followed, and developed in all philosophical works until Stalin's death; and (3) it contains some categories, concepts, and positions which permeated Soviet society and continue to be an integral part of Soviet thought.

The *Short Course* presents the role of the masses in making history and repeats the claims that social and economic conditions determine ideas, that at the turn of the century Russia had already entered on the path of capitalist development, and the like, which we have already seen in their original form and need not repeat here. Lenin's works are frequently quoted, and his *Materialism and Empirio-Criticism* receives especially high praise.

The *Short Course* continues to emphasize the importance of the Party and its mission in the development of communism. Marx's dictatorship of the proletariat is interpreted to mean the dictatorship of the Communist Party. Lenin's insistence on a strongly disciplined party is continued by Stalin, though the Party's role now becomes one of leading the masses not in revolution but in building socialism and communism.

In *Concerning Questions of Leninism* Stalin had pointed out that "in the proletarian revolution the seizure of power is only the *beginning*, and power is used as a lever for transforming the old economy and organizing the new one."[25] Stalin was faced with using power, and he utilized it to bring about forced industrialization with emphasis on the development of heavy industry, collectivization in agriculture, and the elimination of the class of kulaks and of all the bourgeoisie. This development of society was directed by Five Year Plans, the first of which was initiated in 1927. But the development of socialism according to a plan from above seemed hardly compatible with Marx's economic determinism. The *Short Course* gives the justification for it, which consists of a reinterpretation of the superstructure, with emphasis on its active role in social development and in the introduction of the concept of a "revolution from above," that is, a revolution initiated by the state but directly supported from below by the masses.[26] Henceforth, this type of revolution is the means by which progress is to be achieved in a socialist society. Revolutions from below were necessary when the masses were oppressed; if they are being led in their own interests, however, the impetus for revolt from below disappears, though the need for change continues. Moreover, revolutions from below occurred when there were antagonistic classes, the oppressed overthrowing the oppressor. But, supposedly, with the advent of socialism, oppressors no longer exist. Classes remain, such as the peasant class, the transformed proletariat, and the intellectuals. But since none of them oppresses the others, they are "nonantagonistic" classes.[27] The dialectical source of development in socialist society is no longer class antagonism but merely differences, such as between town and country, which will continue—for the dialectic never ends —but which lead to a development directed from above.

A second difficulty which had to be faced was that Marx had claimed that the socialist revolution could not be successful in one country. How could this be reconciled with the existence of the U.S.S.R.? The answer the *Short Course* supplies is that conditions had changed and that while this was true in the nineteenth century it was no longer true in the twentieth.[28] Why this is so is not explained. Rather the claim is made that the October Revolution was a socialist revolution and that it was successful in only one country, proving that conditions had changed. Lenin had introduced the doctrine of socialism in one country, and Stalin developed and acted on it, opposing Trotsky's demands for giving primacy to the active export of international revolution. Stalin did, however, say that the victory of socialism demanded the support and development of revolution in other countries,[29] thereby justifying the export of revolution, and the later Soviet take-over in Eastern Europe after World War II.

The doctrine of the possibility of socialism in one country made it possible for Stalin to proclaim that society had become socialistic in the U.S.S.R., that exploitation had been eliminated and capitalism overcome. This in turn justified the introduction of a new constitution. While exploitation by individual capitalists had been eliminated, exploitation of individuals by the state had clearly not been eliminated, as Khrushchev himself testified in his speech to the Twentieth

192 PATTERNS OF SOVIET THOUGHT

Party Congress. Nor did the achievement of socialism mean that the state would wither away. This supposedly would have happened if the revolution had been successful on a worldwide scale. But one change in doctrine demands another. The doctrine of socialism in one country necessitated the claim that the state would not wither until socialism became worldwide: the army will be necessary for defense against attack by the encircling capitalist world, and penal organs will be necessary to protect socialist property and punish spies, assassins, and wreckers sent into the country by foreign countries.[30]

Among the other concepts found in the *Short Course* which have been part of the everyday jargon of Soviet life are "survivals of capitalism" and "moral-political unity."[31] The first refers to what remains of capitalism in the Soviet Union. Since production and social relations are socialistic, the only survivals of capitalism admitted to be left since 1936 are bourgeois or capitalistic ideas. The existence of these survivals is explained by the fact that consciousness lags behind social being. These survivals are still blamed as the cause for all crime, laziness, or anti-social behavior. "Moral-political unity" refers to the claim that since the U.S.S.R. is the champion of the working masses and is leading them to communism, all its political actions both on the domestic and international scene are morally justified and deserve the moral support of the people. The presence of moral-political unity and of the survivals of capitalism called for increased and sustained activity on the Soviet ideological front; the call was reiterated on the philosophical front, as we have seen, at the 1947 Alexandrov conference.

In "Dialectical and Historical Materialism," the forty-odd pages comprising section two of chapter four of the *Short Course*, we find presented the essentials of "the world outlook of the Marxist-Leninist party."[32] As in Stalin's *Anarchism or Socialism* the discussion of dialectical materialism is divided into a presentation of the Marxist *dialectical method* and Marxist philosophical materialism. This peculiar division of dialectical materialism was followed by all Soviet philosophers until Stalin's death, when they abruptly switched back to Engels' presentation—first of matter, then of dialectics in general and its three laws, and only then of dialectics as a method.

The Development of Soviet Thought 193

Four principal features of the dialectical method are outlined: (1) all of nature forms an interconnected, integral whole, and so any given phenomenon should be considered in its interrelations; (2) nature is in a state of continuous movement and change, and any given phenomenon should be looked upon as developing and changing; (3) there is an onward and upward movement in nature, quantitative changes leading to abrupt qualitative changes, and all phenomena should be considered in this light; (4) internal contradictions, negative and positive sides, and a struggle between old and new are inherent in all phenomena, form the basis of development, and should be sought in the analysis of all phenomena and of social phenomena in particular.[33]

Of Engels' three laws of dialectics this Stalinist presentation includes the interpenetration of opposites and the transition of quantity into quality. Notably absent is the law of negation of the negation. Also omitted is any discussion of categories such as "freedom and necessity," "causality," "space and time," and the like.

According to the *Short Course* the principal features of Marxist philosophical materialism are: (1) the world is by its very nature material, (2) matter is primary, an objective reality existing outside and independent of our minds, while mind is secondary, being a reflection of matter, (3) the world and its laws are fully knowable, authentic knowledge being tested by experience and practice.[34]

Stalin had dialectical materialism reduced to this bare skeleton and the timidity of Soviet philosophers kept them for years monotonously and verbosely repeating these few statements, declining even to adding flesh to the bones.

The discussion of historical materialism in the *Short Course* formally introduced an innovation in theory corresponding to the one Stalin had introduced in practice. Following Marx it explains how social ideas and theories, politcial views and institutions, in short the elements of the superstructure of a society, follow and reflect the material conditions of society. But this, it holds, concerns their *origin*, not their *significance*. For it emphasizes that ideas, theories, and political institutions play an important role in facilitating the development of society. "New social ideas and theories arise only after the development of the material life of society has set new tasks before society. But once they have arisen they become a most potent force which facilitates the carrying out of the new tasks set by the development of the material life of society, a force which facilitates the progress of society."[35] Emphasis on the potent force of ideas is contrary to the spirit of Marx and Engels, but coincides well both with the activistic interpretation of Marxism espoused by Lenin and with Stalin's own action in changing Soviet society from above. In addition, it emphasizes the importance of theory and increases the necessity for indoctrination of the masses by propaganda in order to mobilize and organize them to act according to the plans set up by the Party leader or leaders.

This, Stalin's most basic and lasting reinterpretation of Marxism-Leninism, is found not only in this work but also, as we shall see, in his discussion of linguistics and in his report to the Eighteenth Congress of the CPSU (b), in which he speaks of the moral and political unity of Soviet society, the mutual friendship of the nations of the U.S.S.R., and Soviet patriotism as *"motive forces"* in the development of Soviet society.[36] For classical Marxism the only motive forces were economic. Stalin's reinterpretation not only justified his practice, led to further changes in policy, and increased efforts at moral persuasion and propaganda, but it took the teeth and sting out of the classical Marxist doctrine of historical materialism. It is interesting to note that this basically idealist reinterpretation of historical materialism is made by Stalin, who, unlike Lenin, was a confirmed anti-Hegelian.

Linguistics and the Superstructure

The pervasiveness of Marxism-Leninism throughout the life of the Soviet Union makes the Party an authority in any field in which Marxism-Leninism is at all pertinent. Thus, it was that during his reign Stalin by virtue of his office as head of the Party ruled in a great variety of domains, including not only philosophy but also the arts, many of the sciences, and linguistics as well. Stalin's intervention in the linguistics controversy shows his absolute authority in all realms of thought and confirms the pattern of innovation only from above. Another pattern it exemplifies—and one which is widespread—is that any authoritative pronouncement from above in one field or area of endeavor has direct significance for other areas. *Marxism and Linguistics* opened up discussions not only in linguistics but also in philosophy, economics, and

The Development of Soviet Thought 195

other fields. It is often the case that directives for a general change in ideological policy are given through decrees or decisions made about some peripheral and, to the uninitiated eye, completely unrelated discipline or problem.

N. Y. Marr was a Soviet linguistics scholar who for many years had dominated the field in the Soviet Union and whose work had received high recognition by the Party. His rejection of the comparative methods used by Western linguistics, and some of his own claims concerning the development of language, however, were not completely accepted by all Soviet specialists in the field. In characteristic fashion they were finally subjected to criticism in 1950 in *Pravda*. A debate ensued, and a number of questions were referred to Stalin for his definitive answers. Stalin's replies, printed in *Pravda* on June 20, 1950, occasioned a number of other questions which were similarly answered on June 29, July 11, July 22, and July 28, 1950. By his answers Stalin deposed Marr, but his discussions touched on questions of historical materialism and had far-reaching significance in many areas.

In this collection of articles Stalin reaffirms and clarifies several of the innovations in Marxist-Leninist theory already noted. He reiterates the active role of the superstructure in the development of society, adding that the superstructure is only indirectly connected with production and "therefore does not reflect changes of development of the productive forces immediately and directly."[37] The number of works connected with the impact of social consciousness, morality, and education increased sharply in the Soviet Union in the year following and has maintained a steady rise up to the present.[38] The indirectness of the influence also opens wider the door to the notion of the "relative independence" of development within given fields which had received little consideration prior to Stalin's statement.

Stalin also clarifies the notion of revolution from above. Though antagonistic conflicts no longer exist in a classless society, nonantagonistic ones—such as the differences between town and country, physical and mental labor—do exist, and social development will progress by lessening the distinction between them.[39] He then generalizes the law of the transition of quantity to quality as it applies to socialist society, removing from it its dialectical content in a formulation that smacks of mechanism: "It should be said in general for the benefit of comrades who have an infatuation for such explosions that the law of transition from an old quality to a new by means of an explosion is inapplicable not only to the history of the development of languages; it is not always applicable to some other social phenomena of a basal or superstructural character. It is compulsory for a society divided into hostile classes. But it is not at all compulsory for a society which has no hostile classes."[40] It is understandable that Stalin wished to eliminate the possibility of any theoretician claiming that socialist society like previous societies must be replaced by an explosive leap; but in the change introduced he wittingly or unwittingly undermines the universality of the laws of dialectics which, stated in their generality, are supposed to be exemplified in all of reality without exception.

Besides clarifying and developing previous positions Stalin also utilizes this occasion to introduce a significant addition to Marxist-Leninist theory—to state formally a position which he and Lenin had presupposed in practice but had not clearly formulated in theory—and to open up discussion in many regions of thought.

The fundamental addition to Marxist-Leninist theory arises from his discussion of the superstructure and the base. In accordance with the classical Marxist position he says: "The base is the economic structure of society at a given stage of its development. The superstructure consists of the political, legal, religious, artistic, and philosophical views of society and the political, legal, and other institutions corresponding to them. Every base has its own superstructure corresponding to it."[41] But where does language fit into this scheme? Is it, as Marr maintains, part of the superstructure? Insofar as language is based on thought and thought is secondary, and dependent on matter, does it not follow that language must also be secondary, and thus part of the superstructure? Stalin's reply is an unqualified negative: "Briefly, language cannot be ranked either among bases or among superstructures. Neither can it be ranked among 'intermediate' phenomena between the base and superstructure, as such 'intermediate' phenomena do not exist."[42] In a single stroke Stalin hereby dissociates the categories of base-superstructure from the categories of matter-mind, on which they had previously been modeled. This also creates difficulties for dialectical materialism and the relation of social consciousness and social being, which

Stalin and his successors thus far have ignored. But besides the difficulties it raises in this respect it freed linguistics from the superstructure, unambiguously stated that not every discipline is contained in the dichotomy, and so raised the question of what else did not belong. Mathematics, it seems, is also not class determined. It follows then that mathematical logic, if considered as a part of mathematics, is likewise not class determined and not part of the superstructure. While this did not solve the debate as to the nature of logic it did provide a clear case for the validity of mathematical logic developing independently of superstructural considerations, and we find that mathematical logic started to flourish in the 1950's. A case can also be made for freeing the facts of science from the superstructure, though the interpretation of these facts or theories remains class-bound.

Stalin and Lenin, as seen, both felt free to initiate changes in Marxism and set the pattern of change from above. Could such changes be justified in theory? Stalin, speaking to this point in *Marxism and Linguistics*, formulates a principle of justification. Marxism, he says, is not "a collection of dogmas which 'never' change, regardless of the changes in the condition of development of society . . . Marxism as a science cannot stand still; it develops and perfects itself . . . consequently, its separate formulas and deductions cannot but change in the course of time, cannot but be replaced by new formulas and deductions corresponding to the new historical tasks. Marxism does not recognize any immutable deductions and formulas, applicable to all epochs and periods."[43] Are then the tenets of Marxism-Leninism true? The answer is that Marxism-Leninism is true, but that a formula or conclusion of Marxism-Leninism which stems from the study of one period of history does not necessarily hold for all periods of history: "Two different formulas correspond to two different epochs in the development of society, and precisely because they correspond to them, the two formulas are correct, each for its own epoch."[44] Consequently, though Marx and Engels hold that a socialist revolution could not be victorious in one country alone and Lenin and Stalin claim that such a victory in one country is possible, we do not have a contradiction, for each view is correct for its own period. Likewise, Engels in *Anti-Dühring* says that, after the socialist revolution, the state will wither away. This was true when communism was envisaged

198 PATTERNS OF SOVIET THOUGHT

as something which would be worldwide, but it is not true when the triumph of communism in one country is joined with capitalist encirclement. Stalin's newly formulated principle gives him a means of holding that Marx and Engels are correct and that Lenin and he are also correct, though they seem to contradict one another, for each is correct with respect to his own period. This rule of interpretation is admittedly handy and is prevented from being two-edged (that is, from being used by some to claim that Marx's analysis is obsolete with respect to present-day capitalism) by the fact that only the leaders of the Party are in a position to decide how to interpret the classics and to decide when what they say must be taken in context and when what they say is universally valid.

The final item of significance in *Marxism and Linguistics* is Stalin's reply to the question of whether *Pravda* acted rightly in inaugurating an open discussion on the question of linguistics. Stalin answers in the affirmative and goes on to generalize: "It is generally recognized that no science can develop and flourish without a battle of opinions, without freedom of criticism. But this generally recognized rule was ignored and flouted in the most outrageous fashion. A tight group of infallible leaders, having insured themselves against all possible criticism, began to act arbitrarily and highhandedly."[45] This statement of the necessity for a battle of opinions was taken by Soviet philosophers as a signal for increased debate and criticism, though criticism was not to extend to the bases of Marxism-Leninism. The last two sentences quoted take on an ironic note when read in the light of Khrushchev's exposure of Stalin in almost identical language.

Stalin's Contribution to Soviet Thought

In February 1956, at the end of the Twentieth Party Congress of the Soviet Union, Nikita S. Khrushchev in closed session delivered a now famous speech denouncing the "cult of personality" which had grown up around Stalin and revealing some of the "violence, mass repressions, and terror" which Stalin had initiated and utilized during his reign. The details, though partial, were shocking in themselves, and the fact that the First Secretary of the CPSU revealed them seemed especially surprising. Yet Khrushchev reported less than was widely known in the West, and known by experience—if not

The Development of Soviet Thought 199

in detail at least in general—by a large portion of people in the Soviet Union. Moreover, his denunciation of Stalin was far from thoroughgoing, and his merit "in the preparation and execution of the Socialist Revolution, in the Civil War, and in the fight for the construction of socialism"[46] in the U.S.S.R. was readily acknowledged. Thus, while certain aspects of Stalinism were rejected, many others had become part of the Soviet pattern of thought and were preserved.

After Lenin's death Stalin emerged from the power struggle and helped establish his prestige by identifying himself with Lenin. After Stalin's death a power struggle also erupted. Three years later, almost to the day, Khrushchev helped establish his prestige both by identifying himself with Lenin and by dissociating himself from the Stalinist personality cult which, being a reign of terror, was understandably unpopular. But a careful reading of the speech reveals that Khrushchev dissociates himself only from the violence and terror used against the Party or against Soviet workers, not that used against the bourgeois nationalists, the kulaks which Stalin eliminated as a class, and against many others. The abuses against the Party were decried. In denouncing Stalin, Khrushchev thrust all blame for all abuses upon him and the defects of his personality; he thereby freed the Party and its leaders —especially Khrushchev who did the unmasking—of any taint of evil. At one stroke he cleared the name of the Party and claimed that now that collective leadership had been instituted in the Soviet Union it would be impossible for the crimes of the Stalin era to be repeated. The crimes, he claimed, were perpetrated in violation of Party principles and socialist morality. Thus, Party principles and socialist morality are essentially sound and worthy of adherence. Moreover, whatever was accomplished in positive terms during Stalin's reign is not to be attributed to the person of Stalin but to the Party. Henceforth the Party is to receive all praise for the accomplishments of the Soviet Union; Stalin all blame for its crimes. Khrushchev as the new leader of the Party enhanced his own prestige as well as that of the Party which now, freed of blame, could exercise tighter control in fulfilling the tasks of the future.

In the new *History of the Communist Party of the Soviet Union* Stalin is scarcely ever mentioned. The eulogy of Stalin which permeated the *Short Course* is replaced by a similar eulogy of the Party. But whether the credit goes to Stalin or to the Party during the years of his reign, certain patterns of Soviet thought were established or confirmed, certain doctrines were reinterpreted or introduced which continue to be found in Soviet thought today.

The adherence to the writings of Marx and Engels and the toleration of only Marxist philosophy, initiated during Lenin's time, is continued, though Lenin's writings are added to the list of Marxist classics, making Marxism-Leninism the official Soviet world view. It alone can be taught and propagated in printed or spoken form. Though Stalin's works achieved near-classic status during his lifetime, they have no officially recognized position today.

Stalin continued adherence to Lenin's principles of *partiinost'*. Philosophy is now clearly the handmaiden of the Party, which not only is the ultimate arbiter of disputes and the guardian of orthodoxy but also the guide indicating what theoretical problems need solving. The pattern of change from above, and only from above, seems firmly established, and the post-Stalin period confirms this pattern.

The consequent dichotomy between professional philosophers, concerned with teaching or writing or doing research in the history of philosophy or in special branches of philosophy, and the Party leaders, concerned with the practical aspects of governing the country and directing the expansion of communism, became established during the Stalin years. The Party ideologists bridge the gap and help relate theory and practice—an admittedly new pattern in contrast to the union of theory and action of Marx and Lenin.

Stalin's contribution to the development of *dialectical materialism* was, if anything, negative. The presentation of it in *Dialectical and Historical Materialism* is no longer followed. But the neglect of dialectics, except in their primitive Stalinist exposition, was the pap on which many of today's Soviet citizens were nurtured and undoubtedly forms the bulk of their knowledge of or interest in the subject. The anti-Hegelian atmosphere of the Stalinist period undoubtedly also is at least partly responsible for the considerable number of Soviet philosophers who emphasize the materialist aspects of dialectical materialism rather than the dialectical. It is also responsible for the large number of parrot-like pseudophilosophers

The Development of Soviet Thought 201

and pedagogues, capable of little more than repeating the Party line.

In *historical materialism*, however, Stalin's contributions are important and lasting. The doctrine of socialism in one country and the emphasis on the active role of the superstructure are the two basic changes from classical Marxism which carry with them the others: the possibility of revolution from above, the possibility of society's development being directed by the leaders of the Party, the existence of nonantagonistic differences, the motive power of moral-political forces, and the central position of the U.S.S.R. in the development of communism.

The Stalinist revisions of historical materialism and their implicit negation of the laws of dialectics continue to be exploited without regard to the difficulty they raise for dialectical materialism. There seems to be something of a pattern developing in which dialectical materialism is to some extent divorced from historical materialism. At present Engels and Lenin reign in the realm of dialectics, though several aspects of dialectical materialism are being debated by the philosophers, and an attempt is being made to tighten it up. But at the same time the ideologists continue to revise historical materialism, seemingly oblivious of the difficulties that arise in trying to make both parts of basic Soviet theory compatible.

To the late Stalin period, from 1947 and especially from 1951, can also be traced the ever-increasing emphasis on ideological education and propaganda, and the greater importance attached to and studies made of questions of social consciousness and morality. The rebirth of discussion—within limits—and of increased activity on the philosophical front also date from Stalin's later days.

The New Program of the CPSU

On October 31, 1961, the delegates to the Twenty-Second Congress of the Communist Party of the Soviet Union unanimously adopted its third and most recent Program.[47] The first Party Program (1903) called for the communist revolution; the second (1919) outlined the tasks involved in building socialism; the third Program of the Communist Party of the Soviet Union is a blueprint of future aims and goals as the Soviet Union enters upon its now officially announced era of building a fully developed communist society.

The Program is not a statement of what will necessarily happen in the Soviet Union. Rather, in keeping with the voluntarist approach to Marxism which has been the Party line since Lenin's day, it is a program of action. For Marx, revolution was inevitable, given the material conditions of the proletariat. For Khrushchev and present Party leaders, the material base of a communist society must still be built: the program outlines what they will try to do, both to the base and to the superstructure in the next twenty years.

Marx was concerned with uncovering the laws of capitalism, and in doing so charted what he considered its necessary demise. Lenin was concerned primarily with bringing about the revolution in Russia. But both Marx and Lenin were too far away from the achievement of a communistic society to speak in any detail about the concrete steps leading a society from the first or socialist stage of communism to the final stage of full communism. Both were also extremely vague about what the final stage would be like. The new Program, attempting to remedy this deficiency, proclaims the beginning of a new era in theory and practice.

The Program of the CPSU is not a philosophical document, but it adds new elements to historical materialism and scientific socialism, implicitly sanctifies many of Stalin's contributions to Soviet thought, and prescribes some of the lines of investigation to be exploited by Soviet philosophers. It is in two parts, the first dealing with the transition from capitalism to communism, and the second promulgating the tasks of the CPSU in building a communist society.

The first part of the Program is largely historical. It reiterates the evils of capitalism and the moral aims of communism, in much the same way that Marx had. Though it still calls for revolution ("the possibility of a *non-peaceful transition to socialism* should be borne in mind")[48] and the support of "just anti-imperialist wars of liberation,"[49] it sounds the new line of peaceful coexistence. As the doctrine of socialism in one country had been introduced into Marxism in the face of historically changing circumstances, so the doctrine of peaceful coexistence has been introduced in the face of nuclear warfare. *"Peaceful coexistence,"* the Program reads, "of the socialist and capitalist countries is an *objective necessity* for the development of human society."[50] It also "affords more favorable opportunities for the struggle of the working class in the capitalist countries and facilitates the struggle of the peoples of the colonial and dependent countries for their liberation."[51] To this notion of peaceful coexistence is added the claim that capitalism in its "inexorable process of decay" has entered a new, third stage of crisis, "the principal feature of which is that its development was not connected with a world war."[52] Coexistence, it should be noted, extends only to social *systems*, not to the competing ideologies.[53]

Part Two of the Program begins by defining Communism:

> Communism is a classless social system with one form of public ownership of the means of production and full social equality of all members of society; under it, the all-round development of people will be accompanied by the growth of productive forces through continuous progress in science and technology; all the springs of cooperative wealth will flow more abundantly, and the great principle "From each according to his ability, to each according to his needs" will be implemented. Communism is a highly organized society of free, socially conscious working people in which public self-government will be established, a society in which labor for the good of society will become the prime vital requirement of everyone, a necessity recognized by one and all, and the ability of each person will be employed to the greatest benefit of the people.[54]

There is nothing specifically new in the definition. What is new is that the Program sets a date for its realization. During the decade 1961-70 the U.S.S.R. is to create the material and technical basis of communism. By 1980 the material and technical basis of communism is to have been achieved and "thus *a communist society will in the main be built in the U.S.S.R.* The construction of communist society will be fully completed in the subsequent period."[55] Unfortunately, the meaning of "in the main" is not clarified, and the length of the "subsequent period" is vague enough to extend to eternity.

For the creation of the material and technical base the Program outlines the tasks of the Party and of the Soviet people in industry and agriculture. The patterns of active direction from above and of changing the base according to a plan continue. In addition, the role of the superstructure is stressed even more than under Stalin. Economic management is to increase production by both material and moral incentives.[56] Ideological work becomes an increasingly powerful factor, the paramount task being "to educate all working people in a spirit of ideological integrity and devotion to communism."[57]

To achieve a communist society the Program stresses two main tasks: the construction of the material base to supply the rational needs of all the people, and the development of new men each of whom has a communist consciousness by means of which he acts for the good, not of himself, but of society. The first is difficult enough. The second, according to classical Marxism, should follow the first. But the Soviet experience with socialism convinced the Party that the lag of consciousness behind being—if lag it be—is enormous. The Program, therefore, calls for the production of the new Soviet man, the shaping of communist consciousness by education, art, and literature, by the inculcation of communist morality, and by all other means available. In an unprecedented and un-Marxian act the Program promulgates a moral code by which all are to live. Its main principles are labor for the good of society, collectivism, and socialist humanism.[58] Humanism, hardly central to the Marxist-Leninist writings since the days of early Marx, thus appears prominently once again.

Morality is eventually to replace law, though Soviet law is to become more and more encompassing before it eventually withers away. In a correction of Marx, it is now claimed morality will *not* wither away. The state, as Stalin noted, will not wither away until the complete worldwide victory of communism, but the Program proclaims that the dictatorship of the proletariat has given way to the dictatorship of the working class, which will continue its role of leader in Soviet society until communism is achieved and classes disappear.[59] The Communist Party continues to be the vanguard of the people and has "extended its guiding influence to all spheres of social life. The Party is the brain, the honor, and the conscience of our epoch, of the Soviet people."[60]

The task of philosophy according to this Program is "to firmly defend and develop dialectical and historical materialism as the science of the most general laws of development of nature, society, and human thinking,"[61] to elaborate "the philosophical problems of modern natural science on the basis of dialectical materialism,"[62] to investigate the laws of the development of socialism into communism,[63] and to "uphold the purity of the principles of Marxism-Leninism."[64] To this Khrushchev, in his speech on the Program added: "Guided by the Leninist principle of the unity of theory and practice, the Party must regard the defense and creative development of Marxism-Leninism as its prime duty."[65]

In what has now become a customary pattern, the philosophers responded immediately to the Party directives in the Program. The editorial in the November 1961 issue of *Voprosy filosofii* outlined the tasks of the philosophers in the light of the Twenty-Second Party Congress. These included the analysis of the motive forces of the development of Soviet society, the character of social progress under communism, the role of the subjective factor in social development, and the lines of the progressive development of social consciousness.[66] The philosophical books and articles appearing since then have developed these and similar themes and rarely fail to mention the Party Program. This again verifies the firmly established pattern of the subordination of philosophy to the Party. The Party Program has set the line, in some ways a new line, especially in the fields of historical materialism, which the philosophers are to elaborate, disseminate, and inculcate as component parts of Soviet thought.

Chapter XI
Fundamentals of Contemporary Soviet Philosophy

In 1958 a committee headed by F. V. Konstantinov produced a basic text book in Marxist-Leninist philosophy. It had been submitted to wide discussion before being printed and has since become the standard text for students at all institutions of higher learning, for all party members, and for those members of the intelligentsia interested in independent study. In 1962 a second edition, slightly revised in accordance with the new Party Program, appeared.[1] The text, entitled *Osnovy marksistskoi filosofii* (*Fundamentals of Marxist Philosophy*), is the authorized systematic presentation of dialectical and historical materialism and is a primary instrument of ideological education.[2] It represents the present orthodox position in Soviet philosophy, purged of now unacceptable Stalinist variants of dialectical materialism. As a basic text, already distributed in over 2,000,000 copies, its influence on students, educated laymen, and party members is considerable. Being a text, however, it often represents a safe compromise and does not reflect the differences of interpretation existing among Soviet philosophers. These are to be found in the philosophic journals and monographs, which, though not as widely read, reveal divergencies, disputes, and lines of possible future development. The growing dichotomy—especially with respect to questions of dialectical materialism—between the popular semiofficial texts which remain close to the doctrines of Marx, Engels, and Lenin, as formulated by them, and the more technical philosophical discussions which attempt to clarify and sharpen these doctrines, is a developing pattern of Soviet intellectual life, the consequences of which it is still too early to evaluate.

Matter, Mind, and Modern Physics

The presentation of dialectical materialism in *Fundamentals of Soviet Philosophy* begins with a chapter on "Matter and the Forms of Its Existence."[3] The approach of dialectical materialism is identified with that of science, the primacy of matter over consciousness is claimed to be proved by science, and Lenin's discussion of matter from *Materialism and Empirio-Criticism* is presented in some detail.[4] Matter, which is equated to nature, is infinite, eternal, and in constant motion.[5] Space and time are each said to be "an objectively real form of the existence of matter in motion,"[6] and, like matter, eternal and infinite. Finally, there are not two worlds, one of matter and another of spirit, but only one world which receives its unity from the fact that "at no time or place in the world has there ever been, is there now, or will there ever be anything which is not matter in motion or a product of matter in motion."[7] The sources on which these latter claims are based are almost exclusively Engels' *Anti-Dühring* and *Dialectics of Nature* and Lenin's *Materialism and Empirio-Criticism*.

A great deal has taken place in science since Lenin turned his attention to the problems raised by physics at the turn of the century, and, though the issues are skirted or ignored in *Fundamentals of Marxist Philosophy*, modern physics has created a crisis in Marxist-Leninist philosophy as it has in all contemporary philosophy. The situation is particularly serious in Soviet philosophy, perhaps, because the philosophers are tied to the above stated, dogmatically held positions on matter; but discussion has been vigorous, especially in recent years.

The Soviet popular line often tends to associate Soviet advances in technology with dialectical materialism and to claim for instance that Soviet success with launching earth satellites proves by practice the theoretical positions of dialectical materialism on matter.[8] The ploy is a shallow one, for by similar reasoning American successes in space would prove the validity of various bourgeois, positivistic, or idealistic philosophies of science.

More serious are the claims by Soviet philosophers of science that contemporary advances in physics prove the truth of dialectical materialism. Thus, M. E. Omelyanovsky claims that quantum physics, according to which microobjects evidence both corpuscular and wave patterns, "is permeated by dialectical contradictions. It implies the recognition of contradictions and oppositions in the very objects and phenomena of nature, their union and transitions into each other, the solution of old contradictions and the appearance of new ones."[9] S. T. Melyukhin goes so far as to claim "the history of scientific knowledge displays the following important regularity: all the fundamental problems of natural science, which apply to matter as a whole, have always been defined first in philosophy on the basis of dialectical and materialistic concepts."[10] The patent contradiction of this statement with the history of science is mitigated only if one also holds that "even those scientists, who reject dialectics subjectively, are forced spontaneously (due to the objective content of scientific concepts and theories) to follow dialectical laws and categories, since otherwise they cannot effectively work in the field of science."[11]

The history of science in the Soviet Union during the past two decades gives the lie to the claim that dialectical materialism is either proven by science or is presupposed by it. Not only has dialectical materialism not helped produce any scientific theories, but it has delayed the acceptance of scientific advances made in the West. Thus Academician Pyotr L. Kapitsa, a Lenin Prize winner and a renowned Soviet scientist, said: "Had our scientists back in the year 1954 paid attention to the philosophers . . . we may safely say that our conquest of space, of which we are so justly proud and for which the whole world respects us, could never have been made a reality."[12] And further: "Many of us still vividly remember how some of our philosophers, dogmatically applying the method of dialectics, were proving the unsoundness of the theory of relativity. . . . The physicists would not have been worth their salt had they followed the conclusions of certain philosophers and abandoned work on the problem of applying the theory of relativity to nuclear physics."[13]

From 1951 to 1955 a dispute raged in the pages of the journal *Voprosy filosofii* concerning the acceptability of relativity theory. It was initially considered incompatible with dialectical materialism by a number of Soviet philosophers, who for this reason rejected it as a scientific theory. Any relativization of space or time seemed incompatible with their objectivity and with the objectivity of knowledge. The situation became crucial and embarrassing when the special theory of relativity was experimentally proven. In 1955 the defenders of relativity, among whom were a number of scientists, finally won.[14] Likewise, though some Soviet philosophers originally rejected quantum mechanics because it seemed to set limits to knowledge (the momentum and position of a particle cannot both be known simultaneously), it too has been accepted. In each case the scientific facts could not be ignored, and what took place was a reinterpretation of the meaning of those facts for philosophy. When time and space seemed to lose their absolute quality according to Einstein's theory, it was decided that space and time (contrary to Engels) are indeed relative when considered apart, but that *space-time* is absolute. With quantum mechanics the limits of knowledge were played down and the contradictory and thus dialectical aspect of our knowledge of microparticles was emphasized.

The debate on how to interpret quantum mechanics and relativity theory in accordance with the doctrines of dialectical materialism is by no means finished.[15] Both philosophers and physicists are engaged in it. What precisely is meant by saying that space and time are forms of the existence of matter, and how can this best be fit in with the notion of gravitational fields? How can the concept of antimatter be accommodated by Lenin's definition of matter? Is "matter" to be taken as a transcendental ontological category, or is it to be defined merely epistemologically, or should some intermediate position be adopted? These and similar questions await answers. Solutions are particularly difficult to find when the Party demands that the dated notions of matter, space, and time put forward by Engels and Lenin be preserved and reconciled with contemporary science and that the resultant position be made sufficiently simple for inclusion in textbooks intended for wide ideological education. Yet present discussions in Soviet philosophy of physics are among the most lively in Soviet philosophy today. It is an area in which Soviet philosophers are being forced beyond the position of the classics and in which ideological supervision is limited by the technicalities of the discussion and by the Party's need for the new advances which the developments of physics and technology bring with them. It is also an area in which many of the problems are those shared by all contemporary philosophers of science, and so an area in which Soviet advances might be of particular interest to the non-Marxist-Leninist philosopher.

A second set of difficulties for dialectical materialism concerning matter arises in trying to handle the phenomenon of consciousness. A chapter of *Fundamentals of Marxist Philosphy* is devoted to the problem.[16] But it is again based primarily on Lenin's *Materialism and Empirio-Criticism*, leavened with quotes from Pavlov and Sechenov on the physiological aspects of higher nervous activity.

Consciousness is said to be the highest product and attribute of matter;[17] though a product and function of the brain, it has none of the physical qualities of bodies. Physiological processes and thought or consciousness are one process, the latter being the inner content of the former.[18] Consciousness itself, which is necessarily connected with matter, is not something material. Precisely what this means is yet to be clarified. How a product of matter can be anything other than material, and how it is possible to hold consistently both that matter exhausts all of reality and that consciousness is real but not matter, have yet to be explained. In fairness to Soviet philosophy it should be remembered that the nature and source of consciousness or mind is a topic still hotly debated in Western philosophies today. Most Soviet philosophers, however, have as yet failed to face the difficulties and ambiguities involved in their position.

Categories and Laws of Dialectics

The death of Stalin marked the beginning of a period of renewed interest in dialectics. The Stalinist version presented in the *Short Course* and eulogized during the remainder of Stalin's lifetime was quickly repudiated as untenable confusion. *Fundamentals of Marxist Philosophy* presents dialectics and its laws in four chapters.[19] The first deals with "The Regular (or Law-like) Connection of the Phenomena of Reality." The other three deal in turn with the three laws of dialectics as formulated by Engels: the law of the transition of quantitative into qualitative change, the law of the unity and conflict of opposites, and the law of the negation of the negation. Though preference is given to Engels' formulation of the laws, possibly for their simplicity, Lenin's comments in his *Philo-*

sophical Notebooks are extensively utilized. While nothing substantive is added, the four chapters attempt to systematize the often fragmentary presentations of Engels and Lenin.

Nature, we are told, is in a state of eternal, uninterrupted, and regular (law-like) movement, change, and development.[20] To understand this movement is to formulate laws of the objective development of the real world. The three laws formulated by Marxist philosophy are based on the recognition of the unity of nature and on an understanding of the development of the new from the old because of the internal contradictions of reality. Marxist philosophy thus provides the key for the investigation of all natural phenomena, since these laws are exemplified in all of reality.[21] Moreover, in addition to the laws it also provides a group of categories basic to reality such as "cause and effect," "the individual," "particular and general," "law," "necessity and change," "possibility and actuality"—all of which are treated in some detail—and others such as "essence and appearance" which are merely mentioned.[22]

The treatment of causality is typical of that accorded the various categories in *Fundamentals of Marxist Philosophy*. Almost half of the nine pages devoted to causality are spent summarily presenting and rejecting views of causality such as Kant's and Hume's. Causality in contemporary science receives only one paragraph, in which it is stated that causality holds for the microcosm as well as for phenomena of everyday life. Ultimately, the Marxist-Leninist position on causality which it presents is that enunciated by Engels and Lenin. Causality, we are told, is one of the forms of general and regular connection among all phenomena. Effect and cause are necessarily linked and, given the proper conditions, the one necessarily follows from the other. Everything has a cause, and determinism, though not fatalism, thus has a universal character.[23] Laws express "the necessary, determined relation among things, phenomena, and processes, which flows from their inner nature, from their essence."[24]

Fundamentals of Marxist Philosophy skirts the difficult considerations of the meaning and status of causality in quantum mechanics, in psychology, and the like, in favor of a broad claim that causality, in various forms, is to be found in all phenomena. The claim is vague enough to raise few eyebrows, but so vague as to be of little help in any concrete investigation. Yet this should not be taken to mean that this general text represents the extent of the work of all Soviet philosophers on these questions. For since 1956 there have been a number of articles and monographs concerned with the meaning, number, and systematic interrelation of the main categories of Marxism-Leninism,[25] and with their relation to ideas, concepts, and principles.

The relation of the categories to the laws of dialectics is also a disputed question among Soviet philosophers, though *Fundamentals of Marxist Philosophy* gives no indication of this. Do the categories have ontological or merely an epistemological content? Are laws combinations of categories, and so essentially similar to them, or are they different in kind? Are categories more basic than laws and presupposed by them, or are they instances of the laws and so secondary? Will clarification of the categories lead to reinterpretations of the laws in which they appear, including the three classical laws of dialectics?[26] P. Kopnin, in the article on categories in the recent Soviet *Philosophical Encyclopedia,* discusses the relation of laws and categories, but instead of answering the above questions he rests content with saying merely that "laws form the objective content of the categories. Therefore, without laws there are no categories, and without categories there is no knowledge of laws."[27]

The content of the three chapters on the individual laws of dialectics in *Fundamentals of Philosophy* is already familiar from our study of Engels and Lenin. Only a few additional points need to be noted. In the discussion of the law of transition of quantity into quality (the reverse process is ignored) two forms of development are mentioned, the evolutionary and the revolutionary. Though leaps once again (after the Stalinist period) characterize both forms of development, it is now noted that leaps are not all instantaneous, for some occur over long periods of time, even over whole epochs.[28]

The law of the unity and conflict of opposites still maintains that there are contradictions in things, though these contradictions are carefully said to be not logical contradictions, but contradictory or mutually exclusive tendencies or sides in things. Moreover, contradictions are not abstract but can be found only from an analysis of a given subject in its given conditions.[29] The Stalinist accretion of "nonantagonistic" contradictions, characteristic of socialist society, is maintained.[30]

The law of the negation of negation is restored, with emphasis not on its negative role but on its positive role in preserving what is worthwhile of the old state and in elevating and transforming it to a higher positive level.

Though there is recognition on the part of at least some philosophers of the need for clarifying the content of these laws, little real progress has been made. The laws remain general, vague, and primarily descriptive. Questions concerning the progressive tendency, which evolution evinces and dialectical materialism champions, are little touched. The how and why of evolution are quickly passed over. Creative or emergent evolutionary theories are denied wherever they involve either a first cause, or unknowable "X," or a denial of the principle of causality—and so a denial of the objective knowability of all reality. But reductionism is also denied. What is left seems to be a doctrine according to which life, consciousness, and the like are present in all levels or stages of matter in some analogous or potential way.[31] Varieties of this position have historically been espoused by St. Augustine, Leibniz, and Teilhard de Chardin. But just how such higher qualities are present in lower forms of matter, and the mechanism of their emergence have yet to be seriously discussed questions among Soviet philosophers.

The attempt on the part of Soviet philosophers since 1956 to clarify the categories and the laws of dialectical materialism is not even hinted at in *Fundamentals of Marxist Philosophy*. It is noteworthy. And the consequent development of materialist and dialectical tendencies on the part of individual Soviet philosophers is reminiscent of the 1920's. That there is still much to do along the lines of clarification, development, and enrichment of the dialectical laws and categories, however, is noted even by *Kommunist*.[32]

Logic and Theory of Knowledge

According to Marxism-Leninism, matter is primary and thought is a product of matter, a subjective reflection of what exists objectively. As matter is essentially dialectical and acts in accordance with the laws of dialectics, it would seem to follow that a correct reflection of matter would catch this dialectical character. Therefore, the laws of logic, being based on and reflecting the laws of nature, must be dialectical and knowledge itself must be dialectical. This is Lenin's position in his *Philosophical Notebooks*. He asserts the coincidence *(sovpadenie)* of dialectics, theory of knowledge, and logic. He also sketches a dialectical and quasi-Hegelian theory of knowledge in which, as we have seen, the mind plays an active role in the knowing process. Lenin's copy-theory of knowledge as presented in *Materialism and Empirio-Criticism*, however, was materialistic and almost mechanistic rather than Hegelian; knowledge was purely reflective, and mind had no active role.

Soviet philosophy has fallen heir to this dual inheritance and has tried to preserve it all, incompatible though the elements may be. The result has been general confusion, reflected both in the chapter in *Fundamentals of Marxist Philosophy* on "The Dialectic of the Process of Knowledge"[33] and in the more technical philosophical literature.

According to *Fundamentals of Marxist Philosophy* our thought process (called "the subjective dialectic") is the reflection of the development of phenomena in the material world (called "the objective dialectic").[34] The laws of thought and of being coincide in content, though they differ in form. Dialectics includes both theory of knowledge (epistemology) and logic, which considers the laws of the development of thought. *Formal logic*, "the science of the forms of thought, the rules and forms of movement from one judgment to another,"[35] is concerned with structure and rules of inference and includes the study of the nature of deduction and proof and of the forms of judgments and concepts. It proceeds from the laws of identity, contradiction, excluded middle, and sufficient reason.[36] Formal logic and the principle of contradiction abstract from content, and so from development and from the objective contradictions in the world. "The laws of thought described by formal logic reflect only the simple relations of things,"[37] certain, definite, fixed, and partial aspects of things. They are valid and useful, but not the whole story.

Dialectical logic, while not denying the importance of formal logic, makes clear its place in the study of the laws and forms of thought and goes beyond it in depth and breadth to study thought in all its relations as it reflects the world, its movement, and contradictions. It is concerned with truth, and its laws are the laws of dialectics.[38]

This is as far as *Fundamentals of Marxist Philosophy* goes on the subject of logic. Actually, formal logic was ignored, if not denied, by Soviet philosophers generally in the 1930's. In December 1946, the Central Committee of the CPSU (b) issued a directive that formal logic be introduced into the schools.[39] A dispute arose as to the nature and status of formal logic. After Stalin's pronouncement on linguistics, logic, like language, was freed from its class position. Though formal logic is officially recognized, its relation to dialectical logic, and the nature of dialectical logic itself, are still disputed. For some Soviet philosophers there is only one logic, formal logic, and so-called dialectical logic is another name for theory of knowledge.[40] Others hold that dialectical logic is the only logic worthy of the name;[41] still others hold intermediate positions.[42] But the burden of justifying dialectical logic lies with its supporters, and they have yet to produce anything in the way of rules of reasoning besides the three laws of dialectics; thus dialectical logic at present seems to be essentially equivalent to the philosophy of logic and theory of knowledge.

During this period of debate mathematical logic has been quietly but assiduously developed first by mathematicians and, since the middle of the 1950's, by a growing number of philosophers.[43] Its relation to formal logic is one on which there is as yet no agreement in Soviet philosophical literature.

While mathematical logic is thriving, theory of knowledge has made little progress since Lenin.[44] Some attempt has been made at systematizing the Marxist-Leninist theory of knowledge, but the result is merely an orderly juxtaposition of Lenin's two unharmonious positions.

Lenin's descriptions of objective, absolute, and relative truth are taken over *in toto*.[45] As in *Materialism and Empirio-Criticism* sensation is considered the source of knowledge, which is the reflection of nature, and practice is the basis of knowledge and the criterion of truth.[46] To this is added Lenin's cogitations from *Philosophical Notebooks* on the active function of mind in abstracting and generalizing concrete sense knowledge.[47] The mechanism and nature of abstraction, an explanation of error, a clear-cut distinction between the meanings of "knowledge" and "truth," a clarification of the status and nature of thought in a thorough-going materialism, an explanation of the apparent interaction between mind and body, and a reconciliation of the passively reflective aspect of knowledge and the abstractive activity of mind are all questions which are not even raised clearly, much less answered, either in *Fundamentals of Soviet Thought* or in the technical philosophical literature.

Historical Materialism

There is little divergence between the presentation of historical materialism in *Fundamentals of Marxist Philosophy* and its treatment in the periodical and technical literature. While Stalin's position with respect to dialectical materialism was quickly repudiated, his interpretation of historical materialism has been generally followed. The reason for this becomes clear when we realize that historical materialism is closely tied to the historical development of Soviet society. Stalin's theory of historical materialism could consequently not be denied without implicitly repudiating his practice, that is, the policies of the Soviet Union, most of which were continued by his successors. In general, the modifications introduced into historical materialism since Stalin's death stem primarily from the new Party Program. Party control of historical materialism is stricter than for dialectical materialism, less controversy is tolerated, innovations are almost exclusively from above, and the issues raised for discussion or development are dictated by Party needs. Theory follows practice, and theoretical questions are raised as the development of Soviet society requires theoretical justification. Law, art, ethics, and the like trail behind Party decisions.[48] Thus, with the exception of the Stalinist cult of personality, which has yet to be successfully explained, there is nothing comparable in historical materialism to the difficulties for dialectical materialism raised by developments in physics or logic or cybernetics.

Part II of *Fundamentals of Marxist Philosophy* contains nine chapters devoted to historical materialism, the first four being devoted to a systematic presentation of the basic doctrine.[49]

Since human society is part of the material world, it is governed, as all of reality is, by the laws of dialectics, and the principles and categories thereof pertain to it. But it is a special and qualitatively different aspect of the world, with specific laws also governing its development. In considering the development of society one must consider the will and activity of men—conscious, rational beings acting for ends.[50]

Historical materialism studies society as a whole—the most general laws of social development and life.[51] As a theory it dates from the writings of Marx, which, we are told, produced a revolution in the social sciences. Marx was first to discover the necessary internal relations among social phenomena, thus providing the key to the scientific understanding of law-like development of society. But this claim is supported in the text only by a quotation from Lenin.[52]

The laws of social development are claimed to be objective, independent of man's will and consciousness. These laws, however, as Stalin wrote earlier, are not eternal laws but have an historical character and are applicable in specific historical conditions.[53] The laws of the development of capitalism uncovered by Marx thus do not apply to conditions in the U.S.S.R. Continuing in the Leninist-Stalinist voluntaristic interpretation of Marxism, *Fundamentals of Marxist Philosophy* states that the uncovering of necessary social laws does not lead to fatalism. Though freedom is insight into necessity, this means not that whatever happens takes place necessarily, but rather that man can use his knowledge of social laws, as he uses knowledge of physical laws, to achieve his own ends.[54] Soviet discussions of freedom, even in the technical literature, go no further than this. Questions of individual free will or of the mechanism of choice are still swallowed up in discussions of classes and insight into necessity. The first chapter on historical materialism ends with a reaffirmation of Lenin's notion of party-mindedness (*partiinost'*) and the claim that only the party-mindedness of representatives of the progressive class is objective and can reach objective truth. Unfortunately, as in the classics, these claims are not defended or argued, but are merely stated.

The next chapter discusses material production as the basis of social life and begins, as Marx began, with a discussion of human labor. It is by his work that man produces himself and distinguishes himself from other animals. It is through his work and the social relations it necessitated that human consciousness—and with it thought, language, and ultimately human society—developed.[55] Through his work man changes his society and so himself; love of labor, especially for the development of a communist society, is considered a basic Soviet virtue, and idleness not only a vice but a crime.[56]

Stalin's repudiation of Plekhanov's geographical deviation

(overemphasizing the importance of geography) is maintained,[57] as is the repudiation of neo-Malthusianism. Changes in social life are the result not primarily of geography or population, but rather of changes and growth of the forces of production. Marx's theses that the productive process results in certain relations of production, characterized by forms of property, and that changes in the means of production produce changes in the form of social life are then reiterated and explained. The antagonistic contradictions of capitalism are described in much the same language as used by Marx. New are the description of socialist relations of production and the claims that socialism makes the exploitation of man by man impossible and that state property is the highest form of social property.[58] The Stalinist innovation that there are no antagonistic contradictions under socialism is preserved; the pronouncements of the new Party Program about the U.S.S.R.'s having entered the stage of the full-scale construction of communism are dutifully presented.

The extremely short chapter on the base and superstructure deserves particular mention. For here the interpretation, again strongly Stalinist, stretches the classical Marxist position. While the base is the ultimately determining factor in the development of the superstructure, it is admitted that each part of the superstructure (the state, law, morality, philosophy, religion, etc.) has its own specific laws of development.[59] This assertion has allowed such particular subjects as ethics and aesthetics to make their appearance in Soviet philosophy, instead of being subsumed under historical materialism. Where the general laws of historical development leave off and the specific laws of the particular disciplines begin has not been solved. The lack of a clear-cut line of demarcation between the two is a bone of contention which has caused disputes between historical materialists and specialists in the particular disciplines.

Another innovation in the discussion of superstructures is that not only differences but also common traits shared by many superstructures (such as those of slave-holding, feudal and bourgeois superstructures) due to similarities in their bases (for example, the presence of private property) are stressed. This also supplies a basis of explanation for similarities in the superstructure of capitalistic and socialistic societies and for traits, norms, morals, etc., common to all

Contemporary Soviet Philosophy 219

societies. In like manner, that changes in the superstructure often lag behind changes in the base—so obvious in Soviet society—is also emphasized. Thus, the fact that the socialist mode of production has not yet produced significantly different (more selfless, law-abiding, etc.) men is explained by the doctrine that changes in the base are not immediately reflected in the superstructure, the former changing at a faster rate than the latter.

The last third of the chapter is devoted to an explanation of the active role of the superstructure. The Stalinist line is, of necessity, followed, for the development of Soviet society according to a state plan continues. But just as Stalin muted his statements of *Marxism and Linguistics* with his *Economic Problems of Socialism in the U.S.S.R.*, so the present text mutes the active role of the superstructure by accenting its reflective and secondary character. The state and its laws can strengthen or modify certain economic tendencies, but the state cannot at will determine the economic laws operating in a given type of economy. The ideology and politics of the Communist Party can, however, serve to direct and lead the masses toward the development of a communist society. And, as the Party Program indicated, the role of the superstructure (and so of the Communist Party) will not diminish or wither, but will grow in the Soviet Union during the period of the full-scale building of communism.[60]

Class Struggle and Social Development
The notion of classes has always been central to Marxism. But though class struggles are held to be a motive force of history the classics never presented a clear and unambiguous definition of "class." The authors of *Fundamentals of Marxist Philosophy* begin Chapter XIV with a discussion of the meaning of the term "classes." Classes are not determined by biology, psychology, income, or social functions, but precisely what constitutes a class is never specifically stated. We are left with Lenin's statement that "classes are large groups of men which are distinguished from each other by their places in an historically determined system of social production, by their relations (in great part confirmed and formulated by laws) to the means of production, or by their role in the social organization of work, and consequently by the mode of acquisition and the size of the portion of social wealth which they dispose of."[61]

Marx's doctrine of the history and development of classes from slaveholding to feudal to bourgeois society is rehearsed. But a distinction is introduced between fundamental classes (the two classes which basically split every society into ruler and ruled, exploiting and exploited) and nonfundamental or transitional class.[62] The former include master and slave, lord and serf, capitalist and proletarian. The latter include such classes as those of freedmen, traders, small tradesmen, and the like. The intelligentsia—the group engaged professionally in mental labor—is not and cannot be a particular class because it does not occupy an independent place in the production of material goods. Moreover, though it plays an important part in the class struggle, its members come from and serve different classes. The intelligentsia is thus neither a basic nor a transitional class, but a separate layer or stratum of society. In addition a society can also have numerous "declassed" elements.[63] The resulting distinctions are more adequate for describing the actual elements of society than a simple two-class dichotomy. But the relation of differing groups one to another, the varying mutual influences, the overlap and border-line cases are not considered in the text and are later ignored in favor of the classical position that the conflict of fundamental classes alone determines history.

In the classical vein *Fundamentals of Marxist Philosophy* asserts that class interest is determined by the position of the class in the system of social production (and so proletarian and peasant interests coincided in Russia at the time of the revolution) and that the state is the instrument by which the exploiting class protects its position. The role, importance, and mission of the proletariat receive extended treatment which does not, however, go beyond the position enunciated by Lenin. The elimination of private property is still named as the panacea by which the proletariat frees itself from exploitation and oppression, the recent history of workers in the Soviet Union notwithstanding.

Chapter XV, dealing with social revolution, draws distinctions between socialist and other revolutions and between progress under socialism and progress under other types of social organization. While reforms under capitalism are said to be merely delaying tactics ultimately ineffective in resolving social contradictions, reforms under socialism are considered effective, and revolution is no longer necessary, because the socialist revolution, unlike all other revolutions, eliminates the exploitation of one class by another. The proletariat seizes power in order to repress the remaining exploiters and to lead economic reforms and build a new culture. Though it uses force against parasites, thieves, and other representatives of capitalism, social order is effected primarily by work discipline and education.

To critics who point out that communist revolutions took place not in highly industrialized countries, such as England and Germany, as Marx thought they would, but in backward countries such as Russia and China, an answer is here provided. It is first pointed out that Marx admitted the revolution might begin in a country such as Russia. Then, in accordance with Lenin's thesis that capitalist countries develop at different rates, it is claimed that the revolution takes place in those countries where the contradictions are ripest, producing the weakest links in the chain of capitalism.[64] In a similar manner it is expected that additional countries will individually join the socialist camp, the most likely being the weakest links in the chain—presumably the economically depressed or newly emerging nations of the world. While violent revolutions are not ruled out, the possibility of the proletariat of individual countries taking power by peaceful and even legal means is underlined.

With the victory of socialism, it is claimed, exploiting classes no longer exist in the U.S.S.R. Two classes, the working class and the peasant class, continue to exist, but their relationship is amicable, not antagonistic. The state continues, and, as the Party Program indicated, it is to be strengthened under the period of the building of communism, both to fend off enemies and to organize economic and cultural development.[65] The Party is presented as the sine qua non of achieving communism, in its capacity as leader, guide, and inspiration of the Soviet people.

The chapter ends with the joint affirmation of the contemporary necessity of the coexistence of socialism with capitalism (due to the nature of modern warfare) and of the inevitability of the worldwide victory of socialism. The humanistic aspects of communism, so often ignored in practice since the days of early Marx, appear in the text insofar as peace, work, freedom, equality, brotherhood and happiness for all nations are the stated Party goals.[66] Marx's *Economic and*

Philosophic Manuscripts of 1844 were translated into Russian only in the 1950's. They were officially ignored by the Russians until they driven by interpretations of Lukács and Western scholars to counter the growing early Marxist revisionisms. The result was the expansion of a theory of scientific or socialist humanism equated with communism and, fitting the needs of the times, adopted in the Program of the period of the full-scale production of communism. Soviet humanism, however, is restricted to the builders of communism and is joined with hatred of the enemies of communism. As equivalent to communism, moreover, it is a future goal or ideal and not a present reality.[67]

Social Consciousness, Individuals, and the Masses

Since consciousness reflects being, it was argued in the Marxist classics, social consciousness reflects social being. *Fundamentals of Marxist Philosophy* devotes an extended chapter[68] to a discussion of social consciousness, its forms, and its role.

"Social consciousness" is a term which still awaits precise definition. While it is intelligible to speak of individual consciousness, "social consciousness" is ambiguous. It could mean the sum total of the consciousness of all individuals taken together, or the least common denominator of their views (ideas which they all share), or the ideas and theories generally propagated in their social lives. The last seems to come closest to what is meant by the statement: "Social consciousness is a reflection of the social being of men."[69] Since social being varies according to classes, so social consciousness is said always to have a class character and to be an expression of the interests of a particular class. The various forms of class consciousness include political and legal ideology, philosophy, science, art, morality, and religion. With the exception of morality, which receives extended treatment, the present text adds little to the classical statements. Art, it should be noted, is seen as a weapon in the struggle of classes, and socialist realism is defended on these grounds.[70] Religion is pictured as an instrument of exploiters, and the banner of militant atheism is dutifully, if briefly, waved.

Since 1951 there has been increasing official emphasis on the role of morality in Soviet society, and the importance of morality was underlined by the new Party Program with its

Contemporary Soviet Philosophy 223

moral code of the builders of communism.[71] As Stalin's reign of terror was modified, it became clear that a new form of social control had to replace the rule of force. The substitute was morality, propagated widely, and reinforced by government-molded public opinion and by laws. Moral norms are to increase patriotism, dedication to work, and initiative in a way which force could never do; moral norms are to promote self-sacrifice for the good of society, temper the desire for material goods, and promote collective activity. While the Marxist classics held that morality arose spontaneously as a result of social relations, the exigencies of Soviet life and the fact that communist morality was not developing spontaneously necessitated its inculcation from above. These demands in turn necessitated the development of an adequate Marxist-Leninist ethics, conspicuously absent from the Marxist-Leninist corpus.

In 1961 an officially approved textbook[72] in ethics appeared, and courses in ethics became mandatory in the Soviet institutions of higher education. Textbooks on communist education now contain a chapter on moral education,[73] and the inculcation of the new moral code[74] is the subject of an intensive propaganda and education campaign.

The basic Marxist-Leninist position on morality is presented in *Fundamentals of Marxist Philosophy*. Morality and moral norms are not eternal, but have a social and historical origin and content. Moral rules and men's conception of what is good is based on the needs of a class and so vary from age to age and class to class. The dominant morality of class societies is that of the ruling class. But since it does not answer to the needs of the dominated class it is but superficially held by them and ultimately replaced by a morality of their own. As morality is an expression of social needs, it is not subjective but objective.

Just as two basic classes live side by side in capitalistic societies, so two systems of morality coexist therein. Bourgeois morality, of which religious morality is one expression, is characterized by the principles of individualism and egoism; proletarian or communist morality is characterized by devotion to communism, collectivism, and mutual help.[75] The latter expresses the needs of the development of future society. In a classless society it alone will triumph and be a truly all-human morality. Unlike bourgeois morality, communist morality demands that the individual not separate his personal life from social life, interests, and control. The moral code of the builder of communism expresses not only the simple moral norms which have been recognized as necessary in all societies for thousands of years but also the specific demands of society for the achievement of communism.

The necessity of inculcating communist morality has generated interest in social psychology, the study of man's feelings, sentiments, experiences, habits, thoughts, illusions, and so on.[76] All of these have a class character and as part of social consciousness form the basis for a class psychology. Soviet psychologists, spurred on by the needs of the Party, are turning to the study of social psychology, a subject largely ignored until the past few years. In conjunction with the active role of the superstructure *Fundamentals of Marxist Philosophy* emphasizes the important role of ideas in social development and the necessity of inculcating these ideas in the working masses to help hasten the building of communism.[77]

As Marx insisted and Plekhanov reiterated, it is the masses who make history. Marxist-Leninist teaching on the role of the individual in history remains essentially that of Plekhanov,[78] though this position seems to have been given the lie by the careers of Lenin and Stalin. Historic individuals are those who see most clearly the requirements of social development and place themselves at the head of mass movements. The acknowledged evils of Stalin's reign notwithstanding, the present Party leaders are now leading the masses triumphantly to communism.

Fundamentals of Marxist Philosophy then devotes one chapter to characterizing, caricaturing, and refuting the principal trends of contemporary bourgeois philosophy and sociology, including pragmatism, neo-Thomism, analytic and linguistic philosophy, phenomenology, existentialism, personalism—all of which are classified as various forms of idealism. The Party Program calls for increased diligence in the ideological struggle by refuting ever more strenuously all bourgeois philosophies. The periodical literature is filled with such refutations, which—despite significant exceptions—are becoming generally more polite and often more pertinent than formerly.

The text concludes with a brief eulogy of Marxist philosophy as original, scientific, living, and militant and as the theoretical basis of communism and the actions of the Communist Party. The philosophy between its covers is the philosophy of Marx, Engels, and Lenin. The discussions and controversies it omits may eventually lead to internal modifications or revisions of Marxist-Leninist theory; but nothing indicates that in the foreseeable future such modifications will change the basic doctrine or the patterns of thought developed from the times of Marx to the present.

Chapter XII
Contemporary Practice and Future Prospects

Philosophy and Ideology
"Ideology" in both the Soviet Union and in the West is a much used and a much abused word. The Soviets claim to be involved in an ideological war with the West, a war being waged on many fronts, a conflict in which there can be no peaceful coexistence, and a battle in which the spoils of victory are the worldwide triumph of one social system or another. In the present world context the struggle is evidently real and significant. Yet, surprisingly enough, a number of Western writers claim that the present era is marked by the end of all ideology, with the apparent corollary that the clash of ideologies must also be ending. Unless one side is radically misinterpreting the present situation, the meaning and use of the term "ideology" must be different as it comes from Soviet and from Western typewriters. Three different though related issues are involved in Soviet and Western discussions of ideology. First, there is the question of the nature of the conflict of the opposing world camps. If we are indeed engaged in mortal ideological combat, it would be well to realize this, to understand the field of combat, and to view the situation from the eyes of the opposing forces. This initially necessitates getting clear what the Soviets mean by "ideology." Second, there is the question of whether unreasoned belief held on

Contemporary Practice and Future Prospects   227

authority has given way to scientific and empirical reasoning. If we are interested in the development of Soviet thought itself, it will be helpful to distinguish within it strictly ideological components (or objects of unanalyzed belief, in a Western meaning of "ideology") from those which are philosophical or rational. This will throw light on the status and perhaps on the future of Soviet philosophy, for both the function and the dynamics of development of philosophy and ideology are often different from each other. Both of these problems involve clarification of meaning, which is our concern in this section. They are prior to and distinguishable from the third question, with which they are closely related and often confused, that of the relation of ideology and philosophy to action and to practical politics, dealt with in the following section.

For Marx and Engels ideology referred primarily to the false conceptions or rationalizations of the ruling class used to express and justify existing institutions and practices.[1] In the Preface to the *Critique of Political Economy* Marx equated ideology with the legal, political, religious, aesthetic, and philosophical forms of the superstructure of society.[2] These meanings of ideology have been preserved by the Soviets, particularly with reference to bourgeois forms. But the meaning of ideology has been enlarged and changed to include not only false conceptions or rationalizations but also true conceptions and valid justifications of institutions and practices, at least when these come from the Communist Party of the Soviet Union.

The Soviet *Philosophical Dictionary* defines ideology as "a system of views and ideas: political, legal, moral, aesthetic, religious and philosophical. It is part of the superstructure and as such reflects in the final analysis economic relations. The struggle of class interests in a society with antagonistic classes corresponds to the ideological struggle. Ideology may be a true or a false, a scientific or an unscientific reflection of reality."[3] Marxism-Leninism, it continues, constitutes a true scientific reflection of reality and forms the ideology of the working class, and so of the overwhelming majority of mankind.

The Program of the CPSU emphasizes the struggle against bourgeois ideology and the ideological tasks of the Party in developing communist society. According to the

Soviet meaning of "ideology," the politics, laws, morality, art, religion, philosophy, and other forms of the superstructure of a society express the social relations of that society. Soviet art reflects Soviet society and Western art reflects Western society. The ideological struggle takes place on the level of art to the extent that art reflects opposing systems, educates people in values, and appeals to those still uncommitted to either the Soviet or the capitalist system. Socialist realism is considered to have a positive educative effect on the Soviet people and an appeal to the uncommitted people in the life it reflects. Abstract art is held to reflect the disintegration and confusion of capitalist society and is officially opposed in the Soviet Union. One form of the ideological struggle thus takes place on the cultural level or "cultural front."

Western politicians and political philosophers, in arguing for, defending, and justifying the way of life and government of their society or country are, in the Soviet view, engaged in presenting a political or philosophical ideology. They do so for the benefit of their own citizens as well as for winning uncommitted peoples to their way of life. The Soviets espouse a different way of life, a different political and social system, which they defend and justify. The clash or battle that results is in the Soviet view part of the ideological struggle, a battle of competing systems, ideas, and values. It is a real battle in which, according to the Soviets, no peaceful coexistence is possible because the systems, ideas, values, politics, philosophy, and arts of a society reflect opposing and irreconcilable economic and social systems. They are irreconcilable because capitalism, according to scientific socialism, has within itself the seeds of its own destruction and will inevitably, by reason of the contradictions inherent in it, pass into socialism and communism.

That competition between the Soviets and the West is taking place, that each side does defend and explain its way of life, that the cultural products of a society to some extent do express that society's life can scarcely be denied. And if this is what the ideological struggle consists of, then it does exist. What can be challenged, however, is the Soviet claim that all Western ideology is false and Soviet ideology, Marxism-Leninism, is true.

This leads to the second question concerning ideology. Is it possible to distinguish rationalization from reasoning, be it in defense of one or another political system, value system, or philosophical system? The Soviet answer is that Soviet justifications are valid, but any justification by Westerners of their own system must be a rationalization. This answer is based on the claim that Marxism-Leninism alone represents the ideals and aims of all workers, that it alone is nonoppressive and has no need to rationalize, and that the Communist Party alone is armed with the laws of social development uncovered by Marx and Engels and so it alone can scientifically guide society's development. We have already seen the invalidity of these claims. Yet from this we should not assume either that all Western forms of society or government are justified or that no aspect of the communist system can be justified. There is no logical proof of the claims of the Declaration of Independence and of its self-evident truths, yet this in itself is no reason to give up the way of life which has grown out of it. That communism will ultimately triumph throughout the world is a communist article of faith; yet it might someday come about. The justification for any given claim should in each instance be analyzed for its truth or falsity. Moreover, it should be kept in mind that some arguments or justifications involve preferential value judgements not open to the test of truth or falsehood. The West accuses the Soviets of limiting personal freedom, the Soviets accuse the West of an unjust social system in which some live in poverty while others live in luxury. Each rejects the criticism of the other; yet something may be said in support of both accusations, and both positions involve value judgments rarely made explicit or justified in detail.

With respect to philosophy, the Soviets claim that dialectical materialism is the only true philosophy, though it, like all philosophy, is ideological. There is consequently no attempt to distinguish philosophy from ideology, the first being one of the forms of the second. Philosophy is defined as the science of the general laws of being (nature and society) and of human thought.[4] It is separated from other disciplines by its subject matter, not by its method (which, like that of the sciences, is dialectical) or by its truth claims. Perhaps surprisingly, the extent to which its content is rational is debated by Soviet philosophers.[5]

In the West ideology is generally considered distinguishable from philosophy (and politics, art, etc.).[6] By making certain distinctions between ideology and philosophy we can analyze the status of certain aspects of Soviet thought in order to compare it to Western thought, evaluate it, and follow its developments more intelligently than would otherwise be possible.

Philosophy can be defined as an attempt to understand the totality of reality on the basis of human experience and human reason alone. Its main functions are analysis—of presuppositions and of terms—and synthesis, or the attempt to relate the diversity of experience into a coherent whole. It differs from theology in being based on human reason and experience alone, whereas theology accepts and presupposes divine revelation of what is not naturally knowable by unaided human reason. It differs from the sciences in that its subject matter is both more general and basic. It analyzes the nature and foundation of thought and being (presupposed by the sciences), and it analyzes terms, such as "causality," which are common to more than one of the sciences; it also attempts to unite the results of the sciences into a coherent whole. Any philosophically sound synthesis must be clear and unambiguous, and must contain no unanalyzed terms. It must be logically coherent and nonself-contradictory; otherwise there would be doubt about what it actually said. It should be applicable to the world in which we live. And ideally it should account for all of human experience—or at least be such that it can be developed and expanded to account for new experiences or advances in knowledge as they occur.

Ideology can be distinguished from philosophy in several ways. The component terms of an ideology are often unanalyzed or not clarified, and so are systematically ambiguous. They mean different things in different places within the ideology. Ideologies are not, however, merely poor philosophical systems. In addition to their systematic ambiguity, ideological systems, or statements within the system, are not held on strictly rational grounds, that is, they are not primarily held because of the rational arguments which can be given in support of the system or statement, but because of authority. Ideology is thus dogmatic and immune from critical analysis. A third difference is that whereas the impetus behind philosophy is primarily understanding, the aim of an ideology is not primarily understanding, but action. An ideology states not only how things are, but also what is to be done. As a consequence, its appeal is not only to reason but also to the emotions, and its content is usually stated in such language as to form attitudes and inculcate values leading to a certain desired pattern of action.

This distinction between philosophy and ideology, while certainly different from that made by the Soviets, in some ways overlaps the Soviet usage, especially with respect to the meaning of ideology. Using the above distinction, what in Soviet thought can be considered philosophical and what is strictly ideological?

J. M. Bochenski has suggested that there are three types of statements in Marxism-Leninism: the basic dogma, the systematic superstructure, and the declassified doctrines.[7] The basic dogma contains those statements basic to Soviet thought, held to be axiomatic, and not open either to change or to interpretation. According to our definition, such statements are strictly ideological. Examples of such statements are: "God does not exist" and "the victory of communism is inevitable." The systematic superstructure contains statements—usually of a more abstract and technical nature—which must be verbally held by all communists, but which can be variously interpreted. This is the class into which most of Soviet philosophy falls. An example of a statement of this type is the claim that reality is contradictory. The term "contradictory" can be and is defined in various ways by different philosophers in the Soviet Union. Declassified doctrines are those which, though once considered to be part of the *official* Soviet doctrine, can now be quite freely discussed and developed without Party interference. Mathematical logic, for instance (though not the nature of logic as such), has been declassified in the sense that logicians are free to work in the technical aspects of mathematical logic without reference to official pronouncements either of the Marxist classics or of the Communist Party of the Soviet Union. Precisely which statements fall in any one of the three divisions can be ascertained only empirically by studying and following Soviet usage.

Our previous analysis of Soviet thought makes it clear that the basic statements of Marxist-Leninist philosophy are not open to critical philosophical analysis on the part of Soviet philosophers. Though originally amenable to analysis when formulated by Marx, Engels, or Lenin, they have now been dogmatized and are accepted as proven not because of examined rational arguments but because of the authority of the Party. Any change or reinterpretation of these basic principles can come only from above—from a Lenin or Stalin or Khrushchev—and not from a Soviet philosopher. Thus, it is quite clear that the foundations of Soviet thought are not philosophical in the above meaning of the term, but ideological. For this reason some Western critics claim that there is and can be no such thing as Soviet philosophy, since any system of thought worthy of the name "philosophy" must be based on premises open to analysis, rational scrutiny, investigation, and criticism.

Yet with respect to what Bochenski calls the "systematic superstructure" it seems that at least some philosophical activity takes place. This consists of philosophical analysis of terms and an attempt to handle and answer problems traditionally considered philosophical—such as questions of theory of knowledge. In this connection T. J. Blakeley, for instance, has shown that while some Soviet thinkers approach the problems of theory of knowledge from a dogmatic point of view, quoting the classics instead of presenting arguments for their position, other Soviet thinkers are approaching the problems critically, attempting to systematically clarify the meaning of the terms they use and attempting to give rational arguments in support of their positions.[8] That the latter thinkers operate within a dogmatic framework of dialectical materialism is not to be gainsaid, but within this framework there seems to be good reason for distinguishing their activity from that of their more dogmatic brethren.

These philosophical writings are not found in such works as *Osnovy marksistskoi filosofii* or other textbooks, but in the two philosophical journals *Voprosy filosofii* and *Filosofskie nauki*. But even here they are submerged in a sea of other articles scarcely philosophical at all. Interpretations are always subject to criticism and control by the Party, and the Party issues directives, carried in the journals, concerning those aspects or problems of philosophy with which the philosophers should concern themselves because of the needs of the development of Soviet society. Thus, when the Twenty-second Party Congress emphasized the need of inculcating Soviet values among the people, the "urgent task" of implementing, developing, explaining, and spreading these values was passed on to Soviet thinkers. Though philosophical analysis and speculation is present to a limited extent in the Soviet Union, philosophy as such is clearly subservient and subordinated to Party control and to the Party's needs. Not only is Soviet philosophy part of Soviet ideology in the Soviet meaning of these terms, but Soviet philosophy and philosophers are subordinate to Soviet ideology and ideologists in the Western meaning of these terms, which we have developed. Whether Western philosophers are unconsciously spokesmen for their societies may be debated, but clearly their philosophies and philosophizing are not subordinated to any state, government, or party control or scrutiny, as is Soviet philosophy. That their writings may be less widely known and propagated and consequently less effective than Soviet philosophy in influencing public affairs is the price of separating philosophy from ideology.

Theory, Practice, and Propaganda

Marxism-Leninism has its philosophical components, but in the make-up of Soviet thought these are clearly secondary. Philosophy is subordinate to ideology; theory is subordinate to practice. Yet Soviet practice is infused with theory and can be separated from it only at the risk of falsifying and essentially misunderstanding it, for the reliance on theory to guide practice has been a clear and consistent pattern of Soviet thought from its Marxian beginnings to the present day.

Marx in his eleventh thesis on Feuerbach set out the crux of the communist aim: "The philosophers have only interpreted the world in various ways; the point, however, is to change it." Marx's concern was not, as we have seen, that of an armchair philosopher who wished to understand the world and bask in the contemplation of eternal truths. Marx's aim was a radical alteration of society. The change he sought was not merely change for change's sake. It was change in a definite direction, with an ultimate goal in view—the achievement of a communistic society. He saw, however, that the giving of a goal, the uncovering of the laws of history enabling society to achieve the goal, and the choice of means to reach the goal were all theoretical matters with practical import. He emphasized action, but always action guided by theory. He sought to bring to the consciousness of the working class an insight into its situation and the theory which when implemented would lead to the establishment of communism.

His lead was followed by Lenin, who often insisted that Marxism was not a dogma, but a guide for practical action. The position has been followed consistently by Stalin and his successors, who continue to underline the importance of Marxism-Leninism as their guide in the building of communism.[9]

Among the patterns of Soviet thought which we have uncovered, both dogmatism and change from above are pertinent to a consideration of the relation of Soviet theory and practice. Dogmatism consists in accepting certain statements from the classics as true without rational proof of their validity and in exempting these statements from further scrutiny or investigation. We have seen, however, that Lenin added and changed certain parts of Marx's doctrine, as did Stalin and Khrushchev. Is all of Marxist-Leninist doctrine open to change from above? What is the criterion for those changes from above which do occur and to what extent do any of the doctrines of Marxism-Leninism influence practice if they can be changed? Let us look at these questions in turn.

What constitutes the dogmatic base of Soviet thought, what is kept immune from criticism and interpretation, has varied from time to time in the development of Soviet thought. Yet there seem to be certain doctrines which form a necessary part of Marxism-Leninism, and without which the position would be so radically altered as to be entirely different. In general, these doctrines are not only unverified but practically unverifiable. Some are held on faith or on authority and are at best probable. Others can be neither proven nor disproven by any given state of affairs, and so nothing can happen which either in theory or in practice would require their change. Yet they are fundamental to both theory and practice, and their acceptance colors Soviet action considerably. The most important of these doctrines include the following, taken from both historical and dialectical materialism: matter is all that exists, reality is essentially dialectical, the triumph of communism is inevitable, the aims of communism coincide with the aims of working mankind, the Party is the vanguard of mankind and will lead it to communism.

Materialism, in Soviet thought, implies the correlates of atheism and of the primacy of matter over consciousness. To give up materialism would be to change essentially the whole of Marxist-Leninist theory so drastically that it would no longer be recognizable. Materialism is in the practical realm the basis for militant atheism. In science, relativity theory was initially rejected when it was thought to lead to idealism, for to a Marxist-Leninist materialism is more certain than any findings of physics. Dialectics, though it has had its technical ups and downs in the history of Soviet thought, has always remained an essential component, explaining and justifying revolution, providing a basis for the distinction between mind and matter, and so forth. In the practical realm it seems that it provides something of a method for approaching problems. If all of reality is contradictory, if there are leaps, and if there is a lawfulness to social and historical development—as the laws of dialectics, however interpreted, indicate—then the analysis of any problem should be approached with this in mind. The analysis of any situation, whether of internal or external politics, of science or history, consists in looking for the contradictions, for the different approaches, for the zigzagging line of development, for the qualitative changes. Dialectics does not provide any set answer to any given problem, but it does provide a way of looking at problems. The course of Soviet development has not been rectilinear. The introduction of the New Economic Program in the 1920's and the tendency toward the increased use of material incentives in the 1960's are compatible with the ultimate achievement of a propertyless and classless communist society.

The ultimate triumph of communism and the concomitant demise of capitalism is a cornerstone of Marxism-Leninism. It can only be proven by communism's actually triumphing, which it has not yet done. It can, therefore, be at best a probable occurrence; and to hold it as certain is to hold it on faith. But it is a central component of Soviet thought, and without it much of Soviet action becomes unintelligible. The building of the New Soviet Man who is to live in the new communist society and the concomitant propaganda and educational campaigns make sense only in the light of an ultimate commitment to communism, as does the totalitarian approach by the Party to all aspects of Soviet life. That communism is the aim of mankind gives the Party its moral imperative. And, as Lenin underlined, communism would not be communism without the notion of the dictatorship of the proletariat. The Party is the vanguard of the proletariat leading mankind forward and guarding humanity along the road of its future progressive development.

Without these five components Soviet thought would not be what it is, nor would Soviet action. These then cannot be changed. They set the ultimate goals of action and indicate what to look for in the determination of means. But means are open to change, not arbitrarily from below, but from above. Marx and Engels saw that in some instances legal parliamentary procedure achieved as much as or more than could be achieved by violent revolutionary means. Lenin and Stalin could justify changes in Marxist doctrine, the use of violence against their own people, and secrecy and central control by the Party when these were necessary means to achieve the ultimate end of communism. Where the doctrine of Marx and Engels or of Lenin contained specific predictions, falsifiable by ensuing events, the doctrine was changed where necessary, or modified, as we have seen. For Soviet thought is both dogmatic and flexible, as a guide to action must be.

This conclusion tends to answer our second question. Some doctrines of Marxism-Leninism are not and need not be changed. Others can be and are changed. But changes are made only after careful scrutiny of all aspects of a given situation, and changes in theory are dictated not only by contingent circumstances, short range gain, or power politics, but by contingent situations taken together with ultimate and unchanging goals. Tactics change, ends do not. Any number of alternate courses of action with respect to a particular problem of practical politics is compatible with a given end. But the test of whether a given course of action should be continued is determined by its success in leading toward the desired end. Success is the test of farm policy, foreign policy, and all policy. The acceptance of cybernetics and of symbolic logic came about as a result of their immense value in practice, as did relativity theory and quantum mechanics. By reinterpretation of what they implied, they were made compatible with basic Soviet dogma. The claim that communism will triumph is the basis for claiming that capitalism is in crisis. That capitalist workers are not getting poorer and poorer but are enjoying an increasingly higher standard of living demands not a change in doctrine but a change in interpretation, for acceptance of the fact at face value would tend to undermine the communist claim. Facts thus force

Contemporary Practice and Future Prospects 237

changes in theory where they cannot be refuted and where the changes are not central. Where the changes involved would be central, then the facts are ignored or their import diminished or changed by a new claim, for example, that the present state of workers in capitalism is merely a step forward before going two steps backward when capitalism suffers its inevitable demise.

The relation of Soviet theory and practice is complex. The Soviet theory which is pertinent to practice is not strictly philosophical but ideological. And all ideology, as Marx saw, represents the ideas, views, and aims of the rulers of that society. Communist ideology is the ideology of the members of the Communist Party; communist ideals, goals, and ends are not necessarily the ideals, goals, and ends of all the Soviet people or of all working mankind. Yet if a communist society is to be achieved, not only must the economic base be developed sufficiently for each person to receive what he needs, but men must become radically different from what they are now. They must prefer the good of society to their own good, they must root out the remnants of capitalism, lust, covetousness, greed, envy, anger, sloth, and the desire for possessions or honors. The directing of economic endeavor to produce the wealth necessary for communism can be achieved by Party direction and where necessary by the use of force; but the production of a new superstructure and of a new communist man does not seem possible through the use of force.

Soviet ideology has always provided the ultimate ends in terms of which the Party's policy was explained, defended, and justified at home and abroad. Until the decade following World War II, however, both social control and industrial productivity was achieved largely through the use of force and the threat of force. But with the increase of productivity, force was no longer effective. For initiative, creativity, and improvement in the quality of goods could not be attained through the use of terror. Nor could Soviet society achieve the communist ideal if it were based only on force. Moral re-education, the inculcation of communist values, and the conscious acceptance of the ends of communism are necessary; and all of this falls generally in the realm of ideology. After a brief and abortive attempt at relaxation along the ideological front at home, it became clear that the superstructure of Soviet society had not changed as the base had changed, that there were still many so-called remnants of capitalism, and that ideological relaxation would not lead to the goal of communism in Soviet society. The period of relaxation ended. Since the adoption of the new Party Program, the ideological front at home has been increasingly stressed. All means of education and propaganda have been mobilized and orders have gone out to philosophers, educators, social psychologists, writers, artists, and the like to develop more effective means of inculcating communist values and patterns of action in the Soviet masses.

This does not show that previous attempts at propaganda and ideological indoctrination within the Soviet Union were complete failures, but it does show that they were insufficient to meet the needs of developing Soviet society. Public opinion must be formed and molded if it is to serve as a means of social control. Crime, hooliganism, drunkenness, and parasitism remain in Soviet society. It is hoped that by inculcating communist values and moral norms in all Soviet citizens, such antisocial actions can be practically eliminated. By ideological indoctrination the Soviets hope to increase obedience to law, to secure popular support for both domestic and foreign political decisions, to increase job satisfaction and work discipline, to eliminate selfishness, and to foster new family relations. The appeal of ideology is not only to reason but also to emotions: the end sought is action. As the action and behavior sought become more and more all-inclusive, the motivation required must be more and more internalized to be effective, and action comes to demand widespread conscious belief. The success the Party will achieve in inculcating the requisite degree of belief among the masses remains to be seen. Certain patterns of thought, certain ways of looking at problems have been inculcated among the educated masses. But this is not the same as complete ideological commitment. To believe capitalism is immoral and oppressive is one thing; to sacrifice one's present good for the possible greater good of the members of a future society is quite a different matter, even if there is assent to the proposition that communism is the finest possible form of human society and is the goal of mankind. Yet none of this is in the least incompatible with the fact that ideology remains an important factor in Soviet internal and foreign policy.[10]

Contemporary Practice and Future Prospects 239

Open Areas and Lines of Future Development

The Soviet pattern of thought is both dogmatic and unchanging in certain basic presuppositions, and flexible and changing in large areas of its systematic superstructure. Since change is part of its pattern, we should expect it to continue to change in the future. Moreover, such changes as occur should not be confused with an erosion of ideology as such, if this means either a basic undermining of ideology, or a gradual attrition in its importance in guiding official Soviet practice. There seems at present no reason to hold that a change is under way with respect to the central dogmatic base or to the ultimate communist aims. As we have seen, the basic doctrines are not open to practical falsification and cannot be refuted by empirical claims or discoveries. No practical reason can force their modification, and there are good practical reasons not to change them, since they justify the Party and its actions, give to the Party the prestige of theoretical continuity from the time of Marx, and so forth. Where then can we expect change, and what sorts of change seem most likely? We can throw some light on the answer by examining: (1) the model of the satellites and the dynamics of polycentrism in the development of communism, (2) the "open areas" of Soviet philosophy and the impact of their development on philosophy and ideology, and (3) the interrelation of official ideology and the actual conditions of Soviet life.

1) Until the end of World War II world communism was centered in the Soviet Union. Soviet thought and practice was de facto communist thought and practice, and the Communist Party of the Soviet Union was the only tangible focus of leadership for world communism. The Soviet Union brought communism with its armies into Eastern Europe, but the absolute leadership and authority of the CPSU was challenged, first by Yugoslavia, then by China, and more subtly by some of the European satellites. Under Stalin, as to some extent under Lenin, the aims of communism had become intermingled and identified with the aims of the Soviet Union. Marxism—a German and Western-oriented theory—was slavicized and adapted to the conditions first of Russia and then of the Soviet Union. As Marxism had to be adapted to Russia, so Marxism-Leninism had to be adapted to China and the countries of Eastern Europe. The Leninist-Stalinist doctrine

that countries approach communism at different rates justified differing developments in different countries; but in Soviet theory, the Soviet Union, since it was farthest along on the road to communism should remain the vanguard, head and director of the international development of communism. The Party, used to exercising complete control at home, attempted to exercise it abroad. Marxism-Leninism as the official ideology was imposed, but the crucial element of party-mindedness became ambiguous. Did the Communist Party of the Soviet Union have any clearer insight into the laws of social development than the communist parties of other countries? There seemed little reason to hold this and good reason to hold that local parties were in a better position to judge local conditions and lines of development; and where the leadership of the CPSU was not enforced by arms—as it was in East Germany and Hungary—this tendency flourished. Yugoslavia and China are clear instances of the challenge to control by the CPSU. While detailed studies are necessary in each instance to trace the development of Marxist-Leninist thought in each country, the basic foundations remain constant; tactics, however, and means to achieve the similar ideal of communism differ, as does the impact of nationalism (and with China, perhaps of racism) in each case. Yugoslavia justifies cooperation with the West, China defends a policy of aggressive communist expansion, and the Soviet Union speaks in favor of peaceful coexistence—each on the basis of the Marxist-Leninist classics. The phenomenon of a many-centered communist movement, or of polycentrism, is one which Soviet ideology has not yet squarely faced. We can, therefore, expect some change in ideology to accommodate the irrefutable facts of international life. Changes with respect to collectivization in agriculture or the use of the profit motive in industry will also bring concomitant changes in theory. But none seems likely to necessitate any central change in ideology, for these changes refer to expedient means, not ultimate ends. Any change must be carefully made so as not to cast doubt on the authority of the Party and on the principle of party-mindedness not only theoretically but also in the eyes of the Soviet people.

The development of Marxism-Leninism in the countries of Eastern Europe shows a diversity which could not have been predicted beforehand, and also indicates changes which

Contemporary Practice and Future Prospects 241

may take place in Soviet thought. According to Z. A. Jordan's exhaustive analysis of philosophy and ideology in Poland since World War II,[11] Marxism-Leninism was for a time imposed upon Polish life and thought, upon the universities and presses, in a way parallel to that in the Soviet Union. Yet, though it has remained as the official ideology of the Party and government, it no longer holds complete sway in the realm of philosophy and is now one of several competing schools. Its philosophical demise was brought about by an active and well-trained core of Polish philosophers, trained in logic and philosophical analysis before the war, who subjected dialectical and historical materialism to critical and destructive scrutiny. For a variety of reasons the Polish government allowed a loosening of its control of philosophy and the publication of non-Marxist-Leninist philosophy. There is no reason to expect the Soviet government to do this. But as mathematical logic becomes more widely developed in the Soviet Union and as the work of philosophical analysis taking place—at least with respect to the categories—becomes more widespread, it is possible that some undermining of dialectical and historical materialism, among the well educated, may take place. In Polish Marxism-Leninism, what has given way, according to Jordan, is the subordination of formal to dialectical logic, the claim of *partiinost'*, and the predominantly Hegelian tendency of Marxism. What has resulted is a diversity of Marxist-Leninist views in philosophy: Hegelian and anti-Hegelian, traditionalist and revisionist, positivist and antipositivist.[12] In Soviet thought we already find the seeds of all these tendencies. Lessening of Party control in the Soviet Union seems all that is necessary for the seeds to grow and blossom.

2) Lenin claimed that Marxism-Leninism was a world view, and Soviet textbooks today repeat the claim. It should be remembered, however, that Marx never presented a systematic development of his ideas and that the closest Engels came to doing so was his *Anti-Dühring*. Lenin's works, voluminous though they are, also contain no systematic presentation of the Marxist world view, with the exception of the short pamphlet "The Three Sources and Three Component Parts of Marxism." In the Stalin era the *Short Course* served as the textbook on which the Soviet people were reared, and for a world view this had only the small sketch called "Dialectical and Historical Materialism." Marxism-Leninism was

not in fact systematically presented in any important or widely circulated form until the 1950's, when various systematizations appeared, culminating in the two works, *Fundamentals of Marxist Philosophy* and *Fundamentals of Marxism-Leninism*.[13] Only in the 1950's did Soviet philosophy begin to be systematically divided into the traditional branches of philosophy—ethics, aesthetics, theory of knowledge, etc.—instead of dealing with these topics only under the general headings of dialectical and historical materialism.

It is not surprising, given the way Soviet thought originated and developed, that there are gaps to be filled, and problems which have not even been raised, much less answered. A. Buchholz, writing in 1959, called these areas the "empty domains" and included among them "the question of the meaning of life; the problem of death; intuitive knowledge; and all the questions of the individual and his problems."[14] That these "empty domains" have been seen by at least some Marxist-Leninists is clear from the appearance in 1961 of V. P. Tugarinov's *On the Values of Life and Culture*,[15] and from such statements as those of Adam Schaff, the leading Polish Marxist, to the effect that Marxism may well lose the battle for men's minds unless it can effectively answer questions concerning the individual and his fate.[16]

We can expect to find some interesting developments of Soviet philosophy in these empty domains in the future, for these are areas in which the Marxist-Leninist philosophers and ideologists have no ready answers drawn from the pages of the classics. Consequently, they are areas in which Soviet thinkers will be able and will be forced to break new ground and think through their own solutions. If the few Soviet articles and works concerning values, humanism, and the meaning of life are indicative of what will develop, the answers will be predictably within the already established limits of Marxism-Leninism. But there will be more emphasis on the early works of Marx, since these are practically speaking the only places in the Marxist-Leninist corpus where such problems are at all touched. Moreover, the way the answers may develop need not be very closely cirmuscribed. Leszek Kolakowski in Poland and Georg Lukács in Hungary have given impressive and important answers to some of the questions concerning man and his problems, and have done so within the Marxist framework. It is not beyond expectation

Contemporary Practice and Future Prospects 243

that something similar may yet be forthcoming in the Soviet Union.

The practical need of the Party with respect to questions of social control has led, as we have seen, to the development of many studies in ethics. This development seems likely to continue, and with it a development of such related problems as those of value, happiness, and freedom. The impetus seems likely to arise not only methodologically as Soviet philosophy becomes more systematized, but practically as the Party needs more fully developed theory to guide the development of Soviet society.

Other areas in need of development are aesthetics and ontology. With respect to theory of knowledge, there has been little progress since Lenin. But Lenin's *Philosophical Notebooks*, if fully exploited, could lead to future developments along the lines either of Hegel or of Aristotle, both of whom receive Lenin's approbation.

Candidates for continued immediate development are Soviet formal logic and Soviet philosophy of science (and particularly of physics). As logic and physics have been "declassified," developments in these areas seem reasonably certain, but paradoxically these are perhaps the most likely candidates for undermining official ideology, at least as far as some of the more educated members of Soviet society are concerned. Even if no direct attacks on the classics or on the official publications are permitted, those trained in logic and philosophy of science could apply their knowledge to an analysis of the ambiguous and primitive statements of Marx, Engels, and Lenin, and to Engels' *Dialectics of Nature* and Lenin's *Materialism and Empirio-Criticism*.

3) If erosion is not equated to change there seems little indication that the official ideology will erode in the near future. But the extent to which the Soviet people accept and internalize the official ideology remains a debated question. That there is disparity between what the Soviet citizen is promised in the future and what he experiences in the present cannot be denied. That what he has been promised has changed, that his desire for a better life now and not in the future has been more or less disappointed time and again, that the Party leaders who are supposedly armed with the laws of society's development can time and again be in error (and error sufficiently serious for great leaders like Stalin to be

denounced, and like Khrushchev to be unseated)—all this cannot help but make it somewhat difficult for the ordinary citizen to accept whole much of what the official ideology grinds out for public consumption. Yet this is not to deny that on the whole the Soviet citizen believes in the Soviet government and prefers socialism and communism to what he knows about capitalism. What it seems he has come to discredit are not the long-range promises about communism, but the short-range ones which concern him most directly.

The popularity of existentialism in Poland seems to indicate that Marxism-Leninism does not answer all the questions and needs of Polish citizens, and it is likely that it does not answer those of the Soviet citizens either. Thus, there may well be pressure from below to develop answers. The Soviet attempt to satisfy the increasing demands of the people for more consumer goods and for more adequate housing has already had an effect on Soviet planning and management of the economy. The demands for more direct answers to questions about the meaning of life may likewise eventually be forthcoming.

Ideology and philosophy can go only so far, however, in satisfying people's wants. And if a utopia is promised—as Soviet ideology promises when at long last full-scale communism is achieved—words, philosophies, and ideologies will not make up for actually existing deficiencies. Marx saw this clearly; the Soviet rulers and ideologists may also, and probably do. But whether they can do anything effective about it is not a theoretical but a practical question which time alone can answer.

In sum, the discrepancy between theory and practice, between what Soviet ideology promises and what Soviet practice produces cannot help but limit the extent to which the Soviet non-Party member swallows the daily Party line. This limits the effectiveness of propaganda and ideological education, yet is compatible with an overall general adherence of the people to the basic tenets of Marxism-Leninism and to a belief in the ultimate achievement of communism. Marxism-Leninism is what they have been taught, their patterns of thinking have been formed since childhood, and for the great majority no practical alternative categories or approaches are easily available. If this is so, then to give up their belief or hope would be to live with a void, with no answers or

Contemporary Practice and Future Prospects 245

with complete and thorough-going scepticism—an alternative which few in any society could tolerate.

Philosophical Criticism and the Confrontation of Ideologies
Soviet Marxism-Leninism is a living, vital factor in today's world. It is the official ideology of the leaders of the Soviet Union and is attractive to many within and without that country. Neither static nor atrophied, it may be criticized and rejected, but its existence cannot be denied. It is, moreover, many things, and many things to many people: a world view or an orientation toward all of reality, a philosophical system, a secular religion, a theory of history, of society, and of economics, a program of action, a design for world domination, and a moral projection toward a future utopia. It is all this and more. It claims to be scientific and its exponents claim all its assertions are true.

We have seen both the claims and the basis (or lack of basis) for the claims of the Soviets and of the Marxist-Leninist classics. Clearly much that is basic to Soviet thought is merely presupposed and not proven, much that is built on this basis is ambiguous, vague, and unclear, much of the empirical data contained within it is dated, distorted, or one-sided, and many of its value judgements are neither made explicit nor justified. Nevertheless, as a living, viable, developing body of thought it cannot be rejected in toto as being false or a priori as being untenable. As living, viable, and developing it must be at least partly true, it must account to some extent for the world in which its adherents live, and it must accord to some extent with the structure of man, society, and nature. It should not be merely rejected but studied. The task of separating the wheat from the chaff, the false from the true, is a difficult but necessary one.

Confrontation, as opposed to critical evaluation, is relatively easy. One system can be opposed to another, one society or way of life can be opposed to another, one approach to economics can be opposed to another. The results are simple alternatives given in terms of either/or: either atheistic communism or Christian democracy, either the American way of life or the Soviet, either capitalism or socialism. The approach is holistic, the alternatives clear-cut and apparently mutually exclusive. This is the way of cold war—the way of ideological confrontation. The implied clear dichotomy into haves and have-nots, exploiting and exploited, the moribund and the future-oriented, the false and the true are characteristic of Marx's analysis of society and, following in his footsteps, of the Soviet analysis of the world situation. Willy-nilly it has become characteristic of official Western policy and propaganda as well. Perhaps it is the only practical approach to international power politics. It is not, however, necessarily the way of science and reason, for reality is usually more complex than such easy dichotomies allow.

In general, there are two basic approaches to a philosophical criticism of Marxism-Leninism: external and internal. The first approach consists of criticizing one system in terms of another. This is the approach usually taken by the Soviet philosophers themselves in criticizing other philosophical positions, and it has also been used by Western critics in analyzing dialectical and historical materialism. This type of criticism consists in evaluating Soviet philosophy from the Thomistic or existentialistic or positivistic or other point of view. If Thomism, for instance, is held to be correct, then where dialectical or historical materialism coincides with or approaches the Thomistic position, it would be held to be correct; where it contradicts the Thomistic position, the former must be wrong since contradictions cannot be true together. The technique is not holistic, for it admits that portions of the position being evaluated may be correct. It is effective only to the extent that the position from which the criticism emanates is accepted. Against a defender of the opposing position such argumentation is completely ineffectual, and to a neutral observer such criticism seems to be little more than the comparison of one dubious claim with another.

The second approach avoids these difficulties. Instead of assuming a point of vantage from which to criticize, it proceeds to analyze the given system or position from within for meaningfulness, internal consistency, and validity of argument or proof. It presupposes only the generally accepted criteria of rational consistency which any position must accept if it claims to enunciate anything intelligible at all. It examines terms for clarity of meaning and statements within the system to see whether the statements or what they imply contradict some other statement within the system; it examines presuppositions, uncovers presuppositions not formally stated, and it examines all truth claims in terms of the actual evidence

Contemporary Practice and Future Prospects 247

or arguments afforded. Such analysis presupposes commitment to no particular school. It can be used not only to criticize but also affords the possibility of discussion with those holding the position under review. As a technique, however, it is more negative than positive. It can point out what is not proved and where reasoning is fallacious, but it is a method and not a system and so provides no alternative solutions to questions at issue. Though necessary, it is insufficient of itself to make up for the deficiencies of the answers it scrutinizes.

The history of philosophy has shown that apart from critical internal analysis, it is extremely difficult if not impossible to falsify any of the important systems of philosophy, because the system itself defines truth and establishes the criteria of proof and of evidence which are to be used. One system is better than another if it is clearer, more consistent, and less arbitrary in its choice of basic categories and concepts than another. But systems of philosophy have rarely if ever been definitively refuted. They have tended to fall into disrepute or have been neglected and failed to attract any adherents because they flounder on the rock of adequacy, that is, they prove unable satisfactorily to explain and interrelate the whole of the diverse experience of man and the findings of man about nature and about himself. Philosophical systems and schools, such as the Marxist-Leninist, die slowly, if at all, and when buttressed by the power of the state they may well last as long as the power behind them continues to exert its support. Ironically, it is just this support which most seriously cripples Soviet thought as a philosophical system, for dogmatism is the enemy of reason and the forced uncritical acceptance of the Marxist-Leninist classics and of the authority of the Party significantly limit the field of rational inquiry for the Soviet thinker. The component parts of Marxism-Leninism do not necessarily all stand or fall together. Marxism-Leninism shares its materialism, its dialectics, its naïve realism, and so on with other philosophical systems. Thus, for a communist to lose faith in the Party and in the eventual triumph of communism makes him no longer a communist; but he does not thereby necessarily either give up materialism, atheism, or many of the other tenets of dialectical and historical materialism, nor does he automatically become an anticommunist.

Ideally, philosophical inquiry should seek truth, not

refutation. With respect to Marxism-Leninism we should remember that its roots are Western and that it contains much that is shared by other philosophical positions. The ideal of social justice, of a society in which no man is exploited by another and in which man is a friend to man is an impressive one with roots in the intellectual and religious heritage of the West. To disown it merely because it has become part of the Soviet Party line is to disown our own finer moments. But the means which the Soviets have used thus far, and the extent to which they have approached or are approaching this ideal may well be questioned, as may their continual sacrifice in theory and practice of the value of the individual person on the altar of social development and harmony.

If Soviet thought is true to its pattern it will continue to change from above and to develop. To understand it is to understand a dynamic reality of the world in which we live. To ignore it is to pay the price of ignorance, a price which in these times may well be extremely high.

Notes

NOTES TO CHAPTER I

1. In addition to philosophy Marxism-Leninism includes political economy, the theory and tactics of the international communist movement, and the theory of socialism and communism. See *Fundamentals of Marxism-Leninism* (Moscow: Foreign Languages Publishing House [hereafter, FLPH]), p. 15. Dialectical and historical materialism, which constitute the philosophical basis of Marxism-Leninism, include a philosophy of history, a metaphysics, a theory of knowledge, an ethics, an aesthetics, a philosophy of science, and a theory of man.
2. S. T. Kaltakhtsian, Iu. P. Petrov, "O filosofskom obrazovanii v SSSR" (On Instruction in Philosophy in the USSR), *Voprosy filosofii*, 1963, 8, pp. 61-66. See also *Education in the USSR*, Bulletin 1957, no. 14, U. S. Department of Health, Education, and Welfare, p. 193; and *Communist Education*, ed. Edmund J. King (New York: Bobbs-Merrill Co., Inc., 1963), pp. 1-27.
3. See Chapter XI, section 1. Even the 1961 Party Program stated: "It is essential to develop more broadly and deeply the Michurin line in biology, which is based on the proposition that conditions of life are primary in the development of the organic world." *The Road to Communism: Documents of the 22nd Congress of the Communist Party of the Soviet Union* (Moscow: FLPH, 1961), p. 574. It further stated that science must "firmly defend and develop dialectical and historical materialism" and "uphold the purity of the principles of Marxism-Leninism" p. 575.
4. The Rules of the Communist Party of the Soviet Union require every Party member "to master Marxist-Leninist theory, to improve his ideological knowledge, and to contribute to the molding and education of the man of communist society," *ibid.*,

p. 599. See also *Uchebnye programmy dlia vechernikh universitetov marksizma-leninizma* (Curricula for Evening Universities of Marxism-Leninism) (Moskva: Izd. VPS i AON pri TSK KPSS, 1962).

5. Between 1917 and 1957 more than 366,000,000 copies of the works of Marx, Engels, and Lenin were printed in the USSR. More than 5,000,000 copies of such strictly philosophical works as Lenin's *Materialism and Empirio-Criticism* and more than 2,000,000 copies of Engels' *Anti-Dühring* were published (*Pechat' SSSR za sorok let 1917-1957: Statisticheskie materialy*, Ministerstvo Kul'tury SSSR (Moskva, 1957), pp. 65-67). These figures include publication in all languages. A comparison with figures for the period 1919-47 shows that almost as many copies of these works have been published in the ten years 1947-57 as were printed in the thirty years 1917-47. For the 1917-47 period the total number of copies of the works of Marx, Engels, and Lenin was 198,645,000 with 2,203,000 copies of *Materialism and Empirio-Criticism* and 1,231,000 copies of *Anti-Dühring* ("Sovetskaia kniga za 30 let," *Sovetskaia kniga*, October 10, 1947; Engl. trans., Helen Shadick, *Book Publishing in the Soviet Union*, Washington D.C.: Public Affairs Press, 1948, pp. 21, 23, 24). For details on the number of Soviet philosophers, philosophical dissertations, and philosophical centers, see J. M. Bochenski, "Philosophy Studies," *Soviet Survey*, No. 31 (Jan.-March, 1960), p. 65.

6. See Chapter X, section 1. In 1938 the Central Committee issued a decree concerning the teaching of philosophy, and additional decrees concerning philosophers and philosophy were made in 1944, 1947, 1948, 1956, 1957, 1961, 1962. *Kommunist*, the organ of the Central Committee of the CPSU, regularly reviews, criticizes, and recommends action concerning philosophical publications.

7. See, for example, V. I. Lenin, *Marx-Engels-Marxism: A Collection of Articles* (London: Lawrence & Wishart, 1936), p. 218: ". . . we must understand that without a solid philosophic grounding, no natural science and no materialism can hold its own in the struggle against the onrush of bourgeois ideas and against the restoration of the bourgeois conception of the universe. To hold its own in this struggle and to carry it through to the end with complete success, a naturalist must be a modern materialist, a conscious adherent of the materialism which is represented by Marx, i.e., he must be a dialectical

Notes to Pages 6-26   251

materialist" (from a letter to the journal *Pod znamenem marksizma*, No. 3, March, 1922, p. 9.)
8. J. V. Stalin, *The Foundations of Leninism*, section III (I), "The Importance of Theory," *Works* (Moscow: FLPH), 6, pp. 91-93.
9. *The Road to Communism*, p. 564.

NOTES TO CHAPTER II

1. V. I. Lenin, *Polnoe Sobranie Sochinenii*, 5th Russ. ed., vol. 29, p. 162. English trans. from *Philosophical Notebooks* (V. I. Lenin, *Collected Works*, vol. 38, Moscow: FLPH, 1961), p. 180.
2. Cf. *Philosophical Notebooks*, also Lenin's letter to the editors of *Pod znamenem marksizma*, published under the title "On the Significance of Militant Materialism" in *Marx, Engels, Marxism: A Collection of Articles by V. I. Lenin* (London: Lawrence and Wishart, 1936), p. 219.
3. *Kommunist*, 1956, 17, pp. 100-114.
4. Hegel, *Science of Logic*, trans. W. H. Johnston and L. G. Struthers (New York: The Macmillan Co.), I, pp. 64-65, 119-20.
5. *Ibid.*, p. 65.
6. *Karl Marx-Friedrich Engels Werke* (Berlin: Dietz Verlag, 1962) [hereafter referred to as *MEW*], 23, p. 27; Eng. trans. from *Capital* (Moscow: FLPH, 1959), 1, p. 19.
7. Frederick Copleston, *A History of Philosophy* (London: Burns and Oates Ltd., 1963), VII, pp. 245-46, and Franz Grégoire, *Aux sources de la pensée de Marx* (Louvain: Editions de l'Institut Supérieur de Philosophie, 1947), pp. 133-35.
8. For the best treatment of these figures and of their relation to Marx see Sidney Hook's *From Hegel to Marx* [17].
9. *MEW*, 3, p. 20. For English version see *The German Ideology* (New York: International Publishers Co., 1947), p. 6.
10. Ludwig Feuerbach, *The Essence of Christianity* (New York: Harper and Brothers, 1957), p. xxxiv.
11. *Ibid.*
12. *Ibid.*, p. 201.
13. *MEW*, 3, p. 45 (*The German Ideology*, pp. 37-38).
14. *The Essence of Christianity*, p. xli.
15. *Ibid.*, p. 14.
16. *Ibid.*, p. 20.

17. *Ibid.*, p. 33.
18. *Ibid.*, p. 60.
19. *Ibid.*, p. 155.
20. *Ibid.*, p. 158.
21. *Ibid.*, p. 184.
22. *Ibid.*, p. 185.

NOTES TO CHAPTER III

1. There is no complete edition of Marx's writings. The first attempt to produce such an edition resulted in *Karl Marx, Friedrich Engels. Historischkritische Gesamtausgabe. Werke, Schriften, Briefe* (commonly referred to as *MEGA*), ed. D. Rjazanov and V. Adoratskij (Frankfurt and Moscow). Of the projected forty-two volumes only seven, of Marx and Engels, appeared between 1927 and 1935, as well as one commemorative volume on Engels and four volumes of correspondence between Marx and Engels. *Karl Marx, Friedrich Engels: Werke* (commonly referred to as *MEW*), (Berlin: Dietz Verlag) is in progress, and thirty-two volumes have appeared to date between 1956 and 1965. A complete annotated bibliography of the writings of Marx and Engels has been published by Maximilien Rubel: *Bibliographie des oeuvres de Karl Marx* and *Supplément à la bibliographie des oeuvres de Karl Marx* [6].
2. A portion of it was published in Russian in 1927. In 1932 it appeared in the original German.
3. Riazanov dates it as being written from March to May 1843. I here follow Landshut and Meyer.
4. *MEGA*, 3, p. 33. For English version see Karl Marx, *Economic and Philosophic Manuscripts of 1844* (Moscow: FLPH, 1961), p. 15.
5. *MEW*, 1, p. 378; Engl. trans., Karl Marx, "The Critique of Hegel's *Philosophy of Right*," in *Karl Marx: Early Writings*, ed. T. B. Bottomore (London: C. A. Watts & Co., Ltd., 1963), p. 44.
6. *Ibid.*, p. 390; Engl. trans., p. 58.
7. *MEGA*, 3, p. 33. Engl. trans. from *Economic and Philosophic Manuscripts of 1844*, p. 15.
8. *Ibid.*, p. 39; Engl. trans., p. 21.
9. *Ibid.*, p. 42; Engl. trans., p. 25.
10. *Ibid.*, p. 45; Engl. trans., p. 29.

Notes to Pages 43-59   253

11. *Ibid.*, p. 111; Engl. trans., p. 99.
12. This is sometimes referred to as state capitalism, a term often applied by critics to the USSR.
13. *MEGA*, 3, p. 117; *Economic and Philosophic Manuscripts of 1844*, p. 105.
14. For a discussion of these theses see Chapter II.
15. *MEW*, 3, p. 20 (Engl. trans., Karl Marx and Friedrich Engels, *The German Ideology* (N. Y.: International Publishers, 1947), pp. 6-7).
16. *Ibid.*, p. 21; Engl. trans., p. 7.
17. *Ibid.*, p. 26; Engl. trans., p. 14.
18. *Ibid.*, p. 27; Engl. trans., p. 15.
19. *Ibid.*, p. 28; Engl. trans., p. 16.
20. *Ibid.*, p. 32; Engl. trans., p. 21.
21. *Ibid.*, p. 32; Engl. trans., p. 22.
22. *Ibid.*, p. 35; Engl. trans., p. 26.
23. *Ibid.*, p. 36; Engl. trans., p. 26.
24. *Ibid.*, p. 45; Engl. trans., p. 38.
25. *Ibid.*, p. 46; Engl. trans., p. 39.
26. *Ibid.*, p. 62; Engl. trans., p. 60.
27. Later on Engels gives the name of "historical materialism" to this view of history. "The Marxist conception of history," "the materialist interpretation of history" and "historical materialism" are all used as synonymous terms in the later Marxist literature.

NOTES TO CHAPTER IV

1. From a letter of Karl Marx to J. B. Schweitzer, Jan. 24, 1865. For Engl. trans., see Karl Marx and Frederick Engels, *Selected Correspondence* (Moscow: FLPH), p. 187.
2. *Ibid.*
3. *MEW*, 4, p. 128; Engl. trans., Karl Marx, *The Poverty of Philosophy* (Moscow: FLPH), p. 106.
4. Engels in the Preface to the English edition of 1888 gives the date as 1863. I here follow Rubel's *Bibliographie des oeuvres de Karl Marx*.
5. *MEW*, 21, p. 357; Engl. trans., Marx-Engels, *Selected Works* (Moscow: FLPH, 1958), I, p. 28.
6. *MEW*, 4, p. 462 fn.; Engl. trans., *Selected Works*, I, p. 34 fn.
7. *Ibid.*
8. *Ibid.*, p. 473; Engl. trans., p. 44.
9. *Ibid.*, p. 477; Engl. trans., p. 49.

254   NOTES TO PAGES 60-81

10. *Ibid.*, p. 482; Engl. trans., p. 54.
11. *Ibid.*, p. 493; Engl. trans., p. 65.
12. *Ibid.*, p. 576; Engl. trans., p. 24.
13. *MEW*, 13, p. 468; Engl. trans., F. Engels, "Karl Marx, A Contribution to the Critique of Political Economy," *Selected Works*, I, p. 366. See also *Capital* (Moscow: FLPH, 1959), I, p. 81 fn.
14. *MEW*, 23, p. 12; *Capital*, I, p. 8.
15. This work was first published under the title *Value, Price and Profit*.
16. *MEW*, 23, p. 28; *Capital*, I, p. 20.
17. *Ibid.*, pp. 15-16; *Capital*, p. 10.
18. Eng. trans., from Marx-Engels, *Selected Works*, II, p. 488.
19. *MEW*, 23, p. 791; *Capital*, I, p. 763.
20. *Ibid.*, p. 109; *Capital*, p. 94.
21. *Ibid.*, p. 116; *Capital*, p. 101.
22. *Ibid.*, p. 185; *Capital*, p. 171: "In contradistinction therefore to the case of other commodities, there enters into the determination of the value of labor-power a historical and moral element."
23. *Ibid.*, p. 281; *Capital*, p. 265.
24. *Ibid.*, p. 418; *Capital*, p. 396.

NOTES TO CHAPTER V

1. *MEW*, 21, pp. 291-92; Engl. trans., Frederich Engels, *Ludwig Feuerbach and the Outcome of Classical German Philosophy* (N.Y.: International Publishers, 1941), pp. 42-43 fn.
2. V.I. Lenin, *Polnoe Sobranie Sochinenii*, 5th Russian ed., 26, p. 93; Engl. trans., V. I. Lenin, *The Teachings of Karl Marx* (N.Y.: International Publishers, 1930), p. 48.
3. *MEW*, 22, p. 288; Engl. trans., Marx-Engels, *Selected Works*, II, p. 94.
4. The parts of *Anti-Dühring* that were taken for this pamphlet are Chapter One ("General") of the Introduction, Chapter One ("Historical"), and Chapter Two ("Theoretical") of Part III, which deals with socialism.
5. *MEW*, 23, p. 327; *Capital*, I, p. 309: "Here, as in natural science, is shown the correctness of the law discovered by Hegel (in his "Logic"), that merely quantitative differences beyond a certain point pass into qualitative changes."
6. *MEGA*, Dritte Abteilung, 4, p. 398; Engl. trans., Marx-Engels, *Selected Correspondence* (Moscow: FLPH), pp. 342-43.

Notes to Pages 82-119   255

7. MEW, 20, p. 22; Engl. trans., Frederich Engels, *Anti-Dühring* (Moscow: FLPH, 1959), p. 36.
8. *Ibid.*, p. 35; Engl. trans., p. 57.
9. *Ibid.*, p. 41; Engl. trans., p. 65.
10. *Ibid.*, p. 44; Engl. trans., pp. 70-71.
11. *Ibid.*, p. 55; Engl. trans., p. 86.
12. *Ibid.*
13. *Ibid.*, p. 76; Engl. trans., p. 116.
14. *Ibid.*, p. 81; Engl. trans., p. 122.
15. *Ibid.*, p. 87; Engl. trans., p. 131.
16. *Ibid.*, p. 106; Engl. trans., p. 157.
17. *Ibid.*
18. *Ibid.*, p. 107; Engl. trans., p. 158.
19. *Ibid.*, pp. 131-32; Engl. trans., pp. 193-94.
20. *Ibid.*, p. 262; Engl. trans., p. 387.
21. *Ibid.*, p. 264; Engl. trans., p. 391.
22. MEW, 21, p. 264; Engl. trans., Marx-Engels, *Selected Works*, II, p. 359.
23. *Ibid.*, p. 267; Engl. trans., p. 362.
24. *Ibid.*, p. 272; Engl. trans., p. 368.
25. *Ibid.*, p. 276; Engl. trans., p. 371.
26. *Ibid.*, p. 284; Engl. trans., p. 379.
27. *Ibid.*, pp. 292-93; Engl. trans., p. 387.
28. *Ibid.*, p. 293; Engl. trans., p. 387.
29. *Ibid.*, p. 295; Engl. trans., p. 389.
30. *Ibid.*, p. 300; Engl. trans., p. 394.
31. *Ibid.*, p. 303; Engl. trans., p. 397.
32. *Ibid.*, p. 306; Engl. trans., p. 400.
33. *Ibid.*, p. 307; Engl. trans., p. 402.
34. MEW, 20, p. 327; Engl. trans., Frederick Engels, *Dialectics of Nature* (Moscow: FLPH, 1954), p. 54.
35. *Ibid.*, p. 349; Engl. trans., p. 84.
36. *Ibid.*, p. 485; Engl. trans., p. 286.
37. *Ibid.*, p. 499; Engl. trans., pp. 307-308.
38. *Ibid.*, p. 514; Engl. trans., p. 330.

NOTES TO CHAPTER VI

1. V. I. Lenin, *Polnoe Sobranie Sochinenii*, 5th Russian ed., 42, p. 290; Engl. trans., V. I. Lenin, *Selected Works* (New York: International Publishers, 1943), IX, p. 66.

2. *Ibid.*, 19, p. 313; Engl. trans., V. I. Lenin, *Collected Works* (Moscow: FLPH), 16, p. 269.
3. George Plekhanov, *The Development of the Monist View of History* (Moscow: FLPH, 1956), p. 40.
4. *Ibid.*, p. 44.
5. *Ibid.*, p. 95.
6. *Ibid.*, p. 136.
7. *Ibid.*, p. 226.
8. *Ibid.*, p. 292.
9. George Plekhanov, *The Role of the Individual in History* (New York: International Publishers, 1940), p. 23.
10. *Ibid.*, p. 41.
11. *Ibid.*, p. 48.
12. George Plekhanov, *Fundamental Problems of Marxism* (London: Lawrence & Wishart, 1941), p. 34.
13. *Ibid.*, p. 36.
14. *Ibid.*, p. 51.
15. For Plekhanov's theory of art, see G. Plekhanov, *Unaddressed Letters* and *Art and Social Life* (Moscow: FLPH, 1957).
16. Plekhanov presented his theory of knowledge first in his "Notes" to his translation of Engels' *Ludwig Feuerbach*, which he published in 1892. Fuller statements can be found in his essays "Materialism or Kantianism" (1898-99) and "Once More Materialism" (first published in 1906).

NOTES TO CHAPTER VII

1. V. I. Lenin, *Polnoe Sobranie Sochinenii*, 5th Russian ed., 23, p. 43; Engl. trans., "Three Sources and Three Component Parts of Marxism," *Marx-Engels-Marxism: A Collection of Articles* (London: Lawrence & Wishart, 1936), p. 50.
2. N. S. Khrushchev, *Pravda* (October 1, 1959), p. 2.
3. V. I. Lenin, *Polnoe Sobranie Sochinenii*, 5th Russian ed., 6, p. 9; Engl. trans., *What Is to Be Done?* (New York: International Publishers, 1929), p. 14.
4. *Ibid.*, pp. 24-25; Engl. trans., p. 28.
5. *Ibid.*, p. 40; Engl. trans., p. 41.
6. *Ibid.*, p. 69; Engl. trans., p. 68.
7. *Ibid.*, p. 119; Engl. trans., p. 112.
8. *Ibid.*, p. 141; Engl. trans., p. 131.
9. *Ibid.*, p. 171; Engl. trans., p. 158.
10. *Ibid.*, 8, p. 255; Engl. trans., "One Step Forward, Two Steps

Back," in *V. I. Lenin Selected Works* (Moscow: FLPH, 1947), I, p. 288.
11. *Ibid.*, 11, pp. 103-4; Engl. trans., "Two Tactics of Social Democracy in the Democratic Revolution," *Selected Works*, I, p. 415.
12. *Ibid.*, 18, p. 360; Engl. trans., *Materialism and Empirio-Criticism* (Moscow: FLPH), p. 354.
13. *Ibid.*, 6, p. 135; *What Is to Be Done?* p. 126.
14. *Ibid.*, 33, p. 6; Engl. trans., *The State and Revolution* (Moscow: FLPH), p. 10.
15. *MEW*, 22, p. 519; Engl. trans., Engels, "Introduction to Karl Marx's *The Class Struggle in France, 1848-1850*," *Marx and Engels Selected Works* (Moscow: FLPH, 1958), I, p. 130.
16. *Ibid.*, p. 523; Engl. trans., p. 134.
17. *Ibid.*, p. 525; Engl. trans., p. 136.
18. *MEW*, 4, p. 7; Engl. trans., Preface to the Russian edition of 1882 of *The Communist Manifesto*, in *Selected Works*, I, p. 24.
19. V. I. Lenin, *Polnoe Sobranie Sochinenii*, 5th Russian ed., 33, p. 7; *State and Revolution*, p. 12.
20. *Ibid.*, p. 29; Engl. trans., p. 46.
21. *Ibid.*, p. 84; Engl. trans., p. 134.
22. *Ibid.*, p. 97; Engl. trans., p. 155.

NOTES TO CHAPTER VIII

1. Ernst Mach (1838-1916) was an Austrian physicist who sought to rid physics of metaphysics by restricting it to the study of phenomena or neutral sensible experience, systematized with the help of auxiliary concepts and hypothetical constructions. His influence was considerable and his sympathizers are called "Machians," a term Lenin employs as a synonym for "empirio-criticist."
2. In this number Lenin explicitly includes V. Bazarov (1874-1939, a pseudonym of Vladimir Alexandrovich Rudnev), A. Bogdanov (1873-1928, pseudonym of Alexander Alexandrovich Malinovski), P. S. Yushkevich (1873-1945), N. Valentinov (1878-1964, pseudonym of Nikolai Vladislavovich Vol'sky), and V. M. Chernov (1876-1952).
3. Quoted in V. I. Lenin, *Polnoe Sobranie Sochinenii*, 5th Russian ed., 18, p. xi; Engl. trans., *Materialism and Empirio-Criticism: Critical Comments on a Reactionary Philosophy* (Moscow: FLPH), p. 378, n. 1.

258   NOTES TO PAGES 148-63

4. *Ibid.*, pp. 39-40; Engl. trans., p. 38.
5. *Ibid.*, p. 46; Engl. trans., p. 44.
6. *Ibid.*, p. 50; Engl. trans., p. 48.
7. *Ibid.*, p. 120; Engl. trans., p. 116.
8. *Ibid.*, p. 132; Engl. trans., p. 128.
9. *Ibid.* This is a quotation from Feuerbach.
10. *Ibid.*, p. 103; Engl. trans., p. 99.
11. *Ibid.*, p. 46; Engl. trans., p. 44.
12. For an excellent exposition of the dilemma faced by Soviet philosophers on this point see N. Lobkowicz, "Materialism and Matter In Marxism-Leninism," pp. 430-64, in *The Concept of Matter*, ed. Ernan McMullin (Notre Dame: University of Notre Dame Press, 1963).
13. Lenin, *op. cit.*, p. 257; Engl. trans., p. 251.
14. *Ibid.*, p. 305; Engl. trans., p. 298.
15. *Ibid.*, p. 277-278; Engl. trans., p. 271.
16. *Ibid.*, p. 109; Engl. trans., p. 105.
17. *Ibid.*, p. 146; Engl. trans., p. 141.
18. *Ibid.*, p. 103; Engl. trans., p. 99.
19. *Ibid.*, p. 104; Engl. trans., p. 100.
20. *Ibid.*, p. 138; Engl. trans., p. 134.
21. *Ibid.*, p. 140; Engl. trans., p. 136.
22. *Ibid.*, p. 146; Engl. trans., pp. 141-42.
23. *Ibid.*, p. 131; Engl. trans., p. 127.
24. *Ibid.*, p. 149; Engl. trans., p. 145.
25. *Ibid.*, p. 275; Engl. trans., p. 269.
26. Discussed in *ibid.*, pp. 281-90; Engl. trans., pp. 275-83.
27. *Ibid.*, p. 195; Engl. trans., p. 189.
28. *Ibid.*, pp. 159-61; Engl. trans., pp. 155-57.
29. *Ibid.*, p. 332; Engl. trans., p. 326.

NOTES TO CHAPTER IX

1. V. I. Lenin, *Polnoe Sobranie Sochinenii*, 5th Russian ed., 26, p. 50; Engl. trans., "Karl Marx," *Marx-Engels-Marxism: A Collection of Articles* (London: Lawrence & Wishart, 1936), p. 7; *ibid.*, 23, p. 43; Engl. trans., "The Three Sources and Three Component Parts of Marxism," *Marx-Engels-Marxism*, p. 50.
2. *Ibid.*, 23, p. 43; "Three Sources . . .," p. 51.
3. *Ibid.*, 26, pp. 51-52; "Karl Marx," p. 8.
4. *Ibid.*, p. 53; "Karl Marx," p. 9.
5. *Ibid.*, 23, pp. 43-44; "Three Sources . . .," p. 51.

Notes to Pages 163-66 259

6. *Ibid.*, 26, p. 55; "Karl Marx," p. 11.
7. *Ibid.*, 24, p. 264; Engl. trans., "The Marx-Engels Correspondence," *Marx-Engels-Marxism*, p. 45.
8. *Ibid.*, 23, p. 44; "Three Sources . . .," p. 52.
9. *Ibid.*, p. 45; Engl. trans., p. 53.
10. *Ibid.*, 26, p. 73; "Karl Marx," p. 26.
11. *Ibid.*, 17, p. 22; Engl. trans., "Marxism and Revisionism," *Marx-Engels-Marxism*, p. 75.
12. *Ibid.*, 33, p. 34; Engl. trans., *The State and Revolution* (Moscow: FLPH), p. 54.
13. *Ibid.*, 20, p. 84; Engl. trans., "On Some Peculiarities of the Historical Development of Marxism" (1911): "Our teaching—said Engels, referring to himself and his famous friend—is not a dogma, but a guide to action," *Marx-Engels-Marxism*, p. 85.
14. *Ibid.*, 4, p. 184; Engl. trans., "On the Theory of Marxism" (1899): "We do not by any means look upon the theory of Marx as something final and inviolable; on the contrary, we are convinced that it only laid the cornerstones of the science which socialists *must* advance in all directions, if they do not want to lag behind events. We think that the *independent* elaboration of Marx's theory is especially necessary for Russian socialists since this theory provides only the general guiding principles which in detail must be applied in England in a manner different from that applied in France, in France in a manner different from that applied in Germany, and in Germany in a manner different from that applied in Russia," *Marx-Engels-Marxism*, pp. 64-65.
15. *Ibid.*, 29, p. 162; Engl. trans., V. I. Lenin, *Collected Works*, vol. 38, *Philosophical Notebooks* (Moscow: FLPH, 1961), p. 180.
16. *Ibid.*, p. 160; Engl. trans., p. 178.
17. *Ibid.*, pp. 161, 322; Engl. trans., pp. 179, 363.
18. *Ibid.*, p. 322; Engl. trans., p. 363.
19. *Ibid.*, p. 248; Engl. trans., p. 276.
20. *Ibid.*, p. 215; Engl. trans., p. 234.
21. *Ibid.*, p. 93; Engl. trans., p. 104.
22. See also *ibid.*, p. 215; Engl. trans., p. 234: "It is noteworthy that the whole chapter on the 'Absolute Idea' scarcely says a word about God (hardly ever has 'divine' 'notion' slipped out accidentally) and apart from that—*this NB*—it contains almost nothing that is specifically *idealism*, but has for its main subject the *dialectical* METHOD. The sum total, the last word and es-

sence of Hegel's logic is the *dialectical method*—this is extremely noteworthy."
23. *Ibid.*, p. 131; Engl. trans., pp. 146-47.
24. *Ibid.*, p. 289; Engl. trans., p. 314.
25. *Ibid.*, p. 301; Engl. trans., p. 319.
26. *Ibid.*, p. 98; Engl. trans., p. 109.
27. *Ibid.*, pp. 203, 210, 316-17; Eng. trans., pp. 223, 229, 359-60.
28. *Ibid.*, pp. 202-3; Engl. trans., pp. 221-22.
29. *Ibid.*
30. *Ibid.*, p. 207; Engl. trans. p. 226.
31. *Ibid.*, p. 231; Engl. trans., p. 258.
32. *Ibid.*, pp. 112, 128, 256; Engl. trans., pp. 123, 143, 284.
33. *Ibid.*, p. 124; Engl. trans., p. 138.
34. *Ibid.*, p. 321; Engl. trans., p. 362.
35. *Ibid.*, p. 233; Engl. trans., p. 260.
36. *Ibid.*, p. 99; Engl. trans., p. 110.
37. *Ibid.*, p. 176; Engl. trans., p. 194.
38. *Ibid.*, p. 177; Engl. trans., p. 195.
39. *Ibid.*, p. 194; Engl. trans., p. 212.
40. *Ibid.*, pp. 209, 255; Engl. trans., pp. 228, 283.
41. *Ibid.*, p. 90; Engl. trans., p. 99.
42. *Ibid.*, p. 318; Engl. trans., p. 361.
43. *Ibid.*
44. *Ibid.*, p. 317; Engl. trans., p. 360.
45. *Ibid.*, p. 257; Engl. trans., p. 285.
46. *Ibid.*, p. 330; Engl. trans., p. 372.
47. *Ibid.*, p. 104; Engl. trans., p. 114.
48. *Ibid.*, pp. 83, 85, 180; Engl. trans., pp. 91, 93, 198.
49. *Ibid.*, pp. 135-38, 143-44; Engl. trans., pp. 150-53, 159-60.
50. *Ibid.*, pp. 84, 156; Engl. trans., pp. 93, 175.
51. *Ibid.*, pp. 80, 156, 163-64, 174, 301, 321; Engl. trans., pp. 88, 175, 182, 192, 319, 362.
52. *Ibid.*, pp. 159, 162; Engl. trans., pp. 177, 180.
53. *Ibid.*, p. 172; Engl. trans., p. 190.
54. *Ibid.*, p. 171; Engl. trans., p. 189.
55. *Ibid.*, p. 195; Engl. trans., p. 213.
56. *Ibid.*, 41, p. 308; Engl. trans., V. I. Lenin, "The Tasks of the Youth Leagues: Speech Delivered at the Third all-Russian Congress of the Russian Young Communist League, October 2, 1920" (Moscow: FLPH, 1951), p. 16.
57. *Ibid.*, p. 309; Engl. trans., p. 17.
58. A collection of excerpts from Lenin's other works in which he

Notes to Pages 172-80   261

mentions ethics or morality, usually in passing and rather briefly, has been published: V. I. Lenin, *O kommunisticheskoi nravstvennosti* (Moskva: Gosudarstvennoe izdatel'stvo politicheskoi literatury, 1961).
59. V. I. Lenin, *Polnoe Sobranie Sochinenii*, 5th Russian ed., 41, p. 309; "The Tasks of the Youth Leagues," p. 18.
60. *Ibid.*, p. 311; Engl. trans., pp. 20-21.
61. *Pod znamenem marksizma*, No. 3 (March 1922), p. 6; Engl. trans., "On the Significance of Militant Materialism," *Marx-Engels-Marxism*, p. 214.
62. *Ibid.*, p. 8; Engl. trans., p. 217.
63. *Ibid.*, p. 9-10; Engl. trans., p. 218.
64. *Ibid.*, p. 10; Engl. trans., p. 219.
65. I. Khliabich, "K voprosu ob otsenke filosofskogo nasledstva Gegelia," *Kommunist*, 1956, 17, 106.
66. *Philosophical Notebooks*, p. 18.
67. Sidney Hook, for example in *Marx and the Marxists: The Ambiguous Legacy* [18], p. 76, says: "Lenin's doctrinal emphasis on revolutionary organization and revolutionary will became so pronounced that before he died he left behind him a corpus of teachings which constituted a far greater deviation from the traditions of orthodox Marxism than the Revisionism he so scathingly excoriated."
68. J. Stalin, "Interview Given to the First American Labour Delegation, September 9, 1927," in Lenin, *Selected Works* (Moscow: FLPH, 1947), 1, p. 39; J. Stalin, *Works* (Moscow: FLPH, 1954), 10, p. 97.

NOTES TO CHAPTER X

1. The debate took place primarily in the pages of *Under the Banner of Marxism* (1922-29). A brief account of it can be found in the *Bol'shaia sovetskaia entsiklopediia*, 2d ed., 45, p. 137. More detailed accounts in English are in: N. Berdyaev's "The General Line of Soviet Philosophy," *The End of Our Time* (London: Sheed & Ward, 1933); N. O. Lossky, *History of Russian Philosophy* [31], chapter XXIV; and Gustav Wetter, *Dialectical Materialism* [61], Part one, chapters VI-VIII. Wetter's work gives a detailed discussion of the various philosophical positions. David Joravsky's *Soviet Marxism and Natural Science, 1917-1932* [50] gives the most detailed account of the controversy, considering both its philosophical and its scientific

aspects. Also valuable are Sidney Heitman, "Between Lenin and Stalin: Nikolai Bukharin," S. V. Utechin, "Philosophy and Society: Alexander Bogdanov," and René Ahlberg, "The Forgotten Philosopher: Abram Deborin," all of which are reprinted in *Revisionism: Essays on the History of Marxist Ideas*, ed. Leopold Labedz [53].

2. Thus, J. M. Bochenski, in "Philosophy Studies," *Soviet Survey*, No. 31 (January-March, 1960), pp. 73-74, is able to speak of the Hegelian (dialectical) and the Aristotelian (materialist) schools or tendencies present in recent Soviet philosophy.

3. S. Minin, "Filosofiia za bort!" *Pod znamenem marksizma* (hereafter *Pzm*), 1922, Nos. 5-6, pp. 122-27. He repeated his position in "Kommunizm i filosofiia," *Pzm*, 1922, Nos. 11-12, pp. 184-98.

4. J. V. Stalin, *Works* (Moscow: FLPH, 1954), vol. 11, "The Right Danger in the CPSU (b)," pp. 231-48, and "Industrialization of the Country and the Right Deviation in the CPSU (b)," pp. 255-302. The right deviation, according to Stalin, underestimated the strength of capitalism, opposed an offensive against it, and would lead back to capitalism; the left deviation overemphasized the strength of capitalism and denied the possibility of building socialism in one country.

5. Stalin, *Works*, vol. 11, "Bukharin's Group and the Right Deviation in Our Party," p. 333.

6. *Pzm*, 1921, No. 5, p. 1.

7. *Pravda*, June 7, 1930, pp. 3-4. The article, signed by M. Mitin, V. Ral'tsevich, and P. Judin, was followed by a note which read: "The editors agree with the basic position of this article."

8. Reported in *Pzm*, 1930, Nos. 10-12, p. 17.

9. *Pravda*, January 26, 1931, p. 1. Also *Pzm*, 1930, Nos. 10-12, pp. 1-2 (evidently this issue actually appeared in 1931). It also carries several articles describing the controversy.

10. In both instances a philosophical position was linked with a political deviation, and both the political and philosophical positions—in accordance with the superstructure-base thesis—were traced to their basis in society, viz., social conditions which had not yet been overcome. The social basis for the right deviationist views was the bourgeois peasantry; for the "left" deviationist views, the defeated capitalists. Leon Davidovich Trotsky (1879-1940) was, with Lenin, one of the leaders of the revolution. After Lenin's death he lost the struggle for leadership to Stalin, was exiled in 1928 and later assassinated.

His part in the revolution is officially ignored by the Soviets. According to Stalin, the essence of Trotskyism consists of the denial (1) of the possibility of building socialism in the U.S.S.R. by the efforts of the working class and peasantry, (2) of the possibility of drawing the mass of the peasantry into the work of socialist construction in the countryside, and (3) of the necessity of iron discipline and absence of factions in the Party (Stalin, *Works*, 12, pp. 364-67).

11. Deborin, though demoted from editor in chief, remained listed as a member of the editorial board. He was also allowed to keep most of his other public positions. In 1933 he admitted his mistakes, and though he published a few more articles before his death, they are not philosophically significant.

12. For a summary of the history of the relationship of philosophy and science in the U.S.S.R. see Maxim W. Mikulak, "Philosophy and Science," *Survey*, No. 52 (July 1964), pp. 147-56. A presentation of present controversy can be found in Siegfried Müller-Markus, "Soviet Philosophy in Crisis," *Cross Currents*, XIV (1964), pp. 35-61.

13. For Stalin's biography, see Isaac Deutscher, *Stalin: A Political Biography* [49]; and Bertram D. Wolfe, *Three Who Made a Revolution* [43].

14. J. Stalin, "Anarchism or Socialism," *Works*, 1, p. 302.

15. *Ibid.*, p. 303.

16. *Ibid.*, p. 319.

17. *Ibid.*, p. 322.

18. *Ibid.*, pp. 329-30.

19. *Pzm*, 1942, 11-12, "Filosofskaia nauka v SSSR za 25 let," pp. 95-117.

20. The full text of the directive was printed in translation in *Soviet Studies*, III (January 1952), p. 343-44. A summary with comment can be found in *Soviet Studies*, I (1949-50), pp. 40-51: "Andrei Zhdanov's Speech to the Philosophers: An Essay in Interpretation," J. and M. Miller.

21. G. F. Aleksandrov, *Ocherk istorii novoi filosofii na zapade* (Moskva: Iz. "Sovetskoi Nauki," 1939).

22. *Voprosy filosofii*, 1947, 1, pp. 256-72; Engl. trans., *Political Affairs*, XXVII (1948), pp. 344-66.

23. Khrushchev makes much of this in unmasking Stalin. See his "Special Report to the 20th Congress of the Communist Party

of the Soviet Union" reprinted in pamphlet form under the title *The Crimes of the Stalin Era* (New York: The New Leader, 1962), pp. S55-S56.
24. An English version of its successor appeared in 1960: *History of the Communist Party of the Soviet Union* (Moscow: FLPH).
25. J. Stalin, *Problems of Leninism* (Moscow: FLPH, 1954), p. 156.
26. *History of the Communist Party of the Soviet Union (Bolsheviks): Short Course* (Moscow: FLPH, 1951), p. 467.
27. *Ibid.*, pp. 522-25; *Problems of Leninism*, pp. 777-78.
28. *Ibid.*, p. 543.
29. *Problems of Leninism*, pp. 45, 192-93; see also *History of the CPSU (B)*, p. 259-60, where "just wars" are defined as: "wars that are not wars of conquest but wars of liberation, waged to defend the people from foreign attack and from attempts to enslave them, or to liberate the people from capitalist slavery, or, lastly, to liberate colonies and dependent countries from the yoke of imperialism."
30. *History of the CPSU (B)*, p. 504; *Problems of Leninism*, pp. 796-97.
31. *Ibid.*, pp. 492 and 536, respectively.
32. Chapter 4, section 2 comprises pp. 165-206 of the *History of the CPSU (b)*. It has been reprinted as a separate pamphlet: Joseph Stalin, *Dialectical and Historical Materialism* (New York: International Publishers, 1940), which is more readily available than the *Short Course*. The present quotation is from page 5 of the latter.
33. *Ibid.*, pp. 7-25.
34. *Ibid.*, pp. 15-20.
35. *Ibid.*, pp. 22-23.
36. *Problems of Leninism*, p. 778.
37. Joseph Stalin, *Marxism and Linguistics* (New York: International Publishers, 1951), p. 13.
38. This can be seen in detail with respect to ethics; see Richard T. De George, "A Bibliography of Soviet Ethics," *Studies in Soviet Thought*, III (1963), pp. 83-103.
39. *Marxism and Linguistics*, pp. 27-28; also Joseph Stalin, *Economic Problems of Socialism in the USSR* (New York: International Publishers, 1952), p. 24, in which he characterizes this as a new problem, not discussed in the Marxist classics, but

"one that has been raised practically by our socialist construction."
40. *Marxism and Linguistics*, p. 27.
41. *Ibid.*, p. 9.
42. *Ibid.*, p. 34.
43. *Ibid.*, p. 47.
44. *Ibid.*, p. 46.
45. *Ibid.*, pp. 29-30.
46. *The Crimes of the Stalin Era*, p. S7.
47. The full text of the Program, together with the Report of the Central Committee, Khrushchev's speech on the Program, the new rules of the Communist Party and other related documents is available in *The Road to Communism: Documents of the 22nd Congress of the Communist Party of the Soviet Union* (Moscow: FLPH, 1961). A useful copy of the text of the Program, fully and carefully annotated by Herbert Ritvo is available in paperback under the title *The New Soviet Society* (New York: The New Leader, 1962). The entire issue of *Survey*, No. 38 (October 1961) was devoted to articles dealing with various aspects of the Program and was published in book form as *The Future of Communist Society* (New York: Praeger, 1962).
48. *The Road to Communism*, p. 486.
49. *Ibid.*, p. 508.
50. *Ibid.*, p. 506.
51. *Ibid.*
52. *Ibid.*, p. 470.
53. *Ibid.*, pp. 497-502.
54. *Ibid.*, p. 509.
55. *Ibid.*, p. 512.
56. *Ibid.*, p. 535.
57. *Ibid.*, p. 563.
58. *Ibid.*, pp. 565-67.
59. *Ibid.*, p. 547.
60. *Ibid.*, p. 583.
61. *Ibid.*, p. 575.
62. *Ibid.*, p. 574.
63. *Ibid.*, pp. 574-75.
64. *Ibid.*, p. 575.
65. *Ibid.*, p. 437.
66. "XXII S"ezd KPSS i zadachi sovetskoi filosofii," *Voprosy filosofii*, 1961, 11, pp. 3-15.

NOTES TO CHAPTER XI

1. *Osnovy marksistskoi filosofii* (hereafter referred to as *Omf*), izd. 2 oe (Moskva: Gosudarstvennoe izdatel'stvo politicheskoi literatury, 1962). The 1963 edition is identical. This second edition (it is really the 3rd; the 1959 edition differed slightly from that of 1958) also differs from the first edition in that it lacks a chapter on the struggle of materialism and idealism in the pre-Marxian epoch of philosophy. The chapter on social revolution and development has, however, been expanded. The first edition mentions Stalin as contributing to Marxist thought, but the second edition does not; the second edition gives increased importance to Khrushchev. Though the text has been translated in many languages, no complete English edition exists. For a synopsis of the 1958 edition (and a useful index, lacking in the original) see, J. M. Bochenski, *The Dogmatic Principles of Soviet Philosophy* (Dordrecht, Holland: D. Reidel Publishing Company, 1963). For reviews of that edition see George L. Kline, "*Fundamentals of Marxist Philosophy*: A Critical Analysis," *Survey*, No. 30 (October-December 1959), pp. 58-62; and C. Olgin, "Soviet Dialectical Materialism in Transition," *Bulletin, Institute for the Study of the U.S.S.R.*, VI, No. 11 (November 1959), pp. 3-19.
2. A more popular presentation is found in the first part of *Osnovy marksizma-leninizma* (Moskva: Gosudarstvennoe izdatel'stvo politicheskoi literatury, 1962); Engl. trans., *Fundamentals of Marxism-Leninism* (Moscow: FLPH), which is another widely used text.
3. *Omf*, 1963, Chapter III.
4. *Ibid.*, pp. 69-73.
5. *Ibid.*, pp. 80-81.
6. *Ibid.*, pp. 92, 93.
7. *Ibid.*, p. 110.
8. See for example, *Omf*, p. 66: "These and other discoveries and achievements confirm the truth of dialectical materialism." For a more thorough discussion see Gustav Wetter, "Dialectical Materialism and Natural Science," *Survey*, No. 23 (January-March 1958), pp. 51-59.
9. M. E. Omelyenovsky, "The Concept of Dialectical Contradiction in Quantum Physics," *Philosophy, Science and Man: The Soviet Delegation Reports for the XIII World Congress of Philosophy* (Moscow, 1963), p. 98.

Notes to Pages 208-12   267

10. S. T. Melyukhin, "Dialectical Materialism and the Philosophical Problems of Microcosm," *Philosophy, Science and Man*, p. 174.
11. P. V. Kopnin, "Materialist Dialectics Is a Logic of Modern Scientific Development," *Philosophy, Science and Man*, p. 136.
12. Pyotr L. Kapitsa, "Theory, Experimentation, Practice," *The Soviet Review* (June, 1962), pp. 18-19. The article originally appeared in *Ekonomicheskaya Gazeta*, March 26, 1962.
13. *Ibid.*, p. 19.
14. For a discussion of the debates see Siegfried Müller-Markus, "Einstein and Soviet Philosophy," *Studies in Soviet Thought*, I, pp. 78-87, and his book, *Einstein und die Sowjetphilosophie*, (Dordrecht-Holland: D. Reidel Publishing Co., 1960). For the official statement of the outcome of the debates, see *Voprosy filosofii* 1955, 1, pp. 134-38.
15. In the past several years a number of conferences have been held on the various aspects of contemporary physics including meetings in 1962 and 1963 dedicated specifically to philosophical problems of elementary particles. For more detailed reports on the technical aspects of the discussions see Siegfried Müller-Markus, "Soviet Philosophy in Crisis," *Cross Currents*, XIV, No. 1 (Winter 1964), pp. 35-61; and C. Olgin, "Soviet Views on the Meta-physics of Relativity," *Studies on the Soviet Union*, N.S., 1, No. 1 (1961), pp. 83-114. For discussions on Soviet interpretations of the meaning of 'matter' see Helmut Fleischer, "The Materiality of Matter," *Studies in Soviet Thought*, II, No. 1 (March 1962), pp. 12-20; and N. Lobkowicz, "Materialism and Matter in Marxism-Leninsim," *The Concept of Matter*, ed. Ernan McMullin (Notre Dame: Notre Dame University Press, 1963), pp. 430-64.
16. *Omf*, chapter IV.
17. *Ibid.*, p. 114.
18. *Ibid.*, p. 115.
19. *Ibid.*, chapters. V-VIII.
20. *Ibid.*, p. 145.
21. *Ibid.*, pp. 146-47.
22. *Ibid.*, pp. 148-81.
23. *Ibid.*, pp. 150-58.
24. *Ibid.*, p. 159.
25. The most influential position is that of V. P. Tugarinov presented in *Sootnoshenie kategorii dialekticheskogo materializma* (Leningrad, 1956), *Sootnoshenie kategorii istoricheskogo materializma* (Leningrad, 1958) and in several articles since then.

He divides the categories into three basic types, those of objects, of properties, and of relations, and proceeds to a number of subdivisions. For a discussion of the problem of categories, see H. Fleischer, "On Categories in Soviet Philosophy," *Studies in Soviet Thought* I, pp. 64-77.
26. Some of the literature pertinent to these questions is surveyed by H. Dahm, "Soviet Philosophy's Conception of 'Basic Laws,' 'Order' and 'Principles,'" *Studies in Soviet Thought*, I, pp. 52-63.
27. *Filosofskaia entsiklopediia* (1962), II, p. 474.
28. *Omf*, p. 196.
29. *Ibid.*, pp. 205-22.
30. *Ibid.*, pp. 223-29.
31. See, for example, S. T. Meliukhin, *O dialektike razvitiia neorganicheskoi prirody* (Moskva: Gospolizdat, 1960), reviewed by H. Fleischer, *Studies in Soviet Thought*, II, No. 2 (June, 1962), pp. 157-63; A. S. Bogomolov, *Ideia razvitiia v burzhuaznoi filosofii XIX i XX vekov* (Moskva: Izd. MGU, 1962), reviewed by H. Fleischer, *Studies in Soviet Thought*, III, No. 1 (March 1963), pp. 67-71; and V. S. Tiukhin, "'Kletochka' otrazheniia i otrazhenie kak svoistvo vsei materii" ("The 'Primary Cell' of Reflection and Reflection Itself as a Property of All of Matter"), *Voprosy filosofii*, 1964, 2, pp. 25-34.
32. *Kommunist*, 1964, No. 10 (July), p. 114.
33. Chapter IX of *Omf*. This is the final chapter in *Omf* on dialectical materialism.
34. *Omf*, p. 253.
35. *Ibid.*, p. 254.
36. *Ibid.*, pp. 254-55.
37. *Ibid.*, p. 256.
38. *Ibid.*, p. 257.
39. See chapter X, n. 20. For a general survey of the field, see J. M. Bochenski, "Soviet Logic," *Studies in Soviet Thought*, I, pp. 29-38.
40. Among those holding this position K. S. Bakradze is one of the most outspoken.
41. See, for example, V. I. Cherkesov: *Materialisticheskaia dialektika kak logika i teoriia poznaniia* (Moskva: Izd. MGU, 1962), reviewed by T. J. Blakeley, *Studies in Soviet Thought*, III, 1 (March, 1963), pp. 74-76.
42. See P. V. Tavanets, "Formal Logic and Philosophy," *The Soviet*

Review, V, No. 1 (Spring, 1964), pp. 53-59; also A. X. Kazymzanov, *Problema sovpadeniia dialektiki, logiki i teorii poznaniia (po Filosofskim tetradiam V. I. Lenina)* (Alma-Ata: Izd. A. N. Kazakhskoi SSSR, 1962), reviewed by T. J. Blakeley, *Studies in Soviet Thought*, III, 3 (September 1963), pp. 214-15.

43. A survey of this development is given by G. Küng, "Mathematical Logic in the Soviet Union (1917-1947), " *Studies in Soviet Thought*, I, pp. 39-42. Küng's "Bibliography of Soviet Work in the Field of Mathematic Logic and the Foundations of Mathematics From 1917-1957" [5] is extremely useful. See also the reviews of Soviet logic by George Kline in *The Journal of Symbolic Logic*, 14 (1949), pp. 243-44; 16 (1951), pp. 46-48; 17 (1952), pp. 124-29; 18 (1953), pp. 83-86, and 271-72; 19 (1954), p. 149; N. Lobkowicz, "The Principle of Contradiction in Recent Soviet Philosophy," *Studies in Soviet Thought*, I, pp. 44-51; and D. D. Comey, "Two Recent Soviet Conferences on Logic," *ibid.*, II, No. 1 (March 1962), pp. 21-36.

44. For a discussion of recent Soviet writings in the field, see Thomas J. Blakeley, *Soviet Theory of Knowledge* [47], and T. J. Blakeley, "Is Epistemology Possible in Diamat?" *Studies in Soviet Thought*, II, 2 (June 1962), pp. 95-102. Z. A. Jordan's discussion of "The Materialistic Theory of Knowledge, Theories of Truth and of Universals," Part V of his *Philosophy and Ideology* [51] is also extremely useful. For a critique from the Thomistic point of view, see "The Dialectical Materialist Theory of Knowledge," of Gustav Wetter's *Dialectical Materialism* [61], Part Two, chapter VI.

45. *Omf*, pp. 258-65.
46. *Ibid.*, pp. 266-70, 289-94.
47. *Ibid.*, pp. 271-89.
48. For a detailed analysis of party control with respect to ethics, see Richard T. De George, "Soviet Ethics and Soviet Society," *Studies in Soviet Thought*, IV (1964), pp. 206-17.
49. Chapter X: Historical Materialism as the Science of the Laws of the Development of Society; Chapter XI: Material Production Is the Basis of Social Life; Chapter XII: The Dialectic of the Forces and Relations of Production; Chapter XIV: The Base and Superstructure of Society.
50. *Omf*, p. 299.
51. *Ibid.*, p. 299.
52. *Ibid.*, p. 312.

53. *Ibid.*, pp. 314-15. For Stalin's almost identical statement of this position, see Joseph Stalin, *Economic Problems of Socialism in the U.S.S.R.* (New York: International Publishers, 1952), p. 9.
54. *Omf,* pp. 317-22. For Stalin's similar statement, see *Economic Problems of Socialism in the U.S.S.R.,* p. 11.
55. *Omf,* pp. 331-34. For an examination of the Soviet view of man, see Richard T. De George, "The Soviet Concept of Man," *Iris Hibernia,: 1964: Aspects of Communism,* pp. 14-28 (reprinted in *Studies in Soviet Thought,* IV (1964), pp. 261-76).
56. See "Moral Code of the Builder of Communism" in the Party Programme, *The Road to Communism,* pp. 566-67.
57. *Omf,* pp. 334-40. Though the content of this section in the second edition is virtually identical with that of the first edition, the section title has been changed from "Geographical Milieu and the Development of Society" to "Nature and Society."
58. *Ibid.,* p. 378.
59. *Ibid.,* pp. 389-98.
60. *Ibid.,* pp. 412-13.
61. *Ibid.,* p. 418.
62. *Ibid.,* p. 421.
63. *Ibid.,* pp. 423-24.
64. *Ibid.,* pp. 471-72. This line is also found in the Party Program, *The Road to Communism,* p. 455.
65. *Omf,* pp. 479-80.
66. *Ibid.,* p. 529.
67. For a more detailed discussion of Soviet humanism see the article cited in footnote 55.
68. Chapter XVI: Social Consciousness and Its Role in the Life of Society.
69. *Omf,* p. 530.
70. *Ibid.,* pp. 540-42.
71. For details of these developments and for an analysis of the growing Soviet ethical literature, see Richard T. De George: "A Bibliography of Soviet Ethics," *Studies in Soviet Thought,* III (1963), pp. 83-103, and "Soviet Ethics and Soviet Society," *ibid.,* IV (1964), pp. 206-17; see also George Kline, "Socialist Legality' and Communist Ethics," *Natural Law Forum,* VIII (1963), pp. 21-34. For general discussions of Marxist ethics, see H. B. Acton, *The Illusion of the Epoch* [44], pp. 180-250; Eugene Kamenka, *The Ethical Foundations of Marxism* [19];

Herbert Marcuse, *Soviet Marxism* [54], Part II; K. R. Popper, *The Open Society and Its Enemies* [25], Chapter 22; Maximilien Rubel, *Karl Marx: Pages choisies pour une éthique socialiste* (Paris: Librairie Marcel Rivière et Cie, 1948); and Howard Selsam, *Socialism and Ethics* (New York: International Publishers, 1943).

72. The text is A. F. Shishkin, *Osnovy marksistskoj etiki* ("Fundamentals of Marxist Ethics") (Moskva: Izd. IMO, 1961). For an analysis of its basic contents see Richard T. De George, "The Foundations of Marxist-Leninist Ethics," *Studies in Soviet Thought*, III (1963), pp. 121-33.
73. See, for example, *Osnovy kommunisticheskogo vospitaniia* ("Fundamentals of Communist Education"), 2d ed. (Moskva: Gospolitizdat, 1963), Chapter 8.
74. For the moral code of the builder of communism, see note 56 for this chapter; quoted in *Omf*, p. 550.
75. *Omf*, pp. 544-45.
76. *Ibid.*, p. 557.
77. *Ibid.*, pp. 569-81.
78. *Ibid.*, Chapter XVII: The Role of the Popular Masses and of Individuals in History.

NOTES TO CHAPTER XII

1. *MEW*, 3, p. 46 (*German Ideology*, p. 39); Engels to Mehring (July 14, 1893), *Marx-Engels Selected Correspondence* (Moscow: FLPH), pp. 540-41.
2. *MEW*, 13, p. 9; *Marx-Engels Selected Works*, I, p. 363.
3. *Filosofskii slovar'*, p. 160. This is essentially the same as the definition which appeared in the *Kratkii Filosofskii slovar'*, and in the *Filosofskaia entsiklopediia*, and as the discussion in *Omf*, chapter XVI.
4. *Filosofskii slovar'*, p. 476.
5. See Helmut Fleischer, "The Limits of 'Party-Mindedness': A Selection of Texts," *Studies in Soviet Thought*, 1962 (II), pp. 119-30.
6. For some discussions of the relation of philosophy and ideology see J. M. Bochenski, "Toward a Systematic Logic of Communist Ideology," *Studies in Soviet Thought*, 1964 (IV), pp. 185-205; Thomas J. Blakeley, *Soviet Scholasticism* [46]; George Kline, "Philosophy, Ideology and Policy in the Soviet Union," *The Review of Politics*, XXVI (1964), No. 2, pp. 174-90; Z. A.

Jordan, *Philosophy and Ideology* [51]; George Lichtheim, "Soviet Marxism: From Theory to Ideology," *Survey*, No. 27 (Jan.-Mar. 1959), pp. 69-74; David D. Comey, "Marxist-Leninist Ideology and Soviet Policy," *Studies in Soviet Thought*, II (1962), pp. 301-19.

7. Joseph M. Bochenski, "The Three Components of Communist Ideology," *Studies in Soviet Thought*, II (1962), pp. 7-11.
8. Thomas J. Blakeley, "Is Epistemology Possible in Diamat?" *Studies in Soviet Thought*, II (1962), pp. 95-103.
9. See, for example, section III of Stalin's *The Foundations of Leninism*; any number of Khrushchev's speeches; *Omf*, pp. 31 ff.; *Party Program of the CPSU*, Introduction and Parts II, V.
10. The role of ideology in Soviet foreign policy has often been discussed at length and in detail. See, among others, Zbigniew K. Brzezinski, *Ideology and Power in Soviet Politics* (New York: Praeger, 1962); Bertram Wolfe, "Communist Ideology and Soviet Foreign Policy," *The Realities of World Communism* (Prentice-Hall, 1963), pp. 19-40; Herman Achminov, "Marxism: Dogma or Guide," *Bulletin, Institute for the Study of the U.S.S.R.*, VI, No. 10 (Oct. 1959), pp. 11-22; J. M. Bochenski, "Ideology, Power Politics and Dialectics," *Studies in Soviet Thought*, III (1963), pp. 53-55; Richard Lowenthal, "The Role of Ideology for the Self Preservation of a Totalitarian Regime," *Studies in Soviet Thought*, III (1963), pp. 179-83.
11. Jordan, [51].
12. Z. Jordan, "The Development of Philosophy and Marxism-Leninism in Poland Since the War," *Studies in Soviet Thought*, I (1961), pp. 88-97.
13. The Russian titles are *Osnovy marksistskoi filosofii* and *Osnovy marksizma-leninizma* (see Chap. XI).
14. A Buchholz, "Problems of the Ideological East-West Conflict," *Studies in Soviet Thought*, I (1961), p. 130.
15. V. P. Tugarinov, *O tsennostiakh zhizni i kul'tury* (Leningrad: LGU, 1960).
16. See, for example, his book *A Philosophy of Man* (New York: Monthly Review Press, 1963).

Annotated Bibliography
of Selected Secondary Works

An asterisk before an entry indicates that the title listed is available in paperback according to the June 1965 edition of *Paperbound Books in Print*.

I. *Basic Bibliographies*

1. Bochenski, J. M., and Blakeley, T. J. (eds.) *Bibliography of Soviet Philosophy*. Dordrecht-Holland: D. Reidel Publishing Co. Vols. I-IV and V (Index), 1959-64.
   Lists Soviet books and articles in philosophy from 1947-60.
2. Dossick, Jesse J. *Doctoral Research on Russia and the Soviet Union*. New York: New York University Press, 1960.
   A master list of 960 American, British, and Canadian doctoral dissertations, divided topically. Each section also contains a helpful list of relevant basic books and articles which serve as "aids to further research."
3. Horecky, Paul L. (ed.). *Russia and the Soviet Union; a Bibliographic Guide to Western-Language Publications*. London and Chicago: The University of Chicago Press, 1965.
   An annotated, selective listing of books (with emphasis on those in English) relevant to the political, socio-economic, and intellectual life of the Russian Empire and the Soviet Union.
4. Kolarz, Walter. *Books on Communism; a Bibliography*. London: Ampersand Ltd., 1963.
   An annotated bibliography of books (in English) on communism in general as well as in the U.S.S.R. and other countries. Covers the period 1945-62. See especially section 1: The Theoretical Background. This book updates the previous edition edited by R. N. Carew Hunt, which covers the period 1945-57.

5. Küng, G. "Bibliography of Soviet Work in the Field of Mathematical Logic and the Foundations of Mathematics from 1917-1957," *Notre Dame Journal of Formal Logic*, III (Jan. 1962), 1-40.
6. Rubel, Maximilien (ed.). *Bibliographie des oeuvres de Karl Marx avec en appendice un répertoire des oeuvres de Friedrich Engels*. Paris: Librairie Marcel Rivière et Cie, 1956.
Rubel, Maximilien (ed.). *Supplément à la bibliographie des oeuvres de Karl Marx*. Paris: Librairie Marcel Rivière et Cie, 1960.
Annotated listing of the published works, letters, unpublished manuscripts and dubiosa of Marx with information on date, place, and details of writing and publication. The appendix on Engels is much shorter and not complete. The supplement contains corrections and additions.
7. *Studies in Soviet Thought:*
II (1962), 168-73: "Bibliography of Western Works on Soviet Philosophy."
255-59: "Bibliography of Philosophical Articles in *Uspexi Fizičeskix Nauk* (1918-1962)."
III (1963), 83-103: "A Bibliography of Soviet Ethics."
170-75: "Bibliography of Soviet Historiography of Philosophy: Editions in Russian Translation."
230-42: "Bibliography; Recent Soviet Works on Neopositivism."
IV (1964), 78-80: "Bibliography; Books and Articles by S. L. Rubinštejn."
81-84: "Bibliography; More Writings on Neopositivism."
142-61: "Bibliography; Soviet Publications on Cybernetics."
162-77: "Bibliography; Western Translations of Soviet Publications on Cybernetics."
319-38: "Bibliography; Soviet Writings on Atheism and Religion."
V (1965), 106-13: "Bibliography; Soviet Writings on Atheism and Religion: Supplement."
114-28: "Bibliography; Selected Writings on Nineteenth- and Early Twentieth-Century Russian Thought."

II. The Marxist Period

8. Adams, H. P. *Karl Marx in His Earlier Writings*. London: George Allen and Unwin, 1940.

Annotated Bibliography 275

This little volume contains summaries of all the early works of Marx, many of which have not yet been translated into English.

9. * Berlin, Isaiah. *Karl Marx; His Life and Environment.* 3rd ed.; London and New York: Oxford University Press, 1963.

   An excellent short biography of Marx with critical emphasis on his ideas; 1st ed., 1939.

10. * Bober, M. *Karl Marx's Interpretation of History.* 2d ed. revised. London: Oxford University Press; Cambridge, Mass.; Harvard University Press, 1948.

    A critical and detailed exposition of Marx's social and economic doctrine and of the materialist conception of history; 1st ed., 1927.

11. Böhm von Bawerk, Eugen. *Karl Marx and the Close of His System* and *Böhm Bawerk's Criticism of Marx* by Rudolf Hilferding. Ed. with an Introduction by Paul M. Sweezy. New York: A. M. Kelley, 1949.

    A translation of this well-known 1896 refutation of Marx's economic doctrine, and of the Marxian economist Hilferding's reply.

12. * Carew Hunt, R. N. *The Theory and Practice of Communism; an Introduction.* London: Bles, 1950; New York: Macmillan, 1957.

    A critical study of Marxist theory, the European socialist movement up to 1914, and the development of Leninism and Stalinism up to 1949.

13. Carr, E. H. *Karl Marx; a Study in Fanaticism.* London: J. M. Dent & Sons Ltd, 1934.

    A good introductory biography of Marx with two chapters on Marxism.

14. * Cole, G. D. H. *The Meaning of Marxism.* London: Gollancz, 1948; Ann Arbor: University of Michigan Press, 1964.

    Based on the author's *What Marx Really Meant* (1934). A sympathetic though critical reevaluation of Marx's method and of his basic views on history, society and economics.

15. Cornforth, Maurice (ed.). *Readers' Guide to the Marxist Classics.* London: Lawrence & Wishart Ltd, 1952.

    A program of suggested readings in the Marxist classics with commentaries and summaries of the works suggested.

16. * Fromm, E. (ed.). *Marx's Concept of Man; with a Translation from Marx's Economic and Philosophical Manuscripts* by T. B. Bottomore. New York: Ungar, 1961.

In a long introductory essay Fromm presents a controversial, quasi-existentialistic interpretation of Marx's concept of man as it appears in his early writings.

17. * Hook, Sidney. *From Hegel to Marx; Studies in the Intellectual Development of Karl Marx.* Ann Arbor: University of Michigan Press, 1962.

   This edition has a new introduction. The volume itself traces Marx's early intellectual development and presents the best and most detailed study of the Left-Hegelians who influenced him; 1st ed., 1936.

18. * Hook, Sidney. *Marx and the Marxists; the Ambiguous Legacy.* New York: Van Nostrand; London: Macmillan, 1955.

   A volume of brief critical expositions of and comments on Marx and some of his revisionist and orthodox followers; the second half of the volume contains selected passages from the figures dealt with in the first half.

19. Kamenka, Eugene. *The Ethical Foundations of Marxism.* London: Routledge and Kegan Paul; New York: Praeger, 1962.

   A critical study of the ethics contained in Marx's early works and of its place in his later works, with a brief examination of law and morality in the Soviet Union.

20. * Lichtheim, George. *Marxism; an Historical and Critical Study.* London: Routledge and Kegan Paul; New York: Praeger, 1961.

   An account of Marxist theory since its first formulation, and of the Marxist movement from 1848 to 1948.

21. * Marcuse, Herbert. *Reason and Revolution; Hegel and the Rise of Social Theory.* With a New Preface, "A Note on Dialectic." Boston: Beacon Press, 1960.

   An excellent study of Hegel's philosophy and of the rise of Nineteenth-Century social theory, including that of Marx. First edition, 1941.

22. Mayer, Gustav. *Friedrich Engels; a Biography.* With an Introduction by G. D. H. Cole. New York: Alfred Knopf, 1936.

   This standard biography of Engels is Mayer's German two-volume (1934) Engels biography, rewritten for the English speaking public.

23. * Mehring, Franz. *Karl Marx; the Story of His Life.* Trans. by Edward Fitzgerald. London, 1936; Ann Arbor: University of Michigan Press, 1962.

   Despite the fact that this book was written in 1918 it remains a good introduction to Marx's life and thought.

Annotated Bibliography 277

24. * Meyer, Alfred G. *Marxism; the Unity of Theory and Practice.* Cambridge, Mass.; Harvard University Press; London: Oxford University Press, 1954.
    A brief, elementary exposition of Marxist social science and of its "disintegration" in Western Europe after 1890.
25. * Popper, Karl R. *The Open Society and Its Enemies.* 4th ed. revised. London: Routledge and Kegan Paul, 1962. 2 v.
    The second volume contains extremely critical studies of Marx's method, his socialist theory, and the moral theory of historicism.
26. * Tucker, Robert C. *Philosophy and Myth in Karl Marx.* New York and London: Cambridge University Press, 1961.
    A provocative reinterpretation of Marxism as a religion of revolution, with emphasis on Marx's early writings.

III. Russian Pre-Marxist Philosophy

27. * Berdyaev, Nicholas. *The Russian Idea.* Trans. from the Russian by R. M. French. London: Geoffrey Bles, 1947; Boston, Beacon Press, 1962.
    An incisive study of the major currents of nineteenth-century Russian thought.
28. * Hare, Richard. *Pioneers of Russian Social Thought; Studies of Non-Marxian Formation in Nineteenth-Century Russia and of Its Partial Revival in the Soviet Union.* London and New York: Oxford University Press, 1951; 2d ed. revised, New York: Vintage Books, 1964.
    A good introductory study of the chief Westernizers and Slavophiles with an indication of how they are valued or devalued in the Soviet Union.
29. Lampert, E. *Sons Against Fathers; Studies in Russian Radicalism and Revolution.* Oxford: Oxford University Press, 1965.
    An excellent scholarly, philosophical discussion of the thought of Chernyshevsky, Dobrolyubov, and Pisarev.
30. Lampert, E. *Studies in Rebellion; Belinsky, Bakunin, and Herzen.* London: Routledge and Kegan Paul; New York: Praeger, 1957.
    A detailed discussion of the figures mentioned with an introductory chapter on the Russian intelligentsia.
31. Lossky, Nicholai O. *History of Russian Philosophy.* New York: International Universities Press, 1951; London: George Allen and Unwin, Ltd, 1952.

278   PATTERNS OF SOVIET THOUGHT

A survey of Russian philosophy from the Eighteenth Century. Many short sketches with more extended treatments of a few philosophers.

32. Masaryk, Thomáš G. *The Spirit of Russia; Studies in History, Literature and Philosophy.* 2d ed. revised. London: Allen and Unwin; New York, Macmillan, 1955. 2 v.

First published in 1913. A detailed study of Russian philosophy of history and philosophy of religion with an extended discussion of the rise of Marxism in Russia.

33. * Utechin, S. V. *Russian Political Thought; A Concise History.* New York: Praeger, 1963.

Covers the period from medieval to post-Stalin Russia. The sketches of individual thinkers are short, but the discussion of Slavophilism, Westernism, and Populism are useful.

34. Venturi, Franco. *Roots of Revolution; a History of the Populist and Socialist Movements in Nineteenth Century Russia.* Introduction by Isaiah Berlin. New York: Alfred A. Knopf, 1960.

A full and detailed treatment of the period from Herzen and Bakunin in the 1830's to 1881. Trans. from the Italian, 2 v., 1952.

35. Zenkovsky, V. V. *A History of Russian Philosophy.* Trans. from the Russian by George L. Kline. London: Routledge and Kegan Paul; New York: Columbia University Press, 1953. 2 v.

The most authoritative, readable and reliable history in English of Russian non-Marxist philosophy.

IV.   *Lenin and Russian Marxism*

36. Baron, Samuel H. *Plekhanov; the Father of Russian Marxism.* Stanford: Stanford University Press, 1963.

The first—and a welcome—biography of Plekhanov in a Western language.

37. Fischer, Louis. *The Life of Lenin.* New York: Harper & Row, 1964.

A very readable biography.

38. Haimson, Leopold H. *The Russian Marxists and the Origins of Bolshevism.* Cambridge: Harvard University Press, 1955.

A study of the background and development of the Russian Marxist intelligentsia during the 1890's and the beginning of the Twentieth Century up to 1905. Much biographical detail on Plekhanov, Lenin, P. B. Akselrod, and Martov.

Annotated Bibliography 279

39. Kindersley, Richard. *The First Russian Revisionists; a Study of "Legal Marxism" in Russia.* Oxford: Clarendon Press, 1962.

A study of the philosophical, economic and political theory of Struve and several other Nineteenth-Century Russian revisionists.

40. * Meyer, Alfred G. *Leninism.* Cambridge, Mass.; Harvard University Press; London: Oxford University Press, 1957.

An exposition and analysis of Lenin's political ideas and their implementation in practice.

41. * Plamenatz, John. *German Marxism and Russian Communism.* New York and London: Longmans, Green, 1954.

A critical exposition of Marx's social and political theories and of their transformation into bolshevism.

42. Possony, Stefan T. *Lenin; the Compulsive Revolutionary.* Chicago: Henry Regnery Co., 1964.

A scholarly, reliable biography.

43. * Wolfe, Bertram D. *Three Who Made a Revolution; a Biographical History.* 4th ed. revised. New York: Dial Press, 1964.

Readable biographies of Lenin, Trotsky, and Stalin—their activities, associates, and conflicts—to the October Revolution.

V. *Soviet Period*

44. Acton, Harry B. *The Illusion of the Epoch; Marxism-Leninism as a Philosophical Creed.* London: Cohen and West, 1955; Boston: Beacon Press, 1957.

An excellent exposition, interpretation, and criticism of dialectical and historical materialism and of Marxist ethics, primarily as these are presented in the Marxist-Leninist classics.

45. * Berdyaev, Nicholas. *The Origin of Russian Communism.* Trans. from the Russian by R. M. French. London: Geoffrey Bles, 1937 (new edition, 1948); Ann Arbor: University of Michigan Press, 1960.

A succinct presentation of the Russian background and the development of Russian communism as a secular religion.

46. Blakeley, Thomas J. *Soviet Scholasticism.* Dordrecht-Holland: D. Reidel Publishing Co., 1961.

A study of the method of contemporary Soviet philosophy with a concluding chapter comparing Soviet philosophy and Scholasticism and a large appendix of quotations from Russian sources.

47. Blakeley, Thomas J. *Soviet Theory of Knowledge.* Dordrecht-Holland: D. Reidel Publishing Co., 1964.

A specialist volume which presents developments and variations in Soviet theory of knowledge from 1947 to 1963. The bibliography contains a complete listing of pertinent books and articles in Russian and a short listing of works in other languages.

48. Bochenski, J. M. *Soviet Russian Dialectical Materialism (Diamat)*. Trans. from the German by N. Sollohub and T. J. Blakeley. Dorcrecht-Holland: D. Reidel Publishing Co., 1963.

The body of the work is a concise, penetrating, and critical outline of the sources and doctrines of Soviet Russian dialectical materialism up to July 1956. Two appendixes bring portions of the book up to 1959 and add a wealth of factual material on Soviet philosophical conferences, centers and publications.

49. * Deutscher, Isaac. *Stalin; a Political Biography*. New York and London: Oxford University Press, 1949.

A good biography of Stalin up to the years 1945-46, with emphasis on his political activity.

50. Joravsky, David. *Soviet Marxism and Natural Science, 1917-1932*. New York: Columbia University Press; London, Routledge and Kegan Paul, 1961.

A scholarly study centering on the Mechanist-Deborinist controversy, of which this is the best and fullest treatment available.

51. Jordan, Z. A. *Philosophy and Ideology; the Development of Philosophy and Marxism-Leninism in Poland since the Second World War*. Dordrecht-Holland: D. Reidel Publishing Co., 1963.

An exhaustive presentation of Polish philosophy from 1918-1958. The excellent critique of the Marxist-Leninist theory of knowledge applies to the Soviet version as well.

52. Kline, George L. *Spinoza in Soviet Philosophy*. A Series of Essays, Selected and Translated, and with an Introduction. New York: Humanities Press; London: Routledge and Kegan Paul Ltd, 1952.

A long introductory essay precedes seven articles on Spinoza by such Soviet philosophers as L. I. Akselrod, A. M. Deborin and I. K. Luppol.

53. * Labedz, Leopold (ed.). *Revisionism, Essays on the History of Marxist Ideas*. London: Allen and Unwin; New York, Praeger, 1962.

A series of articles, many of which first appeared in *Survey*, which analyze some of the many diverse interpretations of Marxist theory in its "unorthodox" development.

Annotated Bibliography 281

54. * Marcuse, Herbert. *Soviet Marxism; a Critical Analysis*. New York: Columbia University Press; London: Routledge and Kegan Paul, 1958. (With a new Preface: New York: Vintage Books, 1961.)

    Divided into two parts, Political Tenets, and Ethical Tenets, this book presents an "immanent" critique of Soviet Marxism.

55. Monnerot, Jules. *Sociology and Psychology of Communism*. Trans. from the French by Jane Degras and Richard Rees. Boston: Beacon Press, 1953.

    A partial translation of *Sociologie du communisme* (Paris: Gallimard, 1949). A detailed and extended presentation of communism as a "secular religion" and as a "universal State."

56. Philipov, Alexander. *Logic and Dialectic in the Soviet Union*. Foreword by Ernest Nagel. New York: Research Program on the USSR, 1952.

    Traces the subjugation of logic to governmental authority, discusses the substance of dialectical logic, and presents the Soviet reversal with respect to formal logic following the linguistics controversy.

57. *The Philosophy of Communism*. With an Introduction by Charles Boyer, S. J. New York: Fordham University Press, 1952.

    A translation from the Italian of twenty-three papers on the philosophy of communism given in 1949 at the Pontifical Academy of St. Thomas, Rome.

58. Somerville, John. *Soviet Philosophy; a Study of Theory and Practice*. New York: Philosophical Library, 1946.

    A sympathetic and somewhat popular summary of the Soviet "social outlook" and "world view," with chapters on "Dissemination of Philosophy in the U.S.S.R." and "About Reading."

59. *Soviet Studies in Philosophy*. v. 1–, 1962–. New York. Quarterly.

    International Arts and Sciences Press translations of articles from such Soviet philosophical journals as *Voprosy filosofii* and *Filosofskie nauki*.

60. *Studies in Soviet Thought*. v. 1–, 1961–. Fribourg, Switzerland. Quarterly.

    Volume I contains thirteen articles, some of which are summaries of books which later appeared in the Sovietica series. Continued as a quarterly journal with volume II. Contains articles (primarily in English and German, sometimes in French) on Soviet and East European philosophy, notes and comments, bibliographies, biographies, and chronological listings of philosophical activities in the Soviet Union.

61. * Wetter, Gustav. *Dialectical Materialism; a Historical and Systematic Survey of Philosophy in the Soviet Union.* Trans. from the German by Peter Heath. London: Routledge and Kegan Paul, 1958; New York: Praeger, 1959.

An excellent and detailed historical and systematic presentation of dialectical materialism up to 1956. The author's critical remarks are along Aristotelian and scholastic lines. Generally considered a basic work in the field.

Index

Absolute, 11-13, 16-17, 23-24, 29, 61, 101, 147, 166, 170
Abstraction, 168-69, 215
Adoratsky, V. V., 183
Aesthetics, 31, 119, 242, 249, 256
Agnosticism, 148, 153
"Agrarian Question, The," 185
Akselrod, L. I. (pseud. *Orthodox*), 180
Alexander, 124
Alexander II, 117
Alexander III, 128
Alexandrov, G., 188, 192
Alienation, 11, 13, 18, 27, 29-30, 39, 41-44, 49, 53, 75-76, 169
definition, 41
Anarchism or Socialism, 192
Anthropology, 24-28
Anti-Dühring, 37, 77, 79-93, 103, 197, 207, 241, 250
Aristotle, 6, 95, 149, 166, 187, 243
Atheism, 11, 172, 235
Augustine, Saint, 213

Axe, The, 116
Axelrod, P., 129

Bakunin, M., 20, 22, 57, 114, 116-17
Base, 57, 64-65, 74, 137-39, 189, 196, 203-4, 218-19, 237, 262
Bauer, B., 20-21, 31, 33-35, 45
Bazarov, V. (pseud. of V. A. Rudnev), 257
Being, 23, 83, 95, 158, 214
concept of, 23, 83
Belinski, V. G., 114
Berdyaev, N. A., 115, 117-18
Berkeley, G., 147, 150
Bernstein, E., 109-10, 119, 132
Blakeley, T. J., 232
Bloch, J., 65
Bochenski, J. M., 231-32
Bogdanov, A. (pseud. of A. A. Malinovski), 118-19, 127, 130, 180-81, 257
Bolsheviks, 118, 120, 129-31, 135, 184

Bourgeoisie, 57-59, 87, 91-92, 99, 163-64
Buchholz, A., 242
Bukharin, N. I., 180-82, 186
Bulgakov, S. N., 117-18
Burat, E., 41

Caesar, J., 17, 124, 156
Capital, 10, 22, 36-37, 63-65, 67-70, 72-73, 77, 80, 110, 117, 163, 165, 173, 175
Capitalism, 40, 43, 67, 69-71, 73-74, 80, 117, 130, 132, 136, 175, 192, 218, 220-21, 228, 235-36, 238, 245, 262
  laws of, 73-74, 122, 202, 217
  in Russia, 119
  survivals of, 192
Causality, 83, 105-6, 159-60, 169, 211-12, 220
Chardin, T. de, 213
Chemistry, 84-85, 104, 106-7
Chernov, V. M., 257
Chernyshevski, N. G., 115
China, 239-40
Christ, J., 11, 26
Christianity, 11, 20, 27
Classes, abolition of, 93, 164
  antagonistic, 40, 53, 56-57, 60, 91, 109, 191, 195, 227
  revolutionary, 40, 163
Class struggle, 56-57, 99, 132, 139, 219-22
"Class Struggle in France 1848-1850, The," 36, 141
Coexistence, 162, 202-3, 221, 228
Commodity, 66-68
Communism, 1, 3-4, 6, 22, 41, 43, 45, 50, 54, 57, 59, 62, 70-71, 75, 80, 91, 94, 109, 136, 138-39, 171-72, 174-75, 192, 201, 205, 221, 228, 233, 239, 244, 249
  building of, 176, 187, 190, 201-5, 219, 221, 224, 234, 263
  crude, 43
  definition, 43, 50, 58, 72, 203
  triumph of, 5, 57, 176, 181-82, 228-29, 231, 234, 236
Communist League, 35, 57
Communist Party of the Soviet Union, 2, 3, 6, 172, 176-77, 184, 190, 204, 209, 219, 224-25, 227, 229, 231-33, 237, 239-40, 249
  Central Committee, 4, 10, 173, 183, 187, 214, 250, 265
  and philosophy, 182, 185-89, 194, 198, 200, 247
  Program, 4, 6, 201-5, 216, 218-19, 221-22, 227, 238, 249, 265
Concept, 12
  concrete, 13, 19
  fluid, 14, 168
  static, 14, 168; see also Universals
Concerning Questions of Leninism, 186, 190
Condition of the Working Class in England, The, 79
Consciousness, 11-12, 16, 26-27, 48-50, 53, 82, 96, 102, 106, 133, 148, 151-53, 186, 210, 213, 217, 234
  social, 154, 189, 195-96, 201, 204-5, 222-25
Contradiction, 14, 66-67, 88-89, 167, 208, 218, 221, 228
  law of, 88, 170
  in nature, 88-89, 181-83, 212, 214
"Contribution to the Critique of Hegel's *Philosophy of Right*," 34, 39-40, 45
Contribution to the Critique of Political Economy, A, 36, 63-67, 227
Copy theory, *see* Knowledge as reflection

Index 285

Cosmogony, 84-85
"Critique of the Gotha Program," 37, 71-72
Critique of the Philosophy of Hegel, 22

Darwin, C., 85, 98
Deborin, A. M., 166, 181, 186, 263
Deborinism, 179-84, 186
Democracy, 1, 21, 49, 136, 144
Democritus, 34, 38, 187
Descartes, R., 45, 95, 187
Determination, economic, 51, 54, 59, 73-74, 109, 125, 140, 181, 190
Determinism, 211
  in history, 99, 118, 138-40
Deutsch-Französische Jahrbücher, 21, 34, 39
Development of Capitalism in Russia, The, 129
Development of the Monist View of History, The, 119-22
Dialectical and Historical Materialism, 126, 187, 192-94, 200, 241
Dialectical Materialism, 166
Dialectical materialism, 2-5, 10, 22, 94, 97, 107, 119-21, 127, 130-31, 159-60, 180-85, 187, 190, 192-93, 196, 200-201, 204, 206-16, 229, 232, 234, 241-42, 246-47, 249, 266
Dialectics, 1, 9, 13-16, 18, 44, 53, 63, 73, 80, 82, 88-90, 92, 97-98, 100-101, 107, 162, 164-71, 173, 180-83, 185, 192-93, 201, 214, 235, 247; see also Method, dialectical; Sovpadenie
  laws of, 32, 79, 89-90, 103, 163, 167, 177, 192-93, 196, 201, 210-16, 235
  of nature, 78, 81, 100

  objective, 103, 214
  subjective, 103, 214
Dialectics of Nature, 79, 102-7, 182, 207, 243
Die neue Zeit, 93-94, 97, 110
Distinction Between the Democritian and Epicurean Philosophies of Nature, The, 33, 37-39
Dobrolyubov, N. A., 115
Dostoevski, F. M., 115
Dühring, E., 37, 79, 82-93
Dzhugashvili, J. V., see Stalin, J.

Economic and Philosophic Manuscripts of 1844, 32, 34, 41-44, 162, 221-22
Economic Problems of Socialism in the U.S.S.R., 189, 219
Economics, 55-56, 73, 77-78, 81, 107, 194, 245
Economism, 118
Economy, political, 41, 54-70, 77, 79, 130, 162, 167, 249
"Eighteenth Brumaire of Louis Bonaparte, The," 36
Einstein, A., 209
Elders, 128-29
Emancipation, of man, 40-41, 56, 99, 122
Emancipation of Labor, The, 119, 129
Empirio-criticism, 130
Empiriomonism, 118
Engels, F., 2, 6-7, 10, 20, 22, 32-33, 35-37, 44, 47, 49-50, 57, 59, 65-67, 77-111, 119, 138, 140, 143, 149, 156, 159-60, 162, 174, 176, 180-82, 185, 201, 207, 209, 211, 231, 243, and *passim*
Epicurus, 34, 38
Epistemology, see Knowledge, theory of
Equilibrium theory, 181
Error, 87, 169, 215

286 PATTERNS OF SOVIET THOUGHT

Essays in Historical Materialism, 120
Essays in the History of Materialism, 120
Essence of Christianity, The, 23-29, 34, 39
Estrangement, *see* Alienation
Ethics, 19, 31, 67, 73, 87-88, 94, 97, 109, 171-72, 216, 242-43, 249, 261
Evolution, 85, 98, 167, 213

Fathers and Sons, 114
Feuerbach, L., 7, 13, 18, 20, 22-30, 34-35, 41-42, 44, 46, 52, 79-80, 93-94, 96-97, 114, 120, 129, 165-66, 233
Fichte, J. G., 15, 129
Filosofskie nauki, 232
Forces, productive, 49-50, 52, 55, 60, 64-65, 92, 124-25, 163, 203
Foundations of Leninism, 186
Fourier, C., 91
Freedom, 1, 16, 22, 59, 87-88, 93, 114, 121, 160, 229, 243
of criticism, 132-33
and determinism, 18; *see also* Determinism
and necessity, 17, 87-88, 122, 162, 193, 217
Fundamentals of Marxism-Leninism, 242
Fundamentals of Marxist Philosophy, 206-25, 232, 242, 266
Fundamental Problems of Marxism, 120, 125, 166

Gans, E., 33
General Association of German Workers, 71
Geography, 125-26, 217-18, 270
German Ideology, The, 20, 22, 29, 35, 46-52, 79, 93-94, 100, 162

German Social-Democratic Party, 108
German Socialist Workers' Party, 71
God, 11, 21, 24-29, 41, 53, 84-85, 101, 118, 147, 150, 166, 231, 259
God-builders, 118
God-seekers, 118
Gorki, M., 118
Göschel, K., 19
Grün, K., 46

Hegel, G. W. F., 6-7, 9-20, 22-24, 30, 33, 38-39, 44, 63, 79, 81-82, 94, 98, 100-101, 114, 161, 165-67, 173, 177, 183, 187, 243, 254, and *passim*
Hegelians, 15
Left (Young), 1, 11, 18-22, 33, 44, 46, 52, 80, 93-94
Right, 18-19, 94
Helmholtz, H., 126
Helvetius, C. A., 129
Heraclitus, 81
Herzen, A. I., 114-15, 117
Hess, M., 22, 46
"Historical Destiny of the Teaching of Karl Marx," 161
Historical materialism, 2-3, 5, 10, 46-52, 54, 57, 64-65, 78, 80, 86-87, 92, 97, 99, 100, 107-8, 119-20, 122, 127, 138-39, 152, 154, 157, 163, 187, 190, 193-94, 201-2, 204-6, 216-25, 234, 241-42, 246-47, 249, 253
History, 10, 13, 16, 19, 21, 25, 47, 50, 64, 77-79, 89, 94, 98-99, 167, 220, 245, 249
definition, 50
laws of, 5, 32, 44, 87, 90, 107, 169, 233
materialist interpretation of, *see* Historical materialism
philosophy of, 16-17, 73

History of Philosophy, 166
History of the CPSU, 199
History of the CPSU (b), 187, 189-94, 210, 241
History of West-European Philosophy, 188-94
Holy Family, The, 21, 35, 44, 46, 79, 97, 166
"Housing Question, The," 80
Humanism, 24, 28-29, 43, 45, 62, 162, 221-22, 242
Hume, D., 148, 211
Hungary, 240, 242

Idealism, 10, 13, 18, 20, 22, 24, 28-29, 39, 44, 79, 90, 94-97, 120, 130, 139, 147-51, 153, 157, 165, 235, 257
  dialectical, 22
  epistemological, 25, 147-48
  objective, 12, 147
  subjective, 147
Ideas, source of, 49, 51
Identity-in-difference, 14
Ideology, 99, 133, 169, 195, 205, 209, 219, 222, 226-33, 237-40, 243-48
  definition, 100, 226-28
Imperialism, 130
Individual, role in history, 17, 99, 119, 122-25, 222-25
International Working Men's Association, 22, 36, 80
Introduction to Philosophy, 166
Iskra, 120, 129

James, W., 156
Jordan, Z. A., 241
Judin, P. F., 183
Justification of Capitalism in West-European Philosophy, The, 166

Kamenev, L., 184
Kant, I., 84, 95-96, 118, 148, 150, 211

Index   287

Kapitsa, P. L., 208
"Karl Marx," 161
Kautsky, K., 37, 110
Kedrov, B. M., 188
Khomyakov, A. S., 114
Khrushchev, N. S., 6, 98, 184-85, 191, 198-99, 202, 205, 232, 234, 244, 263, 265
Kireyevsky, I.V., 114
Knowledge, 18, 38, 56, 86-87, 94-95, 98, 147, 158, 163, 209
  hieroglyphic theory of, 126-27, 153
  as reflection, 82, 96, 98, 103, 126, 130, 151-54, 156, 158, 163, 167, 169
  sense, 25
  theory of, 18, 29, 31, 126-27, 130, 146-51, 166-71, 176, 213-16, 242-43, 249, 256;
  see also Sovpadenie
Kolakowski, L., 242
Kommunist, 10, 173, 189, 213
Konstantinov, F. V., 206
Kopnin, P.V., 212
Krupskaya, N., 129
Kuhlmann, G., 46
Kulaks, 190, 199

Labor, 102-3, 217
  division of, 41, 47, 49, 51, 53
  social, 68
Labor union movement, 109, 118, 134
Language, 49, 196, 215, 217
Lassalle, F., 37
Lavrov, P.I., 116
Law, 19, 48, 87-88, 137, 189, 204, 211, 216, 218, 228
Laws, of history, see History
  of nature, 5, 87
  of social development, 169, 204, 217, 219-22, 229, 240
League for the Liberation of Labor, 117, 129

League of the Just, 35
Leap, dialectical, 89, 101, 121, 152, 167-68, 180-82, 212, 235
Leben Jesu, 20
Lectures on the Essence of Religion, 166
Leibniz, G. W. von, 213
Lenin, V. I., 1, 6-7, 10-11, 33, 45, 80, 113, 115-16, 118-20, 126-27, 146-60, 179, 186-87, 190, 200-202, 207, 210, 214-15, 219, 221, 243, and *passim*
and the Party, 128-45
philosophical legacy, 161-77
Leninism, 7, 113, 174, 186
Lenin's Miscellanies, 165
Life, 89
definition, 85
Life of Jesus, A, 11
Linguistics, 189, 194-98, 215
Locke, J., 45, 147
Logic, 10, 13, 15, 63, 165-66, 173
Logic, 13, 18, 107, 119, 166, 169-71, 187-88, 197, 213-16, 231, 236, 241, 243, 260
dialectical, 18, 105, 107, 214; see also *Sovpadenie*
Louis XV, 123
Ludwig Feuerbach, 93
Ludwig Feuerbach and the End of Classical German Philosophy, 77, 80, 93-102
Lukács, G., 32, 222, 242
Lunacharski, A. V., 118
Lysenko, T. D., 3

Mach, E., 118, 146, 148, 257
Man, 11, 18, 41, 60-61, 82, 97, 102-3, 170, 249
nature of, 25-29, 44, 121
Manifesto of the Communist Party, 22, 36, 56-63, 79-80, 108, 117

Marcuse, H., 32
Mark, Saint, 21
Marr, N.Y., 195
Marx, K., 1, 6-7, 9-12, 16-21, 23, 28-30, 77-81, 97-98, 107-10, 122, 127, 140, 156-57, 163, 176, 197, 202, 225, 227, 233, and *passim*
life and writings, 33-37
and political economy, 55-76
young, 31-54
"Marx-Engels Correspondence, The," 161, 163
Marxism, 6-7, 9, 18, 31-32, 78, 100, 107-11, 131, 134, 137-38, 140, 143, 156-57, 162, 164, 174, 179-80, 183, 186, 188, 194, 201-2, 217
as guide to action, 164, 197, 234
legal, 117-18
mature, 72-76
orthodox, 109-11, 127, 184, 206
Russian, 80, 113, 115-27, 146
Marxism and Linguistics, 189, 194-98, 219
"Marxism and the National Question," 186
Marxism-Leninism, 2-6, 9, 18, 32, 54, 60, 127, 131, 157, 174, 177, 184, 188-89, 194, 197-98, 200, 205, 212, 227-29, 231, 233-36, 240-42, 244, 246, 248-49
Masses, 21, 39, 53, 99, 122, 133-34, 137, 143, 163, 176, 191, 222-25
and history, 45
Materialism, 18, 22, 30, 38, 44-45, 79, 82, 90, 94-96, 107, 117, 120, 138, 147-52, 157, 162, 170-71, 183, 192-93, 234-35, 247, 250
crude, 24-25, 140, 180

definition, 24-25, 52-53
French, 45-46, 120
idealistic, 25
militant, 171
Materialism and Empirio-Criticism, 118, 126, 146-61, 165-66, 168, 173, 190, 207, 210, 214-15, 243, 250
Materialist Conception of History, The, 110
Mathematics, 14, 78-79, 81-83, 86-87, 89, 107, 197
Matter, 12, 16, 20, 84, 96, 102, 106, 120, 130, 146-47, 157-60, 186, 193, 207-10, 213, 234-35
philosophical, 156-59
properties of, 158-60
scientific, 158-59
Mechanism, 179-84, 195
Melyukhin, S.T., 208
Mensheviks, 118, 120, 129, 131, 135
Metaphysics, 166
Metaphysics, 18, 29, 48, 104, 147-51, 249, 257
Method, dialectical, 10, 13-16, 18-20, 63-64, 79, 82, 192-93, 259-60; see also Dialectics
Hegel's, 13-16, 63-64, 101
Michelet, K., 19
Mikhailovski, N.K., 116, 120
Mind, 12, 26, 96, 152, 160, 193, 207-10, 235; see also Consciousness
Minin, S., 180
Mitin, M.B., 183, 187
Modern Philosophy, 166
Money, 67-68
Morality, 2, 5-6, 11, 19, 21, 28, 41, 48-49, 60, 67, 69, 87-88, 137, 172-73, 189, 192, 195, 199, 201, 204, 218, 222-24, 228, 261
More, T., 90

Morgan, L., 80
Motion, 84, 88-89, 97-99, 102, 106, 159-60, 162, 167, 180-82, 207
Movement, 15, 193, 211
Mysteries of Paris, The, 45

Napoleon, 124
Narodnichestvo, 115-17, 119, 189
Nationalization, 110, 185
"National Question and Social-Democracy, The," 186
Nature, 11, 18, 42, 103, 166, 170, 193, 211
human, see Man, nature of
laws of, 32, 90, 104, 160, 204
philosophy of, 78
Necessity, 45, 211; see also Freedom
Nechaev, S.G., 116
Negation of the negation, 15, 65-66
law of, 89-90, 103, 105, 163, 193, 210, 213
Neue rheinische Zeitung, 36
Nihilism, 115-16
Nodal point, see Leap, dialectical

Omelyanovsky, M.E., 208
One Step Forward, Two Steps Back, 129, 135
"On Social Relations in Russia," 80
"On the Jewish Question," 34
"On the Question of Dialectics," 166
"On the Significance of Militant Materialism," 171-72
On the Values of Life and Culture, 242
Opposites, law of the interpenetration of, 103-5, 163, 193, 210, 212

Index 289

290 PATTERNS OF SOVIET THOUGHT

Origin of the Family, Private Property and the State, The, 80
Our Differences, 119
Owen, R., 91

Partiinost', see Partymindedness
"Part Played by Labor in the Transition from Ape to Man, The," 102-3
Party, revolutionary, 131-45
Partymindedness, 135-38, 176, 185, 200, 217, 241
Pattern, change from above, 6, 177, 197, 200
  development, 1
  of Marx's thought, 52-54
  of Soviet thought, 7, 180, 182, 200-201, 203, 205, 239
Paulsen, F., 166
Pavlov, I.P., 210
Perception, sense, 23
Personality cult, 137, 184, 198-99, 216
Phenomenology of Mind, 11-16
Philosophical Dictionary, 227
Philosophical Encyclopedia, 174, 212
Philosophical Notebooks, 10, 130, 164-71, 173, 176-77, 182, 210-11, 214-15, 243
Philosophy, 50, 60, 77, 81-83, 95, 100, 107, 130, 137, 162, 180-82, 194, 218, 222, 224, 226-33, 244-49
  and the CPSU, 182-83, 185-89, 194, 198, 200
  rationalistic, 11
  Russian, 7, 113-27
  Soviet, 2-8, 101, 146, 151-52, 154, 157, 173, 179-84, 186-90, 193, 198, 202, 206-25, 239
Philosophy of History, 166
Philosophy of Poverty, The, 55
Philosophy of Right, 35, 39

Philosophy of Right and Law, The, 19
Physics, 84-85, 103, 106-7, 157, 207-10, 216, 243, 267
Pisarev, D.I., 115
Plekhanov, G.V., 97, 117-27, 129-30, 166, 168, 183, 189, 217, 224
Pod znamenem marksizma, see Under the Banner of Marxism
Poland, 241-42, 244
Politics, 48, 228
Pompadour, Madame, 123
Populism, 116-17, 119-20
Poverty of Philosophy, The, 35, 55-56
Practice, 29-30, 153, 160, 170, 174, 193, 205, 216, 233-38
Pravda, 130, 182, 189, 195, 198
"Preliminary Theses in the Reform of Philosophy," 34
Problems of Leninism, 186
Production, means of, 30, 65, 71, 110
  modes of, 92
Proletariat, 40, 45, 50, 53, 56-60, 73, 86-87, 91-93, 99, 111, 118-19, 122, 129, 137-39, 164, 172, 175, 220
  definition, 41
  dictatorship of, 72, 131-32, 143-44, 164, 176, 190, 204, 235
Propaganda, 194, 201, 233-38
Property, common, 67, 90
  personal, 59
  private, 41, 43, 47-49, 53, 59, 65, 75-76, 87, 218, 220
Proudhon P.J., 34-35, 45, 55
Psychology, 28, 119, 187-88, 211, 224

Quantity into quality, law of, 89, 103-4, 163, 167, 182, 193, 195-96, 210, 212

Quantum mechanics, 3, 208-9
Quesnay, F., 34

Realism, 25, 28, 147-51, 154, 247
Reductionism, 181, 213
Relations, productive, 56, 58
  social, 30, 53, 55-56, 58, 121, 124, 152
Relativity theory, 3, 208-9, 235
Religion, 11, 20, 22, 25-26, 29-30, 39, 48, 50, 60, 94, 99-100, 137, 162, 218, 222, 228, 245
Revisionism, 108-11, 119, 138
Revolution, 41, 49, 70, 109, 116, 119, 134, 136, 140-45, 172, 175, 187, 191-92, 197, 220-21
  from above, 190-91, 195
  October, 110-11, 118, 120, 131, 137, 179, 184, 191
  proletarian, 40, 45, 52-53, 56, 60, 74-75, 138-39, 175, 190, 201
  Russian, 62, 78, 131, 136, 142, 164, 202
  theory of, 39-40, 162
Revolutionary Catechism, 116
Rey, A., 161
Rheinische Zeitung, 34
Ricardo, D., 34
Role of the Individual in History, The, 120, 122-25
Rousseau, J.-J., 91
Ruge, A., 20-21, 34-35
Russian Young Communist League, 171

Saint-Simon, C.H. de, 91
Say, J.-B., 41
Schaff, A., 242
Schelling, F.W. von, 129
Science, definition, 56
  division of, 103, 107
  method of, 102-6, 160, 181-82
  physical, 3, 5, 12, 20, 79, 81-82, 98, 102, 160, 162, 172-73, 211; *see also* Physics
Science of Logic, see *Logic*
Sechenov, I.M., 126, 210
Self-consciousness, 13, 44
  critical, 20
Sensation, 147-48, 150-51, 153, 158
  definition, 148-49, 151
Sensationalism, 24-25
Shulyatikov, V., 166
Skvortsov-Stepanov, I.I., 180
Slavophilism, 114-15
Smith, A., 34, 41
Social Contract, 91
Social Democratic Workers' Party, 71, 118, 120, 128-36
Socialism, 71, 77, 79, 81, 110, 116-17, 130, 136, 144, 163, 189, 191, 204, 220, 244, 249
  definition, 72
  French, 90-91, 130, 162
  in one country, 130-31, 175, 191-92, 197-98, 201-2, 262
  scientific, 78, 81, 90-93, 107-8, 117, 119, 132, 164, 202, 228
  utopian, 81, 90-93, 120-21
Socialism and the Political Struggle, 119
Society, 18-19, 39, 89, 219-22, 245
  civil, 40, 50-51
  classless, 61
Sociology, 81
Sovpadenie, 18, 168-71, 177-78
Space, 83, 159-60, 193, 207, 209
Species-life, 42
Spinoza, B., 88, 129, 187
Spirit, 12-13, 16, 19, 45, 53, 207; *see also* Consciousness; Mind

Spirit of Christianity, 11
Stalin, J., 6, 10, 126, 137, 140,
    145, 172-74, 177, 183, 199,
    202, 215-17, 219, 224, 232,
    234, 236, 243, 262-63
    life and writings, 184-201
Starcke, K.N., 93
State, 17-19, 21, 39, 49-51, 60,
    75, 92-93, 109, 136-37, 140-
    45, 164, 218, 221
    abolition and withering of,
    43, 143, 192, 197-98
State and Revolution, 131, 140-
    45
Stirner, M., 20-21, 35, 46
Strauss, D., 20-21
Struve, P.B., 117, 119
Subsistence, means of, 68
*Sudden Changes in Nature and
    in History*, 126
Sue, E., 45
Superstructure, 57, 64-65, 73-
    74, 118, 137-38, 140, 163,
    189-90, 193-98, 218-19, 227,
    239, 262
    active role of, 189-90, 201
*System of Economic Contradic-
    tions, The*, 35

*Tasks of the Proletariat and the
    Peasant Revolution, The*, 131
"Tasks of the Youth Leagues,
    The," 171
Theology, 10, 24-25, 39, 41
Theory, and practice, 174, 216,
    233-38
"Theses on Feuerbach," 29-30,
    35, 46
"Three Sources and Three Com-
    ponent Parts of Marxism,
    The," 130, 161, 241
Time, 83-84, 159-60, 193, 207-
    8
Tkachev, P.N., 116
Tolstoi, L., 115
Trotsky, L.D., 183, 191, 262-63

True socialism, 22, 46
Truth, 1, 20, 94, 101, 154-
    57, 215
    absolute, 91, 154-56
    criterion of, 154, 160
    eternal, 85-87
    meaning, 154-56
    objective, 151, 154-56
    relative, 154-56
Tugarinov, V.P., 242, 267
Turgenev, I.S., 114
*Two Tactics of Social Democ-
    racy in the Democratic
    Revolution*, 129, 135

Ueberweg, F., 166
Ulianov, V.I., *see* Lenin, V.I.
Under the Banner of Marxism,
    7, 131, 171-73, 179-80, 182-
    83, 187, 261
*United States of Europe Slogan,
    The*, 136
Universals, 23, 42, 168-69

Valentinov, N. (pseud. of N. V.
    Vol'sky), 257
Value, judgments, 62, 229
    labor theory of, 67-70, 163
    surplus, 68-69, 92, 163
"Value, Price and Profit," 37
Values, bourgeois, 60
    proletarian, 60-61, 228, 232,
    238, 242
Voprosy filosofii, 188, 205, 208,
    232

"Wage, Labor and Capital," 36,
    63
Wages, Price and Profit, 63
*War Program of the Proletarian
    Revolution, The*, 136
Westernism, 114-15
Westphalen, J. von, 34
What is Property?, 45, 55
What Is to Be Done?, 115, 118,
    129, 131-35

Yugoslavia, 239
Yushkevich, P.S., 257

Zarya, 120
Zeno, 88, 105

Zhdanov, A.A., 188
Zieber, N.I., 117
Zinoviev, G.E. (pseud. of G.E. Radomysl'sky), 184
Zvezda, 130

www.ingramcontent.com/pod-product-compliance
Lightning Source LLC
Chambersburg PA
CBHW021136230426
43667CB00005B/143